WILLIE NELSON
The Outlaw

Also by Graeme Thomson

Complicated Shadows: The Life and Music of Elvis Costello

WILLIE NELSON

The Outlaw

Graeme Thomson

For Louis and Martha

First published in Great Britain in 2006 by Virgin Books Ltd
Virgin Books Ltd
Thames Wharf Studios
Rainville Road
London
W6 9HA

A catalogue record for this book is available from the British
Library.

ISBN: 1 85227 300 3
ISBN: 9 781852 273002

The paper used in this book is a natural, recyclable product
made from wood grown in sustainable forests. The
manufacturing process conforms to the regulations of the
country of origin.

Typeset by TW Typesetting, Plymouth, Devon

Printed in the USA

CONTENTS

INTRODUCTION

I started to hear the songs first, things like 'Funny How Time Slips Away' and 'Crazy'. Then I started to see his name. Back in the days of 45s it was easier to check out who wrote what, and each time I heard a really interesting song, half the time I'd find Willie Nelson's name attached to it.

The minute we looked in each other's eyes I thought, Oh yeah, I know *you*. I might have known him for years and years. Willie is an all American, one of the great Westerners. He's an American patriot, but not in the flag-waving sense. He has a real love and a feel for the soil of the land; a real concern for what you live on. It's a beautiful thing, and really honest. He's dedicated to his ideas and on top of that he's a brilliant musician and a songwriter *par excellence*.

I'm attracted to the man as a character and a player and for his knowledge of music: those wonderful mixtures he has between blues and country and Mariachi. He's got a beautiful bravado. He doesn't mind going off on a flight somewhere in the middle of a song, just taking it and seeing where he ends up, and I admire that. Willie is unique. Nobody else could play like that. Look at the state of his guitar! He has punched holes through it, scraped it away, and it still sounds better than ever. And he's a great singer. Such a wry delivery.

Willie is a great magnet. He brings people together. I met Merle Haggard via him. I was sitting rehearsing with Willie and there was this guy with a baseball cap on – the right way around – and a grey beard, picking like a maniac. I said, 'Your name's not Merle is it?' Yup! It ended up with Merle working with the Stones. Willie pulls together diverse people from every spectrum of music.

It's amazing to see the heart and diplomacy of the man, his dedication and amazing energy; a lovely enthusiasm for music. He's got it all together, very smooth, absolutely beautiful, no sweat. He's an amazing guy. He finishes the show and then spends an hour or more signing every autograph in the audience, It just shows that great patience that Willie has. He should be President. I think we'd be a lot better off.

Willie's a busy man, but he always makes a little space to hang and I always have a great time with him. We're guitar pickers and songwriters and so we can just kick shit around. When I work with him I judge Willie's shows by how many guys he's got rolling behind him in the bus: 'This is a three Frisbee show!' And it's always good stuff, believe me. I'm a connoisseur.

He's been incredibly productive in the last few years and working really hard, but then I don't think he couldn't work hard. If he wasn't working I could imagine him fading away. The road becomes like an addiction: white line fever. On the other hand, there are loads of people out there who want to see what he does and he still feels like doing it. It's really as simple as that.

He has an amazing effect on people, a sort of calmness, but under that there's a hint of real danger if it blows up. He's the most unlikely star – such a recluse in a way. As a man he's actually a bit of a mystery and I don't think he really knows all of himself. All I know is that, although we come from totally different places, I feel at home with Willie.

Keith Richards
Portland, Oregon
November 2005

HAPPINESS

Willie Nelson is talking about happiness.

'Happiness is kind of a decision you make: whether you want to be happy or you want to be unhappy,' he says slowly.

The parts of his face which aren't framed by his loose ponytail are shaded beneath the dark hood of his tracksuit top. He is wearing white socks and green trainers. He looks incongruous in this setting: a modern hotel, all chrome and glass. It has nothing he needs. Beside him one of his London buddies is passed out on the sofa, a victim of the brutally powerful weed Nelson has been smoking for the best part of the afternoon. Or the last four decades, if you prefer. 'Wherever you're at you can decide,' he continues. 'I've decided it's a lot easier to decide to be happy. Otherwise it's a lot of trouble.'

His eyes are almost black, endlessly deep, and they speak volumes about all that trouble and the measures he has taken over the years to banish it. On a table behind him a sleek silver laptop plays music beamed down by satellite from another age, the age when he started writing some of the most simple, sorrowful songs imaginable. He doesn't write those kinds of songs any more.

'I don't like to write negative things,' he says. 'Something that you have to sing every night, if it happened to turn out to be a smash or something that would be the worst thing that could happen to you. I always think of my songs as having a possibility of a happy ending somewhere.' He continues to talk about happiness; about how it evaded him for a long time, how he was confused and succumbed to seeing the world as a dark place.

'My spirituality was always there, but there were other things getting in the way. Then somewhere all of a sudden it was back. I had to work to get there. It was just a matter of living, realising that this works and *this* doesn't work and that positive is better than negative. It's really that simple. And that's where I've been since then.'

There is a loud snap of thunder outside. The stoned, prostrate body lying next to Nelson on the sofa doesn't flicker. He is 72 years old and, like it or not, he has seen plenty of badness in his time. 'You won't get me ever to admit that,' he says clearly. 'I'm not going to give it any energy.'

He used to drink a lot of whisky but it made him negative and brought some kind of deep rage to the surface. So now he smokes prodigious amounts of marijuana each day, the kind of pot that makes most people pass out after two hits. He has 'crazy dreams' without it – some might suggest it is simply reality crashing in on a private world he has shaped and moulded and dreamed into being. He calls it medicine.

He has been on the road since 1950 and he is still out there. He lives his life in a state of almost continual motion, moving from one city to the next with his band, some of whom he has known for fifty years. He sleeps mostly on his bus. It doesn't matter too much where he is as long as there is an audience and a stage. That is his purpose. He has found the life that suits him. A long time ago, making music became something that facilitated the way he wanted to live. It allows him to look neither backwards nor forwards – he simply stares down at a never-ending, immediate present.

'It's not possible for me to do anything other than that,' he says. 'I just have to live here and now. That's all we have, that's all there is, there's no use even arguing about yesterday or tomorrow because I don't know what it is. Well, I know what yesterday was. I have no fucking idea what tomorrow's going to be.'

Keith Richards calls him a man-of-the-soil. Others have called him a Shaman. He has lived a life full enough for ten men and people want him to have big answers. Viewed from this spyhole, he could be a redneck cowboy, a Zen master or simply an old, stoned hippie. Of course, he is really all three, and several other things into the bargain.

'The main thing is, I think we're all the same,' he says. 'People that I've sung to all over the world, there's no difference – from London to Houston. As you get more into it, you realise that this is a Universal thing; the Universal mind and your mind is the same thing. We're all thinking basically the same thing, we're all basically the same person, and once you realise that, everything is kinda simplified. There's a lot of things going on: quantum leaps into the future. A lot of things are happening at quantum speeds.'

He relights his joint, flicks ash on the floor and looks at his buddy next to him, as though he has only just noticed he is there. 'Are you back? Did you make it back OK? You had a good trip?'

There is no answer. 'We lost him. He went out the door.' Willie Nelson smiles. He is happy. It hasn't always been this way.

1. 1933–1950

If Abbott wasn't home it would be hard to love. That applies as truly now as it did back then, when Willie Nelson was born surrounded by the flat blackland cotton prairies of central Texas and the hard white rock that lurks just beneath the ground. Somewhere like Abbott needed a reason to exist, and before baby Nelson grew and put it on the map with his music, the Missouri–Kansas–Texas railroad provided it. In the 1880s a few houses and businesses settled alongside the tracks. Today the old, rusty cotton gin still overlooks the line as it continues to stretch away to its nearest significant points: the little town of West a few miles to the south, the larger town of Hillsboro – the seat of Hill County – about five miles to the north. The railway divides the settlement in half. The Nelsons lived to the east of the line, and the east side in the USA usually equates with poverty. So it proved here, except that everyone was poor. The Nelsons were just that little bit poorer than most.

Abbott is a faceless place, a little bleak without being isolated. The grey university town of Waco lies about twenty miles to the south, while the major conurbations of Fort Worth and Dallas are not far over the northern horizon. Today, Interstate 35 runs right past its outer limits, advertising Czech pastries, cheap motels and gas stations in garish hoardings twelve feet wide. George W. Bush has his holiday ranch nearby, and everything from bumper stickers to baseball hats reminds the traveller that 'Freedom

Don't Come For Free'. This is not the pretty part of Texas. Forget canyons and mountains, or fields of blue bonnets. The route connecting Austin and San Antonio in the South to Dallas in the North is flat, dry and bereft of much in the way of beauty. Abbott is no exception.

In many ways, that I-35 has provided the spine to Nelson's otherwise itinerant life: he has lived most of his 72 years keeping close to this main artery, always happiest with Texan soil beneath his feet. He owns the land on which he was born, and still has a home in Abbott, once owned by the doctor who delivered him. He cut his still-magnificent *Live Country Music Concert* album in 1966 at Panther Hall in Fort Worth. His ranch outside Austin is a mere two hours' drive away. He had spells in San Antonio and Houston as a young married man. The famously nefarious Nite Owl club where he made some of his earliest performances has changed site since the 50s but still occupies a spot on the roadside between Abbott and Waco. It is now only a neglected shell, but even without its scrapping GIs and cheating couples, it still exudes an air of disreputable menace.

What it all adds up to is this: when the huge Lone Star flag of Texas unravels behind him as the opening snare crack of 'Whiskey River' fills the air in concert each night, it is no hollow gesture. Texas – and specifically his early years in Abbott – have made Willie Nelson the way he is, probably even more than he knows or would care to acknowledge.

Abbott's population has fluctuated little over the years, between 350 in Nelson's day to perhaps 300 nowadays. Anyone used to the cramped proportions of a British village would be surprised by the space. Its perimeters stretch and drawl like a Texan getting out of bed, but it's still possible to drive from one end to the other in the length of time it takes to sing 'Crazy'. It is surrounded by cotton fields and farm land, but it has an archetypal heart: the post office, the general store, the lot where the barber once stood and, a little further up the road, the two churches which stand impassively facing each other across the crossroads: one Baptist, one Methodist. The Church of Christ is just a stone's throw away.

Willie Hugh Nelson was born here, perhaps a quarter of a mile south-east of these churches, in the early hours on 30 April, 1933. He once claimed that he was actually born late on 29 April and that it just took his mother a while to alert the doctor, but then maybe he was just hedging his bets: 'Will is always working on his birthday,' claimed his third wife Connie.[1] He was always working on something.

Life was simple. Residents earned their small incomes from agriculture – most predominantly picking cotton, pulling corn or undertaking general farm work – or by providing essential local services: at the grocers, the auto repair shop, the service station, the barbershop or post office. Major shopping was a railroad ride away in Hillsboro or Waco. There were mostly white residents with some scattering of 'coloured' dwellings on the outskirts of the town. It was an era of what has been termed 'benevolent racism': minorities here were not hated or abused, merely denied their civil rights and casually termed 'niggers'. There were other ethnicities too. Even today, a stroll round the centre of nearby West is like walking into a traditional Czech village, and a glance at the old school register of Nelson's classmates at Abbott High School reveals several surnames of Czech origin: Cepak, Janecka, Hutrya, Hlavaty. Poles too, Germans and, of course, Mexicans have all made significant impressions upon Texas. The surname Nelson is apparently of Irish descent.

His parents were no more than children. Ira Doyle Nelson had hooked up with Myrle Greenhaw in Searcy County, Arkansas in the late 1920s. Their families lived close to each other. He was sixteen and she was fifteen when they married in Pindall in 1929. Soon after, they left the slopes of the Ozark mountains and travelled with Ira's parents to Abbott in the neighbouring state of Texas, where they trusted the cotton picking might be better. They all moved into a relatively comfortable two-storey house, typical of the town.

Myrle had some native American blood from her mother's side: when her son unbuckles his hair and lets it hang around his shoulders, you can see the inheritance. She was by all accounts a spirited girl from colourful stock.

Willie Nelson: They were talented bootleggers and moonshiners as well as musicians. My mother told me that her folks used to run hideouts in the mountains where outlaws could come and find safety.[2]

Ira Nelson was a more prosaic soul. His descendants were among the numerous Irish and British immigrants who came to the US in the 1800s, steeped in traditional songs and stories. His father loved music and played the guitar, and his son followed suit. William Nelson was a mechanic by trade, although he had turned to blacksmithing by the time he settled in Abbott. Ira inherited his skill with engines, but when there were no cars to fix he would work on farms and in the fields to earn his pay. It was a tough life, about to get tougher. Their first child arrived on the first day of 1931. They called her Bobbie Lee. Myrle was still only sixteen.

Ira and Myrle were the originators of a domestic pattern which has run like a seam through Nelson family history ever since: early marriage, followed by a break-up, physical abandonment, alcohol or substance abuse, and plain old pain. This is one family which has lived every country music cliché to the full. Nelson caught his share as a child and he has passed it on as a husband and a father. At the time the key moment in his life occurred, he felt it but would have been unable to articulate it.

Myrle left Abbott and her family in 1933 when he was only six months old, the drudgery and confinement of life in a tiny town with two children proving too much for a lively nineteen-year-old. She hit the road unannounced one day, simply walking out and not coming back, joining the endless stream of desperate drifters cut loose from normality by the Great Depression, which had been precipitated by the stock market crash of 1929 and had really begun to bite hard by 1933. She took work wherever she could find it: dancing, waitressing, dealing cards. She sought out high times and bright lights, which in reality would have meant endless road-side honky-tonks and dives. But she was not for turning, and seemed later to possess an admirable recognition of the inevitability of her own impulsive nature.

Myrle Nelson: I left [the kids] with their daddy's folks, because I knew they'd take them to church and Sunday school. I wanted them to stay out of my kind of life – the restaurants and the bars.[3]

In their mother's absence, the children were effectively raised by Ira and his parents, William and Nancy. However, they weren't even allowed the certainty of a complete abandonment. About a year after she departed, Myrle returned to Abbott declaring she had cancer and was all set to die. She apparently came back with the fantastically maudlin and melodramatic purpose of teaching her children a song – 'I'll Be Gone When You Read This Last Letter From Me' – before she passed away. However, she was successfully operated upon and, realising that she was still very much alive and there was presumably plenty more living to do (and many more last letters to write), she promptly went away again. She had already divorced Ira and re-married; she would divorce again and marry a man called Ken Harvey in 1943 before she settled, first in Eugene, Oregon, and then later Yakima, Washington, right out on the Pacific coast. She kept in touch and would even visit, but with a heart-stuttering inconsistency.

Neither was this the last blow. Ira couldn't see much future for himself stuck in Abbott with two children and no wife. By the time his son was four and Bobbie was six, he had forged a new life for himself with a woman called Lorraine Moon, re-marrying and fathering two more children called Doyle and Charles. After fleetingly attempting to merge the two families in the house at Abbott, he decided to call it quits. He loaded his wife and two children into a pick-up truck and headed away in search of something better. They traversed Texas, from Amarillo to Houston, eventually settling in Fort Worth, where Ira found work as a mechanic at the Frank Kent Ford Company. Again, it was sufficiently near in geographical terms for Ira to keep in touch, but not quite close enough.

Jack Clements: I think after he was grown he got acquainted with [his parents] later, but when he was growing up he didn't see much of them.

One can scarcely imagine the extent of the confusion and turmoil this caused a young boy. Still too young to ask the questions or indeed comprehend the answers his mother's disappearances raised, now he faced the realisation that his father seemingly favoured his new family to the extent that he was prepared to ditch his old one. These were, of course, different times and families were by necessity pragmatic, but it was still incomprehensible to a child. To his immense credit, Nelson has never pointed the finger of blame, but it's safe to assume it's an issue that has troubled him deeply through the years.

Johnny Bush: Willie doesn't show his emotions. He guards himself pretty well. I think when he was left by his parents to live with his grandparents at an early age, he might have felt: 'I've gotta get tough.' This is my assumption. I've never heard him say one bad or negative thing against his mom or his dad for leaving him like that – but that's Willie. But [as to] how he really felt inside? He had to have thoughts about why he was dumped like that. I think that's what made him the way he was: 'I can be miserable or I can be happy. I can be tough or I can be weak. It's my choice.'

There can be no question that the legacy of his abandonment has run deep throughout his life. Noting his father's lack of will to do anything significant with his own musical gift, he became determined to be more adventurous, to transcend his surroundings. Not for him the life of a mechanic in Fort Worth, playing the odd gig at the weekend, although for a long time it looked like that was the best he could expect. His mother's lust for life and humour, her energy and intelligence and hospitality would be handed down, but more importantly, he romanticised her departure. She became an outlaw figure, an idealised free spirit. He fantasised about Billy the Kid hiding out with her family in the hills, and she validated in his eyes the seductive if essentially selfish notion of the nomadic life.

In turn he romanticised and mythologised his own life. He escaped into songs, cowboy movies and kung fu comics like most other boys, but in later life he lived out those storylines for real: he has become the cowboy figure in the films, the leader of a succession of rowdy gangs but at heart a heroic loner. And, above all, he has kept moving, happy to accommodate those who wish to travel in the same direction he is going in, but reluctant to stand still and throw his hand in with those who want him to become a fixed point of reference, to be there through thick and thin. It could have gone either way: people who experience that kind of trauma in early life can either overcompensate and smother those around them, or they keep everything at a distance. Myrle's absence taught him not to hold on to anything too tightly, in case one day they might simply disappear.

Willie Nelson: I had to stop thinking that I had a home. You've got to be able to move to the next big town without slashing your wrists.[4]

There were other obvious repercussions. Years later, when the time came for him to marry for the first time, he practically married his mother: Martha Matthews was young, pretty, had native American blood, was as feisty as hell and as likely to settle for a life of domestic drudgery as Myrle had been. Their obvious unsuitability gave further credibility to his already jaded view of male–female relationships. It became a self fulfilling prophecy. 'It was a long time before I ran into any positive relationships between men and women,' he admitted.[5] Almost the first song he ever wrote was a cheating song – part pastiche, no doubt, but also already filtered through the lens of experience. The heartbreak that characterised the majority of his early recorded songs was already there, what he called his 'you-left-me-and-I-want-you-back' kinds of songs. He wasn't even ten.

Connie Nelson: I think he's got a lot of abandonment issues that come from childhood. I really do. Oh my God, it's not at all [surprising]. Waylon [Jennings] told me one time after Willie and I split up that he felt he probably [leaves] before [people] can leave [him]. It was interesting that Waylon had that take on it. I honestly do believe that Willie has abandonment issues.

But he did not lack love. He had his sister Bobbie, with whom he remains almost telepathically close into their 70s, he had aunts who would visit, and he had his grandparents. Nancy and William were known simply as Mama and Daddy Nelson, and they provided the first kind of stability that the Nelson kids would ever have known. It was a tough kind of love: they would be woken in the morning with a bucket of ice water thrown at them, and they had to work hard for their keep. Mama earned money working in the cafeteria of the local school and teaching music, while Daddy worked as a blacksmith, but there was very little going spare. Daddy Nelson was strict, not averse to doling out a beating with a razor strap, but his grandson adored him. When he died of pneumonia Nelson was not yet seven, and it was a devastatingly cruel blow. Another father figure bit the dust.

Willie Nelson: I didn't know what to make of it. It was an almost unbearable situation. I hadn't even had time to grieve for the loss of a mother and a daddy, much less my grandfather.[6]

The kids elected to stay with their grandmother, although financial restraints dictated that they had to leave their two-storey house and move into what would now be classed simply as a wooden shack. Bare earth could be seen through the floorboards. 'They were really raised poor,' recalls Nelson's close childhood friend Jack Clements. 'Everybody was poor back then, but they were poorer than most.' It was 1939, and war was coming, but that all seemed a very, very long way away from Abbott.

As Johnny Bush points out, Willie Nelson got tough. What else could he do?

Nelson paints his early years in cowboy colours, casting himself as the hot-headed young punk who would take back-chat from no one. Quiet, but strong. There is no doubt that kids in Abbott were raised tough, and if you couldn't fight your way out of a corner you were doing yourself a grave disservice, but he is remembered by all as a pleasant boy. It's likely that he was already on his way to mastering the quiet charm that would see him get away with all number of moral felonies through the years with his honour and very often his hide intact. He certainly looked the part: auburn-haired, freckled, brown eyes, protruding ears, skinny and short, occasionally persuaded to don his sailor suit with the red trim and do the cute thing.

When the Nelsons had arrived in Abbott they had joined the Methodist church, and Mama and Daddy Nelson proved to be much stricter upholders of its teachings than their children had been. One of his first really significant compositions as a songwriter, 'Family Bible', is a straight autobiographical recollection of this time, if bathed in nostalgia: the battered Good Book sits on the kitchen table after dinner, Dad reading, Mum singing. His grandparents instilled the basic tenets of decency with some success, but the fire and brimstone preachings which promised a sticky end to those who misbehaved left Nelson cold. He would always be a deeply spiritual man in the broadest sense, but he had no patience for the practical sacrifices and personal denials that conventional Christianity demanded. His upbringing rapidly became defined by twin, opposing forces: the stark good-or-evil religion of the Methodist church as preached by his grandmother, and the typical small-town, yet universal, temptations of girls, alcohol, music and fighting. It's a dichotomy – rather than a contradiction – which has remained throughout his entire life. He has never been a definitive person.

He grew up fast, the way most children did back then. He got drunk for the first time aged nine, courtesy of his father – the two of them colluded so that Ira's mother wouldn't find out and punish her grandson – and by his teens he was well into the usual mix of collective hi-jinks and private self-discovery. The escapades very fairly innocuous. There was a local rivalry with the boys of West, the kind which would be common between any small towns both then and now. He and his friends would meet in the fields out of town and fight, or sometimes turn and run if the odds were against them. He was small – 5′ 7″ at his peak and barely 130 lbs – so he had to learn how to scrap; mostly it was wrestling, but sometimes something more brutally effective was required. Nelson was fascinated by self-defence and martial arts, and would send away for the books on kung fu and jujitsu advertised in the comics he read. He is remembered by all as a personable boy, a good kid, quiet and funny, but he had a foul temper, rarely unleashed but violent in its intensity.

Connie Nelson: He's not real confrontational with anybody unless they get right in his face. Otherwise, he's pretty passive. But the wrong thing at the wrong time and boy! – he's like a locomotive. If you try to cross him or mess with any of his friends or family, that'll get a big rise out of him quickly.

Even now, up close, it is easy to see where that anger lives. It was partly inherited from his mother, and partly a rage that was entirely his own. In later life it would be exacerbated by alcohol, disappointment and people 'fucking up', as his friend Larry Trader puts it, but in Abbott it was born of confusion and frustration. By no means inclined to self-pity, he was quick to feel that he was being attacked and wasn't always able to mask his sense of sadness from his schoolfriends.

Dwayne Adair: I always felt sorry for Willie. We'd pick cotton in the fields and he'd say: 'My momma and daddy are coming down from Fort Worth this weekend.' The next Monday I'd ask him and he'd say, 'No, they couldn't make it.' And he'd look so sad.[7]

He would ride the freight train with friends, or they would wait in the station and rock the train as it passed through. Sometimes a rock would be thrown at the caboose at the back of the train and a federal man would come to the school to investigate. On Hallowe'en he and his friends would gather together and run around the town, pulling the wheels off wagons or stealing outdoor toilets and putting them up on the roofs of buildings.
    They might hunt squirrels or rabbits for eating, or just kill sparrows and feed them to the alley cats. On a Sunday they would fight bumblebees with paddles made from apple boxes. They would play basketball at the local county ground and on Saturday night they might go to the movies in Hillsboro and West. He stayed over at the houses of close friends like Gayle Gregory and Jack Clements, who lived right out in the country, and tried to ride horses. His aunts would sometimes take him on picnics to the huge open expanses of Cameron Park in Waco, where he would stand high up on the sheer rock and look down at the Brazos river. Later there were girls and hitchhiking and trips to Dallas, but mostly it was a self-contained environment.

Jack Clements: There wasn't a whole lot of activities going on. You didn't have a lot of spare time because everybody was poor and had other things to do.

Like everyone else, Nelson worked his way through school. There were constant chores to perform for the family, and in the summertime he picked cotton or pulled corn and packed hay bales, working with the local people. Nelson didn't like too much manual work, especially cotton picking, and would shirk his duties. 'It was a real hard paying job,' he recalled later. 'If like me you picked awhile and sat on your sack awhile, it's not as hard as it was for some.'[8] By the time he was in High school he had landed a more agreeable job, working at the barbershop on the main drag, shining shoes on a Saturday and singing while he shined them. 'They'd tell him not to sing,' laughs Clements. 'They'd say, "Just shine the shoes!"'[9]

Abbott was like most small towns at that time in that it had its own school, despite the fact that the total pupil roll barely exceeded one hundred. The High school is still there on the western outskirts of the town, although none of it resembles how it would have appeared back in the 1940s. Now it's a neat, modern little building, and only the football pitch remains of the original layout. It was known as White Rock Field back in Nelson's day and was not for the faint-hearted. Before the boys played they would throw the rocks off the field, and sometimes at each other.

Sport was a big part of his childhood. He was a decent athlete, the shortest member of the senior boys' basketball team and a passable footballer. He was active in all sports – baseball, volleyball, track, even softball – but that was hardly a reliable indication of aptitude. The school was so small that practically everybody had to take part; there were barely forty boys between freshman and senior. Nonetheless, he must have felt he had something; after leaving school he tried for a baseball scholarship at the junior college in nearby Weatherford, but didn't make the grade.

He served as song leader for the Future Farmers for America, the organisation founded in 1928 to encourage agricultural education throughout the US, and also took an interest in the more creative elements of school. He enjoyed poetry and theatre studies, and when the school came to put on their annual play he was always in it. 'He was,' says Clements intriguingly, 'a pretty good actor even back then.'

Jack Clements: I don't remember him being [unconventional] at school. He was a good student, and he didn't get into trouble or anything like that. That came later! He was an A/B student, probably, but dropped down to a B student by the time we graduated, because he had already started to use up a lot of his time with music.

It was music that really held him. Ira played the fiddle and picked the guitar, of course, and even Myrle had strummed the banjo, but both Nelson grandparents cherished and actually understood music, and had passed it down to the kids. Bobbie always loved the piano: she built one out of cardboard almost before she could speak, then tinkered with a toy one. When she was about five her grandfather finally bought her one for $35, no little sacrifice for a family as financially strapped as the Nelsons, and she would play songs like 'Jesus, Lover Of My Soul' from the Methodist hymnal book one moment, then a pop standard like 'Moonlight

In Vermont' the next. Bobbie would drink up the serious musical theory that her grandparents taught her and quickly learned to read music, but Nelson never did. He was less keen on the theoretical study. He just wanted to play.

His first public performance came when he was just four, reciting a poem at an all-day gospel-singing picnic. He got a nosebleed that dripped all over his white sailor suit. Daddy Nelson bought him his first guitar two years later from a Sears catalogue and taught him how to play the D, A and G chords. It was one of his final bequests, and perhaps his most useful. You can go a long way in country music with those three chords.

Despite the poverty of their circumstances after Daddy Nelson's death, as if by magic a radio appeared in the house, 'a godlike presence',[9] as Nelson remembers it. Until then, he had had to rely on his grandfather and a few old 78s to provide him with music and songs. Now the whole world opened up, or at least the whole of the country. It would be hard to over-emphasise the impact that the radio made.

It was a time when few poor people had cars, television was virtually unheard of, telephones were scarce, and radio opened up a unique and immediate line connecting global events and your own little corner of the planet. There were numerous small local stations that sent their signals over areas of a 70- or 100-mile radius, but it was also the time of the advent of the huge 'X' stations – so called because they all had an X in their names, such as XERA – beaming their 150,000-watt signals from across the border in Mexico and connecting the whole land. 'Border radio' could pretty much play what they wanted without kowtowing to the rather stringent restrictions laid down by the FBC in the United States. It opened up whole new markets for country acts like the Carter Family, and it also opened up a whole world of music for Willie Nelson.

In Texas Bob Wills and the Texas Playboys were the kings of Western Swing, spawning dozens of local imitators. Wills would hit the stage and play for four hours straight, keeping the crowd in his pocket with barely a pause between songs, much as Nelson does today. It was hard, fast country but had elements of blues and jazz interwoven into its fabric. It sounded simple but it was devilishly hard to do well. Nelson learned much of his stagecraft from listening and watching Wills lead the band, hearing how he effortlessly moved from a shit-kicking hoedown to a heart-wringing ballad in the blink of an eye, never once losing the intensity or the crowd. He also learned a degree of professional responsibility from Wills, who kept a twelve-piece band ticking over. It's arguably one of the main factors that has kept Nelson hitting the road so hard in recent times. When your music is keeping food in the mouths and hope in the hearts of literally scores of people, it's hard to quit.

Paul English: If I didn't have Willie, I would die very shortly. I know that. I would go crazy. I would not have a purpose. Right now I feel like I have a purpose in life. We all out here have a job to do and we try to do it. We have a great inspiration.[10]

Before Nelson took his place in Texan folklore, Wills was the local hero, alongside Ernest Tubb, who first landed at the *Grand Ole Opry* in 1943. But Nelson was soaking up sounds from all sides and all sources. Mama Nelson had taught him that 'the definition of music is anything that is pleasing to the ear',[11] and he was testing the theory as he slid along the radio dial. Big bands from Chicago, traditional jazz, crooners like Bing Crosby, as well as the more obvious country – or hillbilly, as it was often known – fare of Hank Williams, Floyd Tillman, Leon Payne, Red Foley, Bill Monroe and live shows from the *Grand Ole Opry*, broadcast by WSM in Nashville. His tastes have never really changed. Sixty years later he would sit in a London hotel and reel off a list of his favourite artists, the ones he still listened to, the ones that still *mattered*, and most of them were the same voices he would have heard on the radio back in his wooden house in Abbott:

Willie Nelson: I like [the old music] because it's good. Well, to me it's better than anything I hear. I haven't heard anything better than Frank Sinatra in a long time. Or much better than Hank Williams or Lefty Frizzel or Johnny Mercer or Hoagy Carmichael. It's hard to beat these guys. Django Reinhardt. Eddie Arnold. Ernest Tubb. I've always thought that you start with a voice and an instrument and you add to it.[12]

The boy was listening, learning and using what he could in practical situations. He was able to find links between Tubb and Sinatra, getting a kick out of the way certain singers phrased different words and made a song their own. He gravitated toward the unusual and the off-beat. He wouldn't have known it, but he was already preparing himself to become a vocal stylist, to find the cracks and spaces in songs which could be filled in a thousand different ways. He had a natural ear and perfect pitch as a singer. He heard blacks and Mexicans singing in the fields and picked up other nuances there, too.

Willie Nelson: I first heard the blues picking cotton in a field full of black people. I realised they knew more about music, soul, *feeling*, than I did. I felt inferior.[13]

It was, he later recalled, 'a great opera'.[14] The Mexican influence in particular was to help shape his unique guitar style. 'He's from a Tex-Mex background, Spanish guitar,' says Merle Haggard. 'There's a lot of Hispanic influences in [his] music.' He adored jazzists like George Barnes and especially Django Reinhardt, and would practise the licks of country pickers like Billy Bird, Bucky Meadows and Hank 'Sugarfoot' Garland from the songs he heard on the radio. Throw into the mix the lyrical

Spanish-style playing he heard from Mexican radio and local players, some of whom lived right across the street from him, and you come to a pretty basic understanding of the three formative musical influences which define his guitar style to this day.

He and Bobbie would play anywhere at the drop of a hat: church meetings, school assemblies on a Friday morning. They would ride together down the Interurban electric train which ran from Dallas into Waco to perform gospel songs together on radio WACO's *Mary Holiday's Amateur Talent Show*.

Jack Clements: They played all the activities at school. Of course, we didn't think anything about it then! It was just another kid who could sing. As long as I've known him he's been pulling the guitar and singing, [but] I don't remember him being that gung ho about it back then. He wasn't obsessed with it. We thought more of Bobbie than we did him because she played piano at just about every function we had.

He played his first proper gig at the age of nine in a bar in West with the local Czech polka group, the John Rajcek Band. He stood on stage and bashed away at an old acoustic guitar, inaudible to all but clearly enjoying himself. He picked up a few dollars, a welcome addition to family funds and certainly enough to risk the wrath of Mama Nelson, who feared for his soul in those rowdy joints. But there was no going back. He performed regularly with the band in the Bohemian beer halls of West, Waco and Ross on the weekends before he was barely into double figures.

His musical apprenticeship really moved to another level when Bobbie married at the age of sixteen. She had known Bud Fletcher only one month. He was 22, good-looking, and a bit of a charmer by all accounts. He had a day job driving a truck for his father, a commissioner in charge of the roads in the Hill County area, and by night he led a band called Bud Fletcher and the Texans. He wasn't much of a singer or a player, but people liked him. Bobbie played the piano, the thirteen-year-old Nelson was on guitar and vocals, even Ira would sometimes sit in. They would practise in Mama Nelson's front room and play Friday and Saturday nights and Sunday afternoons in local venues in West and Waco, many of which were fairly new on the scene in the 1940s. Some, such as the Terrace Club and Scotty's Tavern, weren't too bad, with an Art Deco feel, a bar up at the front and an area for dancing at the back.

At the rather less elegant end of the market were clubs like the Nite Owl, stuck on the roadside between Abbott and Waco. It was run by Marge Lunde and her husband U.J. and Nelson became a patron not long after it opened in 1943. It was not for the faint-hearted.

Jack Loftis: The Nite Owl was a tough joint and was unique in that there was no wash basin in the men's room. I don't know if the ladies' room had one. Waco had an Air Force base in those days and the airmen used to raise hell in the smallish clubs, much to the resentment of central Texas residents. The Lundes put up with no bullshit from the servicemen. True story: Lunde had a Baby Ruth candy box beneath the bar and it contained about six sets of brass knuckles. When trouble broke out in the dance area in the back of the club, U.J. would bring out the 'knucks', pass them out to regulars and the fight would be on – with the Air Force always losing. Mrs Lunde, a stout woman, would also participate. While the fighting went on, Bud, Nelson and the Texans would continue to play. A night without a fight was out of the ordinary.

This was the environment in which Willie Nelson grew up as a performer. There were several of what Johnny Bush would call 'skull orchards', places that existed almost entirely outside of the law and where you could get as drunk as a dog and fight with other like-minded souls. Nelson took to it like a duck to water, and those early bonds ran deep. When Bobbie and Bud had their first child, Randy, Marge Lunde would babysit in the bar while the band played. Much later, in the 80s, Lunde was charged with shooting and killing her brother-in-law. Nelson stood as a character witness at the trial and she walked away free on the grounds of self-defence.

Working with Bud Fletcher and the Texans also took the band to some more prestigious places, like the Scenic Wonderland in Waco which held 3,000 people, and Fletcher even managed to get the band a regular slot on the local radio station KHBR, based in Hillsboro, which really made Nelson feel like a local celebrity. They would head into town on a Sunday morning and broadcast live for an hour or so.

Most importantly of all, it was bringing in the money. Willie was thirteen years old and Bud paid him $8 a show, the equivalent of perhaps $200 today. It was mostly passed straight back to Mama Nelson, with perhaps a little bit creamed off the top, and it proved beyond all doubt that this was what he wanted to do with his life. The money provided for clothes and food and other essentials and helped assuage the guilt that both Bobbie and her brother felt about going so explicitly against her religious wishes by playing music in bars late at night. She firmly believed they were going to hell fast. Nelson was rather attracted to that idea; indeed, he was probably already resigned to it. There were other bands in his teens: the magnificently named Charlie Brown and the Browns, who were led by the father of one of Nelson's early girlfriends, and Joe Massey and the Frontiersmen, to name but two.

He was tasting something new and compelling. He enjoyed playing for people, liked the attention it brought him and the way that he didn't have to work too hard to get it. And he realised early in life that girls like guitar players. His performing instinct undoubtedly helped him with girls, especially as Bud Fletcher and the Texans would sometimes play neighbouring High schools. Fundamentally quite shy, Nelson was awkward with the opposite sex until he realised that he didn't have to do very much more than stand there with a guitar.

At first he had school girlfriends, someone to take to the movies or into town on the weekends, and it was all quite demure until he started playing the night clubs regularly. Then, he would watch the evening shaping up from a safe vantage point on the stage and 'see who was left at the end of the dance'.[15] It's a basic musician's ploy he honed and perfected long into later life. If the girls had had a drink, all the better. Sex was certainly on the agenda. People married young in poor, rural communities anyway, but the process was often speeded up a touch because the girl had already fallen pregnant. Even today, the age of consent remains a pretty loose rule of thumb in Texas in the eyes of the law and, although it had risen from ten to eighteen and then back to sixteen in Texas in the years between 1891 and the end of World War II, it was largely a matter between you and your conscience. Nelson had a fan club of sorts, and it seems he made the most of it.

If the concerts and late nights in honky-tonks were turning his head and opening his eyes to life as an adult, his more creative musical side was a private thing, kept even from his closest friends.

Jack Clements: He'd spend a lot of time [at my house] and at night before we'd go to sleep he'd make up songs about horses or something like that. Of course, I didn't think anything about it. He'd make up songs, but I don't recall him actually putting them on paper.

In fact, Nelson was writing avidly. He had started penning little poems almost as soon as he could write, and into his teenage years he compiled a book of fifteen songs and titled it the 'Songs Of Willie Nelson', complete with index and page references. He was aping his heroes, a common enough conceit for a boy whose head had already been turned by being on stage and on the radio. The songs were called things like 'You'll Still Belong To Me' and 'Starting Tonight', which began, 'Starting tonight/ Your daddy's gonna start living right/ Starting tonight/ I'll never more roam.' Also included was a song called 'The Storm Has Just Begun', which would become one of the first two songs he recorded. It was classic tear-stained country, with some jazzy chords thrown in; it was OK.

He had already decided what he wanted to do, and he couldn't do it in Abbott. In his graduation photograph in the 1949–50 issue of *The Panther*, the school yearbook, he stares out sullenly. He is the only one of the other pupils on the page not smiling, and the only one of the boys not wearing a tie and his Sunday best. He was long gone before it was even taken.

NO SUCH THING AS AN EX-WIFE

W illie Nelson's joint has gone out and he is talking about marriage. He has been married almost continually since the age of eighteen. Indeed, at one point in the early-70s he was married to two people at the same time. 'Well, with marriages, there's nothing perfect,' he says, nodding to himself. 'There's always something a little wrong with it, but you try and live with it the way it is and hope that the next marriage will be better.'

He nods again and takes a swig from a gigantic drum of water in front of him. Nelson has had four wives and still lays some kind of claim on them all, despite the fact that two of them are dead and the other divorced him.

'There is no such thing as an ex-wife, there are only additional wives,' he continues. 'It's an accumulation. It's a fact: there is some reason you married the first one and there's some reason you're going with the next one.'

He has been married to Annie D'Angelo for fifteen years. He calls her his 'current wife'. It's as though he's still expecting another to come along or for something to go horribly wrong. Old habits die hard. He writes his songs without any regard for the signals or messages his wife may interpret in them. In any case, he is sure she doesn't spend much time contemplating the matter.

'My current wife doesn't really worry too much about it. I think she understands that I'm somewhere, and she is somewhere else, and she's not worried about what I'm thinking or writing about. That could no way in the world have anything to do with her. It's completely separate.'

He locks into the kind of eye contact which can make disciples out of people. 'I hope she understands that.'

He maintains eye contact and takes on some more water. There is a pair of white socks under the table in his hotel room, and a small travelling bag on the table. Everything else that matters will be on the bus. His wife is in Hawaii.

2. 1950–1957

The 50s was probably the last era where people could reasonably expect to spend their entire lives in the area in which they had been born. For every wandering Myrle Nelson there were a dozen more who were happy to stay close to the comforts and certainties of home. However, with rapid improvements in transport and a post-war realisation that the world was not quite as large as it once was, the younger generation were beginning to sense wider horizons. Culturally, the notion of travel and discovery was creeping onto the agenda. The Beats were coming: Kerouac's *On The Road* was published in 1957. Marlon Brando and James Dean were reflecting and shaping teenage rebellion in *The Wild One* and *Rebel Without A Cause*, and Elvis Presley was waiting in the wings. Very little of this would have been filtering down to Abbott, Texas, but it was in the air nonetheless. For Willie Nelson, the 50s would be a decade lived on the hoof, consisting of several significant fixed points connected by lines which often meandered, hit dead-ends or double-backed upon themselves, and which – viewed half a century later – occasionally become so entangled they are hard to follow.

All over Texas people were moving, some in pursuit of one vague dream or another, some in retreat from poverty, or attempting to escape the mistakes of their past, or running from responsibility, or in denial over their true identity or destiny. Nelson would fit most of these descriptions at one time or another, and like many other rovers, he was playing music. The first thing any aspiring musician must do is leave the familiar and embrace the notion of constant motion, and it was especially true fifty years ago, before the saturation of television ushered in the rather odd idea of being entertained in your own home by tiny, distant figures on a small screen. Prior to the mass popularity of the 45 single, the 33 album, the cassette, the CD, the Internet, the mp3 or the iPod, not only was the *audience* required to work just that little bit harder to entertain itself, but a musician had to be almost constantly on the move in order to find sufficient numbers to enable him to earn a living. For some reason – its sheer size, its proximity to Mexico, its history, its landscape – Texas seemed to produce more of these wanderers than most places in the States.

Willie Nelson: The question is: why were so many of us [musicians] born down in this part of the country? I really don't know the answer to that, but a lot of us were – and we scattered.[1]

One of the many hundreds of Texan players in the process of 'scattering' was Johnny Bush. Born John Bush Shin III in Houston on 17 February, 1935, Bush was a big baby-faced nineteen-year-old when he first met Nelson in 1954 but, despite their physical differences, each man almost instantly recognised something of the other in themselves.

Johnny Bush: He was a real funny guy, it was one reason why we hit it off: we both had the same sense of humour, a little on the weird side. He was real gutsy, just trying to find his way.

Bush had succumbed to the travelling bug two years earlier when his parents divorced, and headed for San Antonio. He started out as a solo act. He would forever regard himself – and would later demonstrate why he was entirely justified as doing so – as a singer and a songwriter, but he switched to drums because there was more work to be had that way. By 1954 he was singing and drumming with the Mission City Playboys, a local band led by David Isbell, playing San Antonio clubs like the Texas Star Inn, Walter's Ranch House and Al's Country Club; places that sounded a little smarter than they really were.

Johnny Bush: We worked Friday, Saturday and Sunday at Al's Country Club. That was a real joint. An old-fashioned Texas honky-tonk. Today, the word honky-tonk is kinda chic, but if they really knew what a honky-tonk was they wouldn't be using that term today!

Word had got around that Isbell was looking for a fiddle player. One Sunday afternoon a tall, skinny violinist called Cosett Holland walked in to Al's, accompanied by a short, red-headed guitar player he had been playing with locally as a duo. Isbell wanted to hire Holland but wasn't so keen on the guitarist, but he was told that they came as a set. And so Nelson joined the Mission City Playboys in the autumn of 1954. He had come to Al's Country Club by the scenic route. San Antonio is only a three-hour drive south from Abbott, but in the four years since leaving Hill County Nelson had mimicked his mother's wanderlust and traversed great swathes of Texas and beyond in search of a purpose. Along the way he had acquired armfuls of life experiences, not to mention a wife and a daughter.

He had departed Abbott in 1950 with predictable haste. 'Everybody kinda lost track of him for a little while,' recalls Jack Clements. 'He knew what he wanted to do, it just took him a while to get started.' Initially, he had fallen in with his new friend Zeke Varnon, with whom he had become tight in his senior year at school. Varnon was several years older than Nelson – many of his early friends were slightly older boys – and had already been around the block a few times. They egged each other on, taking pride in their near-the-knuckle escapades. Throughout the summer of 1950 and into autumn they moved around, sharing a place in Waco, then spending time in Tyler, about a hundred miles east of Dallas, where Nelson worked with Varnon trimming trees for eighty cents an hour.

They were broke but scraped together enough money for a car, taking off to Fort Worth or Hillsboro or Waco to seek their kicks. Their collective appetites could be encapsulated simply: drinking beer, playing dominoes, chasing girls and seeking out low-level trouble. Nelson was, on the surface, still the quiet, polite young man he had been through school, but already there was evidence of a reckless streak that bordered on the self-destructive. He often seemed not to care much about what might happen to him as a by-product of keeping himself amused.

Zeke Varnon: He had more moxie [guts] in those days than anybody I ever saw. One night we were sitting in Scotty's Tavern, playing dominoes and watching the Monday night fights on TV. A guy at the bar is making comments like he is some kind of expert. Willie says, 'I'll bet you ten bucks on the fighter in the white shorts.' We didn't have a dollar between us. If Willie had lost that bet they'd have beat pure hell out of us.[2]

There are many examples of these kinds of tests. It was a macho thing, most certainly, a little bit of the set-'em-up-and-shoot-'em-down cowboy mentality held over from his Abbott schooldays, but it was more than mere bravado. Plain mischief-making accounts for much of it, but there was something more. It was as if he was challenging the world and he didn't care too much if he lost. A very attractive quality in a young man, but also a pretty desperate one.

Having suffered a painful fall from a tree whilst working, and tired of being broke and having to scrabble for every cent, Nelson enlisted in the

US Air Force in late 1950. The Korean War had begun in the summer of that year, and when he turned eighteen in less than six months' time he would be required to report to the draft board and await military deployment. He preferred to have some choice in the matter and signed up voluntarily. In December he was sent to Lackland Air Force Base in San Antonio to undertake basic training. Straight away he was marched into the barbershop to have his proud pompadour shaved to the skull. There were no barracks, only tents. He was unceremoniously roused for a gruelling run at 4 a.m. every day, and on top of all that it rained constantly. Almost the first thing anyone had said to him when he arrived was: 'You fucked up.' He was inclined to agree.

He wasn't academically cut out to be pilot material. He was always a sharp, bright boy – and an exceptionally switched-on adult – but it was not a sophisticated intelligence. It wasn't measured in certificates or book learning; it was raw and instinctive, and not suited to much beyond manual work, which is all most of the males from Abbott were expected to undertake. Further military training in Wichita Falls led to another relocation to a base near Belleville, just east of St Louis, Illinois, but it could as well have been anywhere. He sloshed around while they worked out what to do with him, drinking, playing poker. He was finally given the choice between being a radar mechanic or a medic. He chose radar but failed to grasp the technical side of it and so was moved to the medics. It sounded grand, but in practical terms it meant a job lifting boxes in Biloxi, Missouri.

His back – already a little out of shape from pulling corn in his schooldays – had been further damaged in the fall from the tree, and the heavy manual work in Missouri exacerbated it. He sensed an opportunity to leave. Although Biloxi had been something of an improvement on Illinois, in that it had given him the chance to play guitar at the Airmen's club and thus also the opportunity to meet and bed some local girls, he was sick of the discipline of the military life and wanted out. Eventually, after nine months in which he felt he had achieved nothing, the state of his back earned him a medical discharge, and by late 1951 he was back living at Mama Nelson's house in Abbott, perhaps a little chastened, playing again with Bud Fletcher and the Texans and anyone else who would have him.

He fell for Martha Jewel Matthews from the stage of the 31 Club on Corsicana Road just east of Waco. She was a regular. Even at sixteen, she loved to go out and dance her way between all the honky-tonks lined up from her home in Waco out to West. She may even have seen Nelson before at the Nite Owl or one of the other regular spots he played. He had certainly seen her: hair so black it was almost blue, eyes like coal, olive-skinned, five feet seven inches tall and every inch of it ready to grab life by the throat. She was the original good-time girl, a teenager before the term had even been coined: loud, fun, a little aggressive, the life and soul of the party and used to getting her own way no matter what.

'Martha did love a good time,' Nelson later recalled. 'She had a lot of friends and she danced a lot.'[3] She was a familiar breed – he could as well be describing Myrle. Their courtship consisted of little more than Martha coming to see him at the 31 Club whenever he was there, or him visiting her at the Lone-Oak Drive Inn on the New Dallas Highway in Waco where she worked as a waitress. Martha's parents were much like Nelson's grandparents: hard-working, fundamentally religious people who frowned upon too much frivolity or carousing. Their daughter defied them frequently to visit the clubs, just like she defied them over her choice of boyfriend. They disapproved of her penniless, rough-around-the-edges guitar player, which may be one of the reasons they wed so quickly. They 'ran away' to Cleburne, a town only a few miles north of Hillsboro, and got married in the basement of the courthouse in February 1952, without either the presence or knowledge of their respective families.

The groom was eighteen. By his own family's standards, at least, Nelson had left it late, but he had known Martha for only a few months, perhaps even weeks, and in hindsight they should both have spent some time taking the temperature of their relationship before running up the aisle. As it was, they were utterly consumed by young love, and not a little lust, and they jumped right in. In time the relationship would fuel some of his most despairing songs and come to confirm his worst suspicions – about himself, and women, and life – but on his wedding day he couldn't believe he had managed to a snare such a sexy, desirable young bride.

Johnny Bush: She was the most beautiful thing. Three-quarters, I guess, Cherokee, raven-haired, brown-eyed, tall. Beautiful. She was the sweetest thing in the world until she got mad or drunk – or both.

Initially ostracised by the Matthews family, they moved in with Mama Nelson in Abbott – always there, always happy to help – and set about fathoming the mysterious art of being man and wife. It was an absolute shock to the system for Martha, whose middle name of Jewel apparently denoted that she was a princess in the eyes of her parents. An only child, she had never even washed a dish before she moved to Abbott and was entirely spoiled rotten. Nobody stood to attention in the Nelson homestead and Martha had little choice but to learn to earn her keep, but life quite quickly became strained.

They had their good times, of course. They both knew how to have fun and made little effort to change their habits. Martha still worked as a waitress and frequented the clubs whenever she could; her husband was still playing around the towns, although he was struggling to get by – what money he made, he quickly spent, a recurring theme from now until far into the future. It would be perfectly normal for him to stand playing guitar on stage with Bud Fletcher and watch Martha dancing on the floor, or even working behind the bar, in the same club. It sounds cosy but they were so young they struggled to cope with the reality of it.

Willie Nelson: Anybody she would look at, I'd be pissed off. Anybody I'd look at, she'd be pissed off. We were extremely jealous of each other, seeing just how much we could do to each other and get away with it.[4]

Both of them, particularly Martha, thrived on the tension, but it was exhausting. Nelson effectively began testing the strength of Martha's love. He liked women and they liked him, and he felt a certain security in having his wife shouting accusations of infidelity – or at least inappropriate flirtations – at him. He was also a product of his time and place: he never would be first in line for any awards for his contribution to the feminist cause, and he felt that as long as he was earning a little money and providing some kind of home for them both he could pretty much do what he wanted. On the other hand, Martha was so striking and attracted so much attention he could hardly believe that she could be faithful. After all, his role models had not been promising. He was well versed in the mechanics of abandonment and deep down had very few expectations that someone as beautiful and flighty as his wife would stick around for the long run. He loved her, but he was already preparing for the worst. He needed options.

They were mere teenagers, and singularly ill-equipped to iron out their differences in a sensible manner. They left Abbott and headed for Eugene, Oregon in late 1952 to stay with Myrle and her husband for a while, seeking pastures new and trying to earn a little more money. They financed the trip by taking a job delivering a car from Texas to Eugene. It was not a happy journey. The marriage had settled into a routine of rows, accusations, periods of intense fun, sex and even romance, then more rows again. Martha was not impressed by her husband's inability to keep even the most menial of jobs. 'He lost more damn jobs in a month than most people have in a lifetime,' she later said. 'All he wanted to do was pick that damn guitar.'[5] His musical career had effectively gone nowhere in the three years since he had left school – indeed, he was earning less now than he had been when he was thirteen and working beer halls with Bud Fletcher. In Eugene, Nelson worked as a plumber for a while and played briefly with a band on the *Hayloft Jamboree* programme on the local radio station, KUGN. Martha continued to wait tables; it soon became apparent there was little reason to stay long.

Martha fell pregnant and the couple returned to the open arms of Mama Nelson in Abbott to await the baby. She was born on 11 November 1953, in hospital in Hillsboro, and christened De Lana Nelson. The birth of his first child caused Nelson to be physically ill in the hospital. Whether he was scared of the implications or simply squeamish is hard to say. But it caused him to think a little harder about the future, that's for sure.

Since its creation in 1845, Baylor University has made its home in the series of distinctive, austere red-brick buildings which sit amidst 750 acres in the centre of Waco. It houses the premier collection of the poet Robert Browning's life works in the domed, somewhat ostentatious surroundings of the Armstrong Browning Library, and attracts some of the most prestigious academics and writers in the world through its doors on visiting lectures. As you might expect from the largest Baptist university in the world, it is a conservative campus, broadly Christian in thought and deed. This was even more emphatically the case in 1954. Waco itself was in a state of mild shock. Its population of 85,000 was in the process of dusting itself down following the deadly tornado of 11 May 1953, which killed 114 people and virtually destroyed the city centre. Even today as you drive around there are huge gaping holes in the city's fabric where a building was destroyed by the tornado and never rebuilt. A visitor can't help wondering whether the storm knocked much of the personality out of the place as well.

There may have been no dancing, no sororities or fraternities, no smoking inside the student centre and very few ethnic minorities at Baylor, but one obvious incongruity was the high proportion of military ex-servicemen among its 6,000 students, perhaps as high as twenty per cent. This would be a remarkable statistic today, but was fairly ordinary back in the 50s. Following World War II, the American GI Bill programme paid a weekly wage to ex-servicemen if they wanted to pursue further education. The men on the GI Bill brought a little bit of the real world into the Baptist propriety of the campus. Many of them were in their twenties, had families, would drink, smoke and swear. Nelson became one of their number on 9 March 1954, when he cashed in his GI Bill chips and signed up for the full fifteen-hours-per-week course for the spring quarter of the academic year.

What was he thinking? Clearly a 22-year-old guitar player with no house, no money, no steady job, a wife and a newborn baby would – to a greater or lesser extent – be aware that he needed to stop messing around with his life. Even if self-improvement was not his basic motivation, it would have got Martha, back waitressing in West, off his case for a while. Equally, he might simply have been running out of ideas and taken an easy option. The campus was only a few miles down the road from Abbott and he had his weekly $26 of GI money to support him. He later claimed he had some vague idea of becoming a lawyer, but in reality all his short stint at Baylor succeeded in doing was cementing, once and for all, his determination to work in music.

Willie Nelson: I was there long enough to realise that I really wanted to play music more than I wanted to be a lawyer. But I had a good time while I was going there. I had some good teachers, and in class I made some new friends.[6]

One of these new friends was Jack Loftis, who originally hailed from Hillsboro and went on to become a respected journalist and editor of the

Houston Chronicle. Loftis recalls a polite young gentleman, reserved and clean-cut with his short hair, jeans or khakis, never once, to his knowledge, associated with trouble. He was a bit of a loner, playing dominoes and drinking with 'whomever was available' at the Rendezvous on Fifth Street when he should have been studying. Someone who was amiable and popular but a little unknowable. Nelson often joined a carpool with Loftis and others who lived back north up the I-35, and the one thing they quickly found out about him was that he was hooked on music. Waco was a thriving hub at the time: the likes of Slim Whitman, Faron Young, the Maddox Brothers and Hank Thompson had all been recent visitors to the city's clubs, which attracted students and general citizens alike from all over central Texas. Nelson was a little further down the ladder, still playing long nights in honky-tonks throughout his time at Baylor, still hooking up with Bud Fletcher's band and even taking the Interurban railroad up to Hillsboro to pick his guitar on street corners.

Jack Loftis: There was never a doubt that music was his main interest. I never thought he would be ambitious enough to leave central Texas, but that was about par for the course for all of us back then. He was playing pure country honky-tonk songs of that era. I remember he liked Bob Wills and the Texas Playboys, as did just about everyone else. His [voice] was quite ordinary. Most of us thought Willie was great, but few ever dreamed he would become an icon.

His classic wisecrack about his time at university was that 'he majored in dominoes',[7] and it's true that he was largely absent from his classes the whole time between his enrolment until his premature departure on 10 July 1954, halfway through the summer quarter. But among the six courses he took – which ranged from business and plane trigonometry to history – was one which held some genuine significance: Speech and Radio 105, an introductory study of radio and TV. He had definite ambitions to become a disc jockey, whether as an end in itself or as a means to getting his songs heard. Many singers in those days served an apprenticeship working in radio, and taking a course on speech and radio was a conscious move. Nelson has been – and can be – a sight more calculating than he is often portrayed. 'I do recall his talking about his plans to drop out of Baylor and seek work as a disc jockey or musician,' says Loftis. He was, in fact, about to do both.

His presence was barely missed, and is hardly celebrated even now. He is not a student that the university remembers with any pride, and indeed a Willie Nelson concert scheduled to be held on campus in 1988 was cancelled by the university president: 'It is our hope that he will use his influence in the future to strengthen the moral fibre of our nation,' he announced, unamused by his public endorsement of marijuana. 'Our concern for the health and well-being of the American people is an overriding one.' It was one of the rare instances where Nelson vented his fury in public. 'Maybe the guy felt sanctimonious, like his hallowed hall was too good for me,' he responded. 'It makes me mad. Waco is my home town.'[8]

He and Martha and little Lana headed south for San Antonio, where Johnny Bush, the Mission City Playboys and the delights of Al's Country Club were waiting. He found a city like no other. Home of the Alamo, it is a bustling, colourful, cramped place, filled with noise and music and wearing its history on its sleeve. Built on the banks of the San Antonio river in south-west Texas, it is defined by its geography. Mexico is a mere two hours away, and many Texans drive down to Laredo or another of the grey border towns to regularly stock up on cheap cigarettes and alcohol. It is, perhaps surprisingly, America's ninth largest city, with a population nearing 2,000,000, well over 50 per cent of which are of Hispanic origin.

Nelson came here in 1954. He has previously stated that he arrived in San Antonio in 1953, but Johnny Bush recalls that baby Lana was already several months old when they first met and that Nelson mentioned he had recently attended university – it's likely the date has simply become confused in the mists of time. The city already had a distinctive flavour, with a heavy Mexican presence as well as many native Americans. San Antonio was undergoing a growth spurt, in the process of virtually doubling its population every ten years, and it was home to about 500,000 residents. It was by far the biggest place Nelson and Martha had ever lived, and its temptations and trials weren't perhaps the best influence on their marriage. Martha was always suspicious of her husband's activities, and though she was wrong in the beginning, she 'wasn't wrong for very long',[9] according to Nelson.

There was simply little that could be done. Nelson was discovering quite quickly that he wasn't really cut out for marriage. Without the support network of family and old friends, Martha was left literally holding the baby most of the time, and she resented the late nights he spent playing in clubs, getting up to God knows what. She wanted to be out there too, and not necessarily with him. They would fight almost constantly upon his return. The family were living in a large house in Florida Street in the south side of the city, shared with other members of the Mission City Playboys: steel player Carl Walder and his wife Dottie had a couple of rooms at the front, the Nelsons were holed up in the back, and Cosett Holland hung some curtains to screen off the dining room and set up his bed in there. It was not a particularly serene environment for the fiddle player. Walder and his wife fought almost as frequently as Nelson and Martha, while he was stuck in the middle, hiding behind his curtain.

Johnny Bush: Usually, Willie prompted it. She took it out on him, and I think toe to toe she could have probably whipped him. I've seen the battle scars several times. He'd come to work with scratches and Band-aids. She thrived on it, [but] I don't think he liked it so much – maybe he did, or he wouldn't have stayed with her as long as he did. They [could be] great together, but it was World War III about two or three times a week. I drove up one day and got out of the car, and I looked up [to see] Willie running out of the back door full throttle, and a pot was following him. He was outrunning the pot. When he saw me he turned, and when he turned the pot went straight into the garage. He looked at me and said, 'She loves me. Gimme a cigarette.' It didn't seem to bother him at all that she was mad enough to throw a pot which could have really hurt him. That went on all the time. But there were a lot of laughs, too, it wasn't all like that.

A proper job helped a little. Nelson became the morning disc jockey at KBOP radio station in Pleasanton, a small, rural town about thirty miles south of San Antonio. Just as almost every little backwater in the 40s and 50s had a dance hall, so many of them also had a local radio station. KBOP was founded in February 1951 by Dr Ben Parker, a chiropractor by trade, and operated on a modest scale. His wife Mona was the engineer.

KBOP was considered one of the first small-town country music stations in Texas, an antidote to the slicker sounds of big band music and Frank Sinatra types which WOAI would play in San Antonio. It could broadcast over a hundred-mile radius on a good clear day, and built up a decent-sized audience. Nelson got the gig through sheer chutzpah. He overstated his credentials, exaggerated his experiences at KHBR in Hillsboro, bluffed his way through the technical side, and in general thoroughly messed up his audition. However, Dr Parker loved him. They had a very fond and close relationship for many years, a little reminiscent of father and son. He was hired on the strength of his personality as much as anything else – people just liked him, his mix of shyness and mischief. Also, the station had very few other options.

Charlotte Ramsay: Most people know if they wanted to make it as a DJ they had to start at the little stations, because they'll hire anybody! Just about anybody could pass the test. So you're pretty lenient about who you hire.

His wages were $40 a week, a small but decent enough salary. His job was to open the station at dawn each morning and stay on air for about four hours until the next DJ came along. Programming was half in English and half in Spanish; Nelson worked the English side of the fence. There wasn't much room for improvisation. In those days, programmes were typed up in advance and you were effectively told what your programme would consist of prior to going on air. There was no room for shock jocks; all air space was logged and signed for. Advertising was king, and there would only be time for a couple of country songs before he had to read out some adverts. It was very commercial and competitive. Once he came off air one of Nelson's other tasks was to sell air space, though he had little appetite for that. But it was work and it was in the music industry, and in many ways he was lucky just to have a job at all.

The task of opening at the station at daybreak could hardly have been given to a less capable candidate. He was playing weekends with the Mission City Playboys and often didn't get off stage until one in the morning. Then he would go home and grab some sleep – or sometimes stay up through the night – and try to get down to Pleasanton for 4.30 a.m. Dr Parker and his wife would wake up and turn on the radio in their bedroom, waiting to see if he had made it. More often than not he hadn't, and the residents of south Texas were greeted with a grave silence when they switched on their sets as they headed off to the fields or into town. Trying to get him up in the morning was, according to his wife, 'the damnedest thing you ever saw. He could sleep through a darn tornado.'[10]

Johnny Bush also started working sessions at the studio. They were all in and around each other's business – Bush had his own sideline band, Johnny Bush and his Hillbilly Playboys, which Nelson was 'exclusively managing' – and Nelson managed to find room for his friend at KBOP. Bush's weather forecasts were legendary: 'I had a very scientific method. I'd just look out the window and report what I saw. I was 100 per cent.' He and Nelson and another DJ called Red Hillburn each had a fifteen-minute slot which they were supposed to fill each week by finding interesting musicians to play and interview. The three of them quickly turned these spots into a little self-publicising scam.

Johnny Bush: Red would go on and do his fifteen minutes, and have Willie as his guest. Well, I would do my show and have Red as my guest. Then Willie would come on and do his fifteen minutes show, and have me as his guest. Out of three of us, we would get thirty minutes each. It was troubadour style.

This went on for three or four weeks, until Dr Parker finally put his foot down; he came in and informed them that if they didn't go out and actually interview someone else, they were all fired. It was an empty threat. He loved them, and Nelson loved the work – if not the hours – and the tiny bit of local celebrity it gave him. Indeed, it was such a secure job that at some point Martha, Lana and Nelson left San Antonio and rented an apartment in Pleasanton itself, perhaps in a bid to get him to work on time.

Aside from playing with the band and working on the radio, he was trying to work on his own material. The very first songs he ever recorded were taped in the KBOP studio in early 1955. As a DJ, he had the perfect opportunity to record a demo for next to nothing, using old reel-to-reel tape from previous broadcasts. With just his voice and an acoustic guitar, he cut 'The Storm Has Just Begun', written back in Abbott a decade earlier, and 'When I've Sang My Last Hillbilly Song'. Neither was a particularly inspiring effort, nor did they have the virtue of being distinctive. They followed traditional country structures and Nelson had yet to find his true voice – he sang on the beat and with little flair, with none of the jazzy phrasing or metre-messing which later made him stand out. He sent the recordings to Charlie Fitch, the producer at the influential local label SARG which had already released two singles by Dave Isbell on which Nelson played guitar.

Johnny Bush: They naturally turned him down. I still have that old tape. He used an old studio tape – of a farm market report – and you can hear it in the background! At the time, my impression of him was as a guitar player. I even made a comment to him one time that he ought to stick to playing the guitar and let me do the singing. I liked his playing better than his singing. He never forgot that! Knowing Willie like I do, why would he give a damn what I thought one way or the other? But even to this day he still brings it up. But you listen to that tape and you can see why I said that.

The KBOP demo of 'The Storm Has Just Begun' does throw in a few neat jazz moves on the guitar which were somewhat out of the ordinary for the genre, but nobody in south Texas was looking for the next Django Reinhardt. However, it meant a lot to him that he was a good guitar player. He will still claim that it is what he works hardest at, recognising it as a discipline that was endlessly variable, limitlessly expressive, and ultimately unmasterable.

Merle Haggard: Knowing him personally, he's studied that bugger like I have. He would be sitting there and we'd both have the same blank looks on our faces about how to understand it. It is a monster.

Nelson was disillusioned with the rejection, especially as it hadn't been the only one. For several months he had been sending his songs not just to SARG but to other labels as well. Nobody was interested. He walked into KBOP and told Dr Parker, 'I've had it, I'm not going to do it any more,' and threw a sheaf of his songs into the bin in disgust. Parker pulled them out and said: 'A lot of people aren't famous until they die. It's going to take you a long time. You're very talented, don't give it up. Keep your day job, but keep doing what you're doing.'

He perhaps held this advice too closely to his heart. To observe the years between 1955 and 1958 from this distance is like looking at a hamster on a wheel. The locations change but the song is on repeat. There he goes: heading into a new city, picking up some DJ work, working nights with any band he can find, arguing with Martha about money and women – she would always feel that there wasn't nearly enough of the former and a few too many dalliances with the latter – until the only thing that could be done was to move on, in the hope that their life somehow wouldn't follow them. But bad luck proved less easy to shake off than bad debts. 'They were,' recalls Johnny Bush, 'wild and desperate times. We were all struggling just to make a living.' Each time the rent was due, it was time to move.

Charlotte Ramsay: Willie was always broke and he was always in trouble. Not so much in trouble with the law, but with the bills and stuff. He had a little apartment and an old car and he was just really not doing well. At that time he didn't have much to offer.

But for the first time in his life he had something approaching a career. After Pleasanton he moved his family to Fort Worth, back into familiar central Texas territory and close to his father Ira and his second wife Lorraine. He moved into a three-room apartment and quickly found work at a tiny 250-watt station called KDNT in Denton, about sixty miles north of Fort Worth. If anything, it was a step down from Pleasanton. The station had been built in a burned-out building and when the copywriter walked into the control room her footfall would knock the arm off the record.

He worked there for about nine months, earning $40 a week, until a better job came along at KCNC in Fort Worth itself. KCNC was still a local station, but it was a city station and it was much more professional. Nelson worked the morning shift and then presented an afternoon show called *The Western Express*, where he could perform for the opening half-hour of the three-hour show. He began to enjoy himself and the response from the public seemed to indicate that they enjoyed him too, but things were still rocky. One of the songs Nelson wrote around this time was called 'Too Young To Settle Down' and it was all too autobiographical. Johnny Bush had married and moved back to Houston for a spell, and he and his wife would travel up to Fort Worth to see them. He was impressed by the strides his friend was making in his career, but rather dismayed at the state of his marriage. Martha had become pregnant again in the late spring of 1956, but nothing had changed.

Johnny Bush: He was doing rather well. On the Fourth of July weekend [of 1956] we went up to visit for a few days, and Willie was good. He was a very popular DJ and all the musicians knew him. During that week, Willie was showing me some guitar licks, and Martha said, 'Willie, put up the damn guitar.' He just ignored her and kept playing. 'I *said*, put up the damn guitar, we wanna visit.' After the third time I heard this noise, this missile coming through the air. It was a bottle of hair tonic. She threw it at him and he ducked, it hit the lamp, went through the lampshade and smashed the light bulb. And he looked up at me and said: 'Well, John, I guess we should put the guitars up, we've done enough for today.'

On another occasion he came home late. He had played a poker joint where he was making $8 a night – the same wage he was picking up when he was thirteen – and then stopped at the 811 Club for a pot of coffee and a game on the pinball machines which paid out in cash. He got home and walked through the door to be met once again with a hail of pots and pans, Martha's favourite means of showing her displeasure. He seemed to take it all. For a man with a lethal temper, he knew where to draw the line.

Paul English: He was the kind of guy who would never hit back. Martha would beat him up and he'd never fight back. I learned a lot from things like that.

Home was only marginally safer than the clubs he was playing. Fort Worth was like Sodom and Gomorrah twinned with Dodge City. Actually, its closest comparison was Prohibition-era Chicago, riddled as it was with gang feuds, violent crime, prostitution, drugs and guns. Fort Worth had risen up as an annex to oil-rich Dallas, just a few miles to the east, and was the equivalent of a down-at-heel outhouse tacked on to an elegant townhouse. It had its mainstream establishment venues such as the Skyline or the Rocket Club, but the real centre of the action was Jacksonboro Highway, a five-mile strip of nightclubs and throbbing neon which conducted itself in the manner of some Wild West town from the previous century.

There were several murders, frequent stabbings, nightly fights, and all manner of attendant dangers. One beer joint was called the County Dump, next to the real dump and without even a telephone. The stage at the Mountaineer Club was situated behind the bar for safety reasons, while the S&S Club was subject to a boycott by its regular musicians because playing it was such a hairy experience: many players, including Nelson, were hit with beer bottles. The club responded by putting chicken wire across the front of the stage to protect the musicians – and the fights went on. Another club was simply called the Bloody Bucket. It made the Nite Owl back near Abbott look like the Albert Hall.

Nelson learned a lot in Fort Worth. He refined the economical stagecraft of Bob Wills to even greater lengths: stop for no one, say nothing, keep your head down or at least your eyes straight ahead. He played with black and Mexican musicians for the first time, which brought a few extra strings to his bow. He added more overt jazz and blues songs to his repertoire onstage. He saw that there really were no boundaries to music.

Willie Nelson: When you played a club in Texas back then, you had to do 'San Antonio Rose' and you had to do 'Stardust', because those people didn't know what was country and what wasn't. They [hadn't] been educated that music is separated. Back then, you just took requests and if you knew the song you played it.'[11]

He also smoked pot for the first time and – like many steady drinkers – found it a little pointless: it would take years for that particular love to take hold. He became accustomed to the company of criminals, and found that they could be fun, as well as useful and helpful. He has always loved cutting deals and has scant regard for authority. His essential moral core was formed in Abbott, but his adult code of honour was really established in the bars of Fort Worth.

He loved the drama and the loyalty. Later, in the 70s, he would befriend the Hell's Angels, entranced by these big, violent, frequently highly intelligent men with their codes and sentimental brand of fraternal love. His Family Band have fulfilled much the same purpose over the years. What he could never seemingly find in a conventional family of husband, wife and children, he found in the cowboy stereotypes of male bonding. In Fort Worth, he would judge people as he found them and make few assumptions. He liked being on the outer edges of criminality and recognised the echoes of old-time Wild West values: loyalty, courtesy, do-unto-others. He liked to sit back and watch them at work and play. It was Damon Runyon in oil country. He began to carry a gun in his guitar case; everyone else did.

But his luck was failing. 1956 was the time of Elvis Presley and rock 'n' roll hysteria. Those who disliked rock 'n' roll became more firmly entrenched in their views and upheld the populist status quo of Pat Boone and Doris Day, but many nightclubs had to start booking acts which reflected the changing times. The teenager was arriving, and he was powerful. The rawness of old-time country had been superseded by something new and wonderfully vibrant, and eventually country music would give up the ghost and dissolve into the saccharine, polished gloop which spewed out of Nashville with production line monotony for much of the next decade. Willie Nelson would later feel the impact of that, too, on a more significant level, when he set up shop in Music Row. But for now rock 'n' roll was simply a contributory factor in a whole host of reasons which ensured he couldn't make ends meet.

There would always be a place in Texas for the old-fashioned honky-tonks and skull orchards of Fort Worth, but there was less work to go around and someone in his position was not at the front of the queue. Also, the dangerous nature of the country clubs meant that there was little media interest in who played there. The bottom line was: even with his DJ-ing and his moonlighting, he was still flat broke.

Johnny Bush: Between jobs if he got broke he would hawk his guitar for rent and grocery money. Then a [gig] would come up and he wouldn't have the guitar to play the job. That happened more than once.

With Martha and Lana and their unborn baby in tow, he picked up sticks again. The hamster prepared himself for a few more circuits of the wheel. He tried San Diego but he couldn't play unless he paid $100 to the union. They headed back to Oregon, this time to Portland, where his mother was now living. They stayed with Myrle for a while then moved into a house on 148th Street, across the Columbia river in Vancouver. His second daughter was born there on 20 January 1957, and they called her Susie. There was more DJ work with KVAN on Main Street. He called himself Wee Willie Nelson – other DJs included Shorty the Hired Hand and 'Cactus' Ken DeBord – and was a great success, by all accounts, although the wage was meagre. He played a little. For about six months he was a member of Roger Crandall and the Barn Dance Boys, even appearing on local musician Heck Harper's TV show, and would check out whoever happened to be playing at the Frontier Room club across from the radio station. On the surface, things seemed good, but still it wasn't happening the way he wanted it to. It was slow work in the North.

Willie Nelson: I don't know if you could call it a [music scene] or not. There were a few good bands around that I used to go and play [with], whenever I could find a job somewhere around Portland or Vancouver.[12]

Whatever he earned he spent. It was all getting a little too depressing. Almost within six months of Susie being born, Martha was pregnant again. Nelson would tell his wife that everything was going to be all right, and she would reply: 'Ain't nothing goin' to be all right.' He asked, or rather he told KVAN that he needed an extra $100 a week or else he would have to leave. Then leave, they said. He had recently interviewed the songwriter Mae Axton on his show. She was the composer of 'Heartbreak Hotel' and was on tour with Hank Snow, handling his PR. He cornered her afterwards and played her some of his own songs, and she told him what he already knew: he was in the wrong place. He left town with the same question he had been carrying around in his head for the past seven years: where was the right place?

LABOUR PAINS

Willie Nelson is talking about writing songs.

He has been doing it for nearly seventy years and yet still finds it an odd, uncomfortable experience, somewhere between a drag and a beautiful compulsion.

'It's kind of like labour pains,' he says. 'When something comes along, if it worries you enough then you have to write about it. That's good. I want to be worried by it. You gotta do it. It's labour pains.'

Something seems to occur to him. ''Course, I don't have to write.'

Once upon a time he had to write. Once upon a time it put food on his table, but more than that, he had to write because the things that were happening to him demanded some kind of release. He leans back on the sofa, exhales, and looks deep into the past. It's not possible to follow him. He remembers what worried him into writing songs like 'Crazy' and 'Night Life', but he doesn't want to remember out loud.

'Oh, you could pin me down,' he sighs. He stands up and readies himself for the bathroom. 'I probably wouldn't be able to tell you whether it was a Thursday or not. They were either my experiences or yours, you know? That's what I always wrote about, what I knew about or saw.'

He is still standing up, his hand on the door knob.

'I knew pretty early in life that what I'm thinking is not that far from what you're thinking, and what makes you happy, laugh or cry, is probably going to make me happy or laugh or cry. Once you realise that you're the same as the audience, then everything else is pretty simple. You just do what you like.'

He doesn't write too much any more. One or two truly great songs slip out each decade, but most of the time he just jots down what he calls 'mind farts'. He has chosen to become an interpreter – as much of his own songs as other people's – rather than a creator. More than anything, he is a communicator. A point of connection.

'If you're a singer you can get up in front of an audience and sing songs that you know communicate,' he explains. 'It doesn't matter whether you wrote them or not. I play "Stardust" and "Georgia On My Mind" because I know that these songs are not only great and I love to sing them, but probably more important is the fact that everybody in that audience will like them. Whether they've ever heard them or not, they're going to like it.'

He smiles. 'You don't have to write 'em. Just sing 'em.'

He looks suddenly relieved. He opens the door and disappears from view.

3. 1958–1961

W hat does it mean to an artist when he plays a song almost fifty years after he wrote it? What does it signify to him? When Willie Nelson slips 'Night Life' into his medley of old classics in concert each night, is he immediately transported back to the stretch of highway between Houston and Pasadena where he first pieced together the song in his head; is his sleeve still tugged by the lure of the clubs which kept calling him, despite the infidelities, marital fights, hangovers and numerous small humiliations which they meted out in return? Does he feel the phantom pains of those draining days on the road somewhere in the pit of his stomach, or is he – to borrow Brian Eno's classic analogy of onstage detachment – simply thinking about his laundry?

More than any of these things, the fact that the song has stood up to almost five decades of constant wear and tear and who-knows-how-many performances tells him that he has created a timeless piece of art. It tells him he has succeeded. Up until the point when he wrote it, Nelson had offered up nothing out of the ordinary, nothing truly special. He was concentrating primarily on being a performer and – probably more than anything else – a guitarist, and though he could write songs at the drop of a hat, he was spending too little time on the craft to create anything that transcended mere competent imitation.

Willie Nelson: When I was playing clubs in Texas, before I went to Nashville, my songwriting was secondary then. I was earning a living as a singer and guitar player.[1] I didn't come up with anything I thought was worth anything until I was 20 to 25 years old.[2]

He left a slight but useful trail of evidence behind him, which largely backs up his analysis. Following on from his failed demos at KBOP in 1955, he had made a handful of slightly more polished recordings. Back in Vancouver in 1957 he'd cut a single, again using equipment which he could access through the radio station, recording it in a friend's garage and paying for it to be issued independently under his own label: Willie Nelson Records.

In a typewritten, KVAN-headed letter to Don Pierce, the president of the Nashville-based record company Starday which was pressing it for him, he wrote: 'This is the kind of label I would like to have if possible: background in black and letters in yellow.' He accompanies his note with a crude sketch of the record, with the words Willie Nelson prominently displayed, and signs off: 'P.S. Check enclosed.' He was only 24 and clearly rather excited. 'It was,' he later admitted, 'a magic thing.'[3]

The songs he cut in Vancouver were his own 'No Place For Me' and Leon Payne's 'Lumberjack'. He sold the single hard over the airwaves on his radio show for $1, and for your dollar you also got a slick black and white autographed photograph. He always had an eye for a good deal, and it eventually shifted about 500 copies. 'No Place For Me' is very reminiscent of Johnny Cash's early Sun sides, 78 seconds of boom-chicka-boom, drenched in reverb, with bass and pedal steel buried in the mix. It nonetheless displays a believable sense of disaffection with his life and his wife: 'Your love is as cold as the north wind that blows/ And the river that runs to the sea,' it begins, before concluding: 'I can see this is no place for me.' Payne's 'Lumberjack' – which name checked Eugene, Oregon and was probably included with an eye on the local market – was forgettable fare, a logging song with 'Rawhide'-style whip cracks interspersed throughout.

He recorded again over a year later. He had by now left Vancouver for Texas, making a few hopeful detours in Missouri and Denver before arriving back in Fort Worth in 1958 with the intention of giving up on music and settling down. Martha gave birth to their third child, Billy, on 21 May, and Nelson knew in his heart that he couldn't support his family on what he was making. He took a job selling encyclopedias door-to-door. He enjoyed it, and with his easy grin and quiet charm, he was good at it. He tried to forget about the clubs and knuckle down, coming home at five o'clock to have his dinner before turning the television on.

He tried, but he was kidding himself. Soon enough, he was back prowling the joints of Jacksonboro Highway once again, and even returned to clubs like the Nite Owl and Scotty's, literally back where he started. If Martha could get a babysitter she would happily join him; she was, after all, still only 22. He was doing a little commercial radio work from Fort Worth for XEG, one of the huge 'X' stations transmitting from over the border in Monterey, Mexico. A surviving spool of him reading a leadenly scripted advert appealing to songwriters to send in their own songs – and $10, of course – does little to eulogise his talents as a DJ.

He was a little lost, and seemed to veer back towards the comfort of religion. Whether his spell at Baylor a few years earlier had ignited something slow-burning, or whether it was the influence of his father and Bobbie – who was now also living in Fort Worth – isn't clear, but he was baptised into the Metropolitan Baptist Church and began teaching Sunday School in the mornings. It offered some peace and tranquillity among the chaos. He would head to church just hours after singing through a storm at some dive or other on the strip. Mama Nelson would have been appalled at the dissonance, and she was not the only one. The preacher of the church told Nelson that he disapproved of his lifestyle and asked him to give up the honky-tonks and the music and the nights spent dodging bottles behind chicken wire.

Willie Nelson: I tried to explain to them that the plumber was in there putting in the commode; he was getting his money and nobody was bitching about him. Same with the electrician stringing the lights. But the guy who was up there singing his ass off, he couldn't sing in beer joints and churches, too.[4]

An astute preacher would have recognised that for Nelson, the joints were not simply a place of work; they had become essential to his life. He couldn't escape them even if he wanted to. In disgust, he ditched formal religion and instead re-affirmed his commitment to making music – he wrote the wonderful 'Family Bible' around this time, trying to reconcile his warm spiritual feelings with his love of music. From now on he would mould his beliefs into something that suited and reflected his own lifestyle and choices. His spirituality became the very definition of a broad church.

He made his first professional quality recording in early 1959. A DJ friend based in Cleburne called Hank Craig had contacts with H.W. 'Pappy' Daily, who ran 'D' Records in Houston. The new label was designed to discover new talent and had recently had a hit with George Jones's classic 'Why Baby Why'. Nelson also had a vague connection with 'D' records: Daily had previously founded Starday records, the company who had pressed Nelson's Vancouver songs. Nelson started cutting singles for Daily. He sold half of the rights to one of the songs, 'Man With The Blues', to Craig in order to pay for the first session, which took place in the Manco studio in Fort Worth in early 1959.

For the first time Nelson featured with a full band of local musicians behind him. It was a tight little song, driven by nifty walking bass, and a clever enough lyric about a man who offers unhappiness as a speciality, like a salesman proudly hawking his finest wares. 'The Storm Has Just Begun' was the other song recorded. Fifteen years after it was written, the addition of sickly sweet backing vocals from the Reil Singers, trilling in something just less than unison, didn't help improve what had been a landmark composition for a teenager but merely an average song for an adult.

The record did nothing of any note, but it did, improbably, create some interest in the B-side. Billy Walker, a Waco-born musician whom Nelson knew well, re-recorded 'The Storm Has Just Begun' as 'The Storm In My Heart' for Columbia, and it was released as a single in April 1959, becoming a minor regional hit in Texas. It was a small vindication, and an indication that he was on the right track. His second recording for 'D' Records marked further improvement: 'What A Way To Live' was another step forwards, Nelson's confident, breezy vocals leading the way, although the mood is plaintive: lyrically it contained the essence of some of his landmark compositions – it documents a dissolute lifestyle with a certain characteristic proud resignation – but lacks the spareness and economy. On the flip side, 'Misery Mansion' was a self-explanatory and bleakly enjoyable exercise in self-loathing, utilising the cold, rudimentary fabric of an empty home to accentuate his heartache. He would revisit that particular idea again. It boded well.

In 1959, in the metropolis of Houston something at long last clicked in Nelson's songwriting. In a short spell he wrote the songs which were to change his life: 'Night Life', 'Crazy', 'Mr Record Man', 'Funny How Time Slips Away'. He wrote them quickly and simply, and they have endured. What happened? Initially Houston had seemed like just another stop on the line. Another hustle. Nelson knew the city well enough: like most places in Texas, he had passed through, slept on floors, mooched around. Bolstered by Billy Walker's success, which he felt legitimised him as a songwriter, he tried to persuade Starday to get one of their acts, Frankie Miller, to record 'Family Bible', but Dan Pierce wasn't keen. Lana was now almost six, Susie was two and Billy had just turned one. Work was proving hard to come by and Nelson was pushed to some drastic measures.

Jack Clements: When we were in High school, Willie played with Charlie Brown and the Browns on the weekend. Charlie got divorced and went to Houston, and he was playing in a nightclub when Willie showed up with his three kids. He told Charlie, 'I've got a problem here. I've got no money, I'm out of work, I've got to get a job.' Charlie said, 'I'll give you some money and you can play for me two or three times a week.' This went on for about a week until the manager said, 'Charlie, you're going to have to fire that boy. He can't sing and he's frightening off all the customers!'

He tried the same stunt at the Esquire Club, out east on the Hempstead Highway. The band at the Esquire was headed by Larry Butler, a well-known Texan musician whom Nelson knew a little. He turned up and asked if there were any vacancies in the band. He was told no. So Nelson offered to sell him some songs. To his immense credit, Butler refused to take them, although they would have cost him just $10 each. He knew they were good – they included 'Family Bible' and 'Mr Record Man' – but his conscience wouldn't allow it. Instead, he loaned Nelson $50 and sent him on his way. With the money, he was able to rent an apartment in Pasadena, an eastern suburb of Houston, and buy some food. Later, when a vacancy arose at the Esquire, Nelson was hired to play guitar in Butler's band six nights a week. Soon, he found some more work as the Sunday morning sign-in DJ on KCRT radio in Houston.

He also became tight with Paul Buskirk, an extraordinarily talented guitarist and mandolinist who had settled in Houston and opened the Paul Buskirk School of Guitar. Buskirk had already had a long and prestigious recording career, and indeed played on Nelson's 'What A Way To Live' session for 'D' Records. He offered Nelson work teaching at his guitar school, which he happily accepted, although he struggled to keep ahead of the students. In return, Nelson offered him 'Family Bible'. The legend states that the two were having dinner in a Pasadena bar. Nelson had no money with which to pay and so he leaned across the table and began singing 'Family Bible' to Buskirk. 'This is a tune you'll like,' he smiled. 'I'll sell you this one.' Buskirk offered to give him $50 for it – and pay the bill. It was a deal.

Selling songs is almost unheard of now, but it was fairly common practice back in the 40s and 50s. It was a simple process. A budding songwriter took a flat cash fee, which bought the purchaser the right to put their name on the song and pick up any royalties that it might accrue in the future. It was a small gamble on behalf of the buyer, perhaps, but a much bigger exploitation of a poor songwriter who was desperate enough to flog his best songs for a pittance just to make ends meet in the here and now. Floyd Tillman had sold one of his classics, 'It Makes No Difference Now', for $300 to Louisiana Governor Jimmie Davis in 1937. It became a country hit for Cliff Bruner and a pop hit for Bing Crosby, and was later recorded by Gene Autry, Bob Wills, Ray Charles, and Diana Ross and The Supremes. His was not the only such tale. Nelson, utterly hopeless with money and not one to ever take the long view, was ripe for the picking.

Buddy Killen: Back then, writers were really struggling to make a living. It was very, very tough. Unfortunately, sometimes writers struggle or might be a little bit frivolous with what they do earn. Willie in the beginning was [part of] those days, so he felt he had to sell off some rights to survive.

Buskirk took the song to Claude Gray, a singer also signed to 'D' Records, who liked it and duly recorded it. The credit was split between Gray, Buskirk and Walt Breeland, Buskirk's business partner, who presumably raised the bulk of the funds. Nelson's name was nowhere to be seen on the record. That Gray's recording of 'Family Bible' went into *Billboard*'s country Top 10 was a mixed blessing: on the one hand, it gave him the confidence to know he could write a song which had mass, popular appeal within its genre. On the other hand, he had traded in a considerable sum in royalties for a flat $50 which, given his lifestyle, didn't go far and indeed had already been spent. Buskirk has sometimes been portrayed as the villain in this tale, the exploitative older man taking advantage of his stymied friend, but as he later pointed out, 'We were all poor and [that] was a bunch of money – a bundle – to gamble on an unheard of tune.'[5] Nelson said he never regretted it.

Johnny Bush: Up to a point he [took his marriage and responsibilities seriously]. He was responsible in the respect that he always tried his best. The one thing he had to sell was his songs. He needed the money at the time and they had the money. Willie is a very positive thinker. This is his philosophy: if I can write songs good enough for people to buy, then I can write other songs – and he did.

Nelson saw song-selling as a quick way to make ends meets. It was a hand-to-mouth philosophy, but it was the best idea he had at the time. Indeed, it may even have spurred him on creatively. Always a reluctant writer when times have been good, he has often needed the promise of money or the threat of trouble to get him going. Where previously he may have dragged his heels and viewed his writing as an indulgence when there were mouths to be fed, now he had a real purpose.

Following the sale of 'Family Bible', there is not necessarily a sense of him writing to order, but he had one eye on the cash register. He focused. Driving between Pasadena and the Esquire club in Houston and back every night, he finally made the breakthrough. 'Night Life' came in fits and starts as he sat silently at the wheel. It had all the economy of the oldest of blues song – nothing was wasted. Its mood is best summed up as a kind of heroic loneliness, a simple and almost defiant acceptance of what he is. It is written without melodrama or shame, and could only have come from a man who had spent the best part of a decade seeking solace in the most transient places and who now finds himself alone in the early hours with nowhere to hide. Despite the fact that it became a hugely successful song, it sounds like someone who has given up on trying to write what he thinks a record company might like to hear and is simply pleasing himself. It became a kind of template for Nelson's early songwriting: a Texan haiku.

Rodney Crowell: It's so economical and powerful at the same time, distilling it down to that one true sentence: 'When the evening sun goes down/ You will find me hanging around/ The night life/ Ain't no good life/ But it's my life.' That's sort of like Hemingway to me! When it's distilled down to that much truth and simplicity, then it accesses to the power of the universe. It becomes archetypal.

The music too was superb, flitting between blues and jazz and country, with a lovely slice of musical onomatopoeia in the bridge as Nelson invites the listener to 'listen to the blues they're playing' then reels off a burst of pure Delta blues guitar. It was restrained, intimate and enormously powerful. It went on to sell over 30 million copies in over 70 different versions. And he sold it for $150.

Surprisingly, 'D' Records didn't want 'Night Life'; Nelson thought it was because it wasn't a straight country song, but they were a label with a diverse stable. More likely, 'Pappa' Daily just didn't see much commercial mileage in it, despite the fact that everybody locally knew that he had already written a hit in 'Family Bible'. Although under contract to Daily's company, Nelson decided to throw in his lot with Buskirk and Freeland. He may have thought he was driving a hard bargain by upping his asking price three-fold when he sold them 'Night Life', but $150 was a paltry sum, denoting a desperately struggling man. It paid at least for the independent session recorded in Houston's Gold Star studio in the spring of 1960, with the same musicians who had cut 'What A Way To Live'. The A-side was 'Night Life' and the B-side 'Rainy Day Blues', a straight, hard blues riding on after-hours saxophone and Nelson's confident vocals. Bobby Bland would have been impressed. It was a long, long way from 'The Storm Has Just Begun'. The record was released by Rx under the guise of Paul Buskirk and his Little Men featuring Hugh Nelson, a pretty lame attempt at throwing Daily off the scent.

It made no waves, but the dam had burst. In the next few weeks he also composed 'Crazy' and 'Funny How Time Slips Away', two more deceptively simple minor miracles of songwriting. He had the good sense to hang onto them, despite the fact that he was mired in debt and had been fired by the radio station for missing too many Sunday calls. He was, he later admitted, 'broke, tired, drunk and unhappy'.[6] It could almost be his motto for the entire decade. But he had to admit that his misery was letting through some marvellous songs. It was a dangerous precedent, for now he believed he could only write when he was dramatically blue. He swallowed hard and made up his mind: Nashville or bust.

There were several cities in the United States which could have ended up being Nashville. Places like Shreveport, Louisiana; Dallas, Texas; Chicago, Michigan; Springfield, Missouri; Wheeling, West Virginia. In the 30s and 40s they all had huge 50,000-watt radio stations and massively popular

Saturday night jamborees, broadcast live across the nation on radio. In Nashville, of course, it was the *Grand Ole Opry*, which broadcast from the Ryman Auditorium on WSM from 1925 onwards. But there were many others. Shreveport had the *Louisiana Hayride*, the show where Hank Williams became a star, beamed over 28 states on KWKH. Chicago had the *National Barn Dance* on WLS; Wheeling had the *Wheeling Jamboree* on WWVA.

Any one of these cities could realistically have become Nashville, but crucially, it was the Tennessee city which first added a substantial recording element to the equation. The record companies built studios and established offices there. By the 50s it had indisputably become the place to be for any aspiring country music singer, musician or songwriter; the other radio shows effectively became nurseries, building talent locally then sending it onto Tennessee to swim with the big fish. During this period, everyone coveted an affiliation to the *Grand Ole Opry*. It was almost impossible to make it without one. The acts came to Nashville, went on the show, had hit records and then went on the road. It drew Hank Snow from Canada, Billy Walker from Texas and Jim Reeves from Shreveport. Later, with the growth of television and the diversification of radio, it became possible to have hit records without ever playing the *Opry* – Buck Owens never played it, Charley Pride broke through without it – but that time was a few years hence.

When Willie Nelson drove into town in mid-1960, with his 45 pressing of 'Night Life' clutched hopefully in his hand, he was entering a city already working towards having every angle of the country music business covered. The record companies owned all the studios, they provided the musicians, they often picked the songs and would overdub willy-nilly. Essentially, what the musician laid down in the studio was a mere template for what might be released on record. It was a ruthlessly unromantic system, and an era which pre-dated any notion of the musician as an Artist. This was about control. Control meant money and money meant work; the rolling out of product – like a factory rolls out carpet by the yard – was regarded as paramount. There was little time or opportunity to get precious about what was being done in the studio.

Interestingly, although he came to resent the confines of the Nashville system, Nelson remains a product of his generation: he is a resolute opponent of any preciousness or high-falutin' claims when it comes to his work. If you are looking for an artist who sweats blood over his music or who spends months locked in studios seeking inspiration, then look elsewhere. He is more likely to add a vocal on his bus and think no more of it. The difference now, of course, is that he is in complete control.

One of his frequent gripes throughout the 60s was that he couldn't use his touring band on his records. This was commonplace. The live band and the studio band were kept firmly delineated. The musician would go on his merry way around the country with his band or, if budgets were tight, pick up local players in clubs as he passed through different towns. There was no tour money, no label support. It was a tough game. Mere road musicians weren't entrusted with the 'Nashville Sound'. Records were traditionally cut in two- or three-hour sessions with professional session men and a company-appointed producer, then the label would pick the best songs, produce them and put them out. It encouraged a certain level of quality control, but it also bred a blanket uniformity of sound.

By 1960, the stark, emotionally raw style of Nelson's heroes like Lefty Frizzel and Hank Williams was going out of fashion. Williams had been dead seven years, and the era of pop-country was looming. The great, dark spaces of yore were filled with strings and featureless backing vocals. The big ambition was to score a crossover hit into the pop charts. The album had not yet really taken off as a concept in country music and the single was still king, ready to feed the jukebox and the radio stations all over the nation.

Buddy Killen: They were only selling singles, it was before album sales. It was a local thing. If you had 100,000 or 200,000 albums in the 60s you were really cooking. It hadn't crossed over.

Nelson arrived in Nashville primarily as a songwriter. Many country acts wrote their own songs, but none were averse to cutting other people's material if they smelled a hit. It was before the days of 'cover versions'. People in the industry cared about who was writing the songs, of course, but nobody buying the records did. The artist was the important part of the marketing process, and the songwriter was strictly behind the scenes. Most good songwriters were signed up to publishing companies like Tree or Pamper, who paid them a weekly wage set against future royalties to write songs which they could then get other people to record. The bigger the star the better. The composer would then get a small share of the royalties from sales, and also royalties from radio play and performance, the latter calculated by the Broadcast Music Inc., or BMI. It was a system designed to favour the big fish and penalise the small fry.

Buddy Killen: When I signed Roger Miller in 1957 I gave him $25 a week – and [for that] I also got his BMI royalties. Back in those days the rate was two cents per record, and the label would often say: 'We're not going to put this [record] out unless you give us a [lower] rate: a cent or even a half a cent.' Back in those days, people weren't getting rich off hit records.

If the *Grand Ole Opry* was Nashville's flagship, Tootsie's Orchid Lounge was the engine room, the place where ideas and personalities mixed with smoke and alcohol to dream alive the music which kept the whole industry afloat. Situated on Fifth Avenue, Tootsie's literally backed on to the Ryman Auditorium, and became a home from home for practically every famous face in country music. Roger Miller, Hank Cochran, Faron Young,

Webb Pierce *et al* could be found hunkered down in the booths or playing in the back room at all times of day and night. It was run by 'Tootsie' Bess, a big, maternal woman with a three-inch hat pin to keep trouble-makers at bay. If she knew you and liked you, you could run up a bar tab and settle at the year's end.

The place was nothing much to look at: 'Just a dump that served beer,' says Ray Price. 'Just a beer joint.' But it was jumping. All the acts at the *Grand Ole Opry* played two shows, and would wander over to Tootsie's for a drink before, between and after. It was a Mecca for writers and musicians. Although the industry itself was something of a cartel, there was a real camaraderie amongst fellow musicians. David Zettner first visited Tootsie's with Nelson in the mid-60s and paints a vivid picture of a typical night in the bar.

David Zettner: Willie grabs me and says: 'Welcome to Nashville. Let's go to Tootsies!' That night Willie and [steel player] Jimmy Day decided to have a jam session. There was this old coloured lady that worked there back then, and she would cook this great bowl of chilli for everybody. Lord Jesus, we started phoning around, and Jimmy got me in the car and we went to get Buddy Emmons, the steel player. Before we knew it there was maybe fifteen awesome pickers coming in: Jimmy and Buddy, a guy named Curly Chalker who was an incredible steel player, they were just grabbing them out of the nightclubs. Boots Randolph came in with his sax. Johnny Bush was there. At the same time, Willie would get on the phone and call people like Roger Miller and all his writing buddies, and they'd get over to drink and write. By now, we're into day two of the jam session: been up a whole night. Willie and them would come in about every three hours and go: 'Hey, we've got one here! We got one!' And all the musicians are like, 'Oh, Goddamn singers! We don't care about words!'

It's little wonder that Tootsie's was where Nelson naturally gravitated upon his arrival in Nashville. He had left Houston and deposited Martha and the kids with her mother in Waco for about ten weeks while he went to explore the city. He cheated on his wife a little, now a fairly routine distraction, cashed in favours, looked up old contacts and found places to stay, including a spell with Billy Walker and his wife Boots. He eventually told Martha to come up on the bus with the children and join him in the autumn of 1960. He had found them their most desultory home yet, an old three-room trailer house next to a graveyard in Dunn's Trailer Court on Nashville's east side. It cost $25 a week and it was grim.

At first it was the usual drill: fights and disappointments. Martha – the waitress to end all waitresses – quickly got two jobs: at the Hitching Post, a bar across the street from Tootsies, and at the nearby Wagon Wheel. It was the closest she could get to having a good time. She earned the money, paid the babysitter and watched as Nelson went out to Tootsie's every night and got drunk in the name of making music biz contacts. Nashville was a tough city to crack. It was full of people like him, aspiring stars or desperate songwriters on every corner, and what seems like obvious talent in hindsight was less apparent to the naked eye back then.

Ray Price: They didn't understand him at first. And you don't do very well until you get that big hit. When you get that big hit, everybody all of a sudden recognises it, saying, 'Oh well, we knew he was going to do it!' [But] at that time it was hard to get started anywhere.

He approached Starday with 'Night Life', hoping they would release it as a single or perhaps hire him as a staff writer. They weren't interested. He hung around Toostie's waiting for a chance to show what he could do. Songs like 'Night Life' and 'Crazy' were not straightforwardly country, and although people could see that he could write, not everyone was sure he could sell. He would hang around and drink anyway, work his natural charm on the place. Not really a natural drinker – it made him aggressive, depressive and prone to blackouts – in many ways Toostie's was a dangerous place for him to spend a lot of time. It was a haven for musicians and a necessary place for him to visit if he was to interest anybody in his songs, but it was also an environment which perpetuated the myth of the hard-living, self-destructive songwriter. He accentuated his behaviour accordingly, and may even have felt that he had to live up to the words of 'Night Life'. He was finally amongst his heroes and he wanted to emulate and be equal to them in every way: in song, in drink, in women.

Willie Nelson: Well, the myth can get in the way, all right.[7] I think a lot of people got to thinking that everybody had to do the same thing Hank Williams did, even die that way if necessary. And that got out of hand. Of course I did [that].[8]

He went from being merely unhappy with his lot to being depressed and a little ashamed. Martha had scuffed around after him for nearly ten years, dragging up the children, staying at home while he worked and partied, and she had nothing to show for it but an old trailer home and an unhappy marriage. She had wanted him to come to Nashville, but this was not the kind of reality she had envisaged. She started drinking a lot of whisky as well, and the fights got nastier and more physical. The most famous Martha story recounts the time her husband came in drunk and she tied him up with the children's skipping ropes before beating him up with a broom handle. It has been turned into a comic vignette over the years, but it was a bleak little episode at the time. There were other, similarly violent occurrences. She attacked him with a knife, and on a separate occasion, a fork; whether she every tried to get him with a spoon is unrecorded. In

Nashville, they nicknamed her Dynamite. Only once, according to her daughter Susie, did Martha claim her husband retaliated with his fists. It was a vicious cycle: Nelson would disappear for days to escape Martha's wild moods – he disliked confrontation and distrusted his temper; Martha would react with escalating fury each time he went off and left her alone to fend for the kids.

Johnny Bush: The depression came after he went to Nashville. He was living in some trailer park and it was cold, and he was trying to get his songs published and she was waiting on tables. He was going to these guitar pulls trying to get his songs recorded, and he'd come in drunk and broke and they'd get into it.

The bottom line was that he didn't want to be at home, and he didn't want to be responsible for his family if it meant he had to change his ways. That laid-back facade masked a hard, determined, selfish streak. He would smile benignly and say 'OK' to most things, but he would do what he wanted nonetheless, and then try his level best not to be around to face the consequences.

Two things happened to lighten the skies. Late in 1960 Nelson finally got the break he had dreamed of. Hank Cochran was a hot young songwriter who had recently co-written 'I Fall To Pieces' with Harlan Howard, which was about to become a big hit for Patsy Cline. Cochran was a staff writer for Pamper Music Company, co-owned by the musician Ray Price and his manager Hal Smith. One night in Tootsie's, Nelson sat down and sang a whole host of songs in front of Cochran and Howard and several more of his peers. As he ran through 'Touch Me', 'Night Life' and 'Funny How Time Slips Away', Nelson sufficiently impressed Cochran for him to recommend him to his bosses at Pamper. They 'ummed' and 'ahhed' over the finances for a while, until they finally agreed to pay Nelson $50 a week to write songs for the company.

Willie Nelson: I broke down and cried. Martha cried, the kids cried, Hank cried. We were so happy. It was a real big deal for me.[9]

It was the culmination of a decade's endeavour. He would never need to work outside of music again. It wasn't a great wage, but it was enough to get by on and get them out of the trailer park. In the winter of 1960 the family moved to a rented red-brick house in Goodlettsville, a northern suburb of Nashville where Pamper had their office, and Nelson settled down to write songs for a living. Almost immediately he struck gold.

Very few writers have ever been able to articulate the mundane truth of loneliness quite like Willie Nelson. He can make the abstract physical, the inanimate come alive. He can even make the furniture talk. 'Hello Walls' is the truest example. Even the means of its composition is a lesson in creating something precious out of the most ordinary base metal: he was sitting in the garage at the Pamper offices, with just a window, a door, a guitar, and the walls closing in. He was staring into space. Ten minutes later, he had a song. 'Hello walls/ How are things going for you today/ Don't you miss her/ Since she upped and went away?' he sang, later conjuring up the magnificent, pathetic image of a teardrop in the corner of the windowpane. Its wit didn't dilute its poignancy. Its mundane imagery didn't overwhelm its humanity. It was a classic.

'Hello Walls' announced him as a songwriter with a unique perspective, but it wasn't a *cri de coeur*. It was an inspired piece of off-the-cuff craftsmanship, a song firmly within the Nashville parameters of measured, acceptable unhappiness. Country music always found room for sad songs, and it didn't always require the writer to believe what he was singing. 'Hello Walls' was grief-lite, and none the worse for that. Nelson once wrote a never-recorded song with Harlan Howard called 'Wanted: One Mother' ('For one little boy/ Who cleans up his room/ Puts away all his toys') which effectively lampooned the whole tears-in-my-beer country stereotype, even if the subject matter strayed dangerously close to home.

But he was writing dozens more quality compositions around the same time, and many of them were emotionally much nearer the knuckle. He cut raw, guitar-and-voice or stripped down band demo versions of these new songs for Pamper, recordings that wouldn't see the light of day until years later. These included 'End Of Understanding', 'Face Of A Fighter', 'A Moment Isn't Very Long', 'Home Is Where You're Happy' and 'And So Will You My Love'. Most of the songs document a litany of despair, a catalogue of heartache and confusion which was, for the most part, too downbeat for public consumption in 1961. 'No Tomorrow In Sight' – which begins 'The children are sleeping/ Our talk can begin' and then proceeds to gets *really* morose – is a straight slice of autobiography. For all the salty anecdotes and embroidered tales passed down through the years, this bleak, brilliant, but ultimately suffocating music remains the best source of divining the depths of Nelson's unhappiness in his first year in Nashville.

Willie Nelson: I was writing my life, what I saw around me. You've got to live the life, I don't think you can write those sort of songs otherwise. Or even sing them. Ain't nobody that good an actor.[10] And I was writing it from a dark, shady side, I guess. I was going into one relationship out of another, all kinds of domestic bullshit. Over the years it produced a lot of music, that's for sure, but it was a hard way to do it.[11]

Pamper sent 'Hello Walls', alongside another Nelson original, 'Congratulations', to Faron Young, one of the hottest stars in Nashville. Legend has it that Young had already been given a sneak preview of the song in Tootsie's almost as soon as it was written. Within days of hearing it, he cut the song on 7 January 1961, for the A-side of a Capitol single. By May, 'Hello Walls' had reached No. 1 on the *Billboard* Country charts. It stayed there for nine weeks, and even passed over into the pop charts. A few weeks earlier, on 21 April, Billy Walker had recorded 'Funny How Time Slips Away', a beautiful, regretful essay about how what goes around eventually comes back around. It made No. 21 on the country charts in October. Around the same time, Patsy Cline was – reluctantly – gearing up to record her version of 'Crazy', finally persuaded of its worth by her husband, Charlie Dick, whom Nelson had befriended.

Willie Nelson: Charlie Dick and I and Hank Cochran were drinking beer at Tootsie's, and after Tootsie's closed they decided it was time to wake up Patsy and play it for her. I was hesitant to get out of the car. I stayed in the car and in a little while she came out and made me come in the house. This was like two or three in the morning. She recorded it the next day.[12]

He had arrived. Those who looked deep enough into those dark eyes might have seen an unusual expression lurking within them. It took a moment to recognise it as relief.

WHO GIVES A DAMN?

Willie Nelson is talking about making records.

He has made so many records over the years he has lost count, but it's somewhere around two hundred and fifty, he thinks. And he has never quite got it right.

'The records kind of happen on their own,' he says. 'Over the years, they just happen. I've never been able to really make the records I wanted to make and do everything exactly the way I wanted to do it.'

What he means is that he believes that the true essence of what he does can only really be captured when he steps upon the stage with his band. Each record is simply a miniature, a tiny little piece of the whole picture.

At least now he can record whatever he wants. In his early years he was at the mercy of what his record companies thought might sell and that was a hard pill to swallow.

'If you believe in your music, then you should do it the way you want to do it,' he says. 'At least it means you have the freedom to do it the way you want to do it. Doesn't mean it has to sell. Regarding whether it's commercially good or not, well, who gives a damn?'

And it sounds so obvious and simple that he laughs.

4. 1961–1965

I t is entirely typical of Willie Nelson that he agreed to become the bass
player in Ray Price's backing band, the Cherokee Cowboys, despite the
fact that he had never even played the instrument before, indeed never
even held one in his hands. As usual, he had simply shrugged and said 'OK'
when asked, happy to cross the rickety bridge when it came into view. He
was – not uniquely in Nashville – living a double life: successful writer,
journeyman musician, and he was shrewd enough to take his chances
when they came. Opportunities as a performer were far harder to come by
in Nashville than they were in Texas; there were fewer venues and the
competition was fierce.

He had already played with country guitarist Bobby Sykes' band for a
little while upon arriving in the city and now, in the few months between
the recording and release of 'Hello Walls', he went happily out on the road
with Price. The Cherokee Cowboys' previous bassist – Donny Young, soon
to relaunch himself as Johnny Paycheck – had quit, and Price had asked
Nelson if he wanted to play bass. He might have agreed without
deliberating too long over the consequences, but he learned quickly.

Ray Price: When we got off the first tour Willie said, 'I betcha didn't know
I couldn't play bass!' and I said, 'Yeah, I knew on the first night!' But he's
a good guitarist, so he could play bass all right.

Having managed to pull off a convincing impersonation of a professional bass player, the only other tasks required of him in the Cherokee Cowboys were easy: wear a gaudy Nudie suit and sing a few songs when the spotlight swung in his direction. Bob Wills' classic 'San Antonio Rose' and Harlan Howard's 'Busted' – which would shortly be recorded by Johnny Cash and Ray Charles – were specialities.

He was paid $25 a night and he needed it. The rent on his new house was $85 a month; royalties took a little while to accrue and then be paid; and Martha continued working two jobs to make ends meet. Above all, his social expenses were high and he was still scuffling around. Indeed, when he returned from his first stint on tour with Price and the Cherokee Cowboys, he offered to sell his writer's credit on 'Hello Walls' to Faron Young for $500, even though the song had now become a hit and was on its way to generating thousands of dollars in royalties and BMI payments. It was an astonishingly misguided piece of short-term thinking, illustrating just how terrible he was at handling his finances and the lengths he would go to secure even the quickest of fixes. Thankfully, the idea was given short shrift by Young.

Faron Young: I made him raise his hand and swear to God that if I loaned him some money, he wouldn't sell [it], and then I loaned him $1,500. His first [royalty] check – seven or eight weeks later, for something like 600,000 copies sold – was $20,000.[1]

In fact, it was around $14,000, which would tally with a basic two per cent writer's royalty rate on 600,000 single sales. Other sources say that Young loaned him only $500. Nevertheless, when the bumper check arrived, he ran into Tootsie's and gave Young a big sloppy French kiss for saving him from what may perhaps have been the biggest mistake of his life. Then he went back on tour with Ray Price and lived like the 'King of Spain'. He bonded particularly well with Jimmy Day, Price's steel guitar player and a veteran of Hank Williams' old band, not to mention Tootsie's. Day probably saw more of the royalty money than Martha, who was at home, furious, working and raising the kids while hearing stories filtering back through the Nashville grapevine about Nelson's incessant partying and fiscal recklessness: booking into penthouse suites in high-class hotels, flying first class on commercial airlines instead of taking the bus with the band, generally just blowing the cash as quickly as he could. He also abruptly abandoned his writing. It seemed a little too much like hard work now that he had made his big breakthrough. He had what he wanted: money in his pocket and the chance to have some fun on the road.

Martha Nelson: Willie's attitude was that now he had a job with Ray Price, he didn't give a damn what anybody thought of his music. He couldn't be bothered, now that he had some hit songs.[2]

It was a time of excess for almost all concerned. Nashville was crammed full with young men from mostly poor backgrounds who suddenly had access to a lot of cash and didn't know what to do with it. Or rather, they did know what to do with it. Alcohol remained the main source of escapism. Cocaine and LSD were rare as hen's teeth, and marijuana was still generally uncommon. Pills were prevalent. Cheap 'speed' like Benzedrine kept things going, sometimes nicknamed 'LA Turnaround' for its rare ability to get you to California and back without having to worry about anything so rudimentary as sleep. Mixed with alcohol it made for an aggressive combination. There were stories about Roger Miller staying up for days, handing out sage advice to his peers: 'Don't keep your pills in your pockets with your loose change. I just swallowed a nickel.' Nelson enjoyed himself but he was no more excessive than most.

Ray Price: He wasn't all that wild. He wasn't into drugs or anything. He drank beer or drank whisky a little bit. He was a rounder, somebody who drinks and parties and just has a good time, but all of us were pretty wild when we worked the nightclub circuit. [And women]. That happens too, when you're young!

Nelson's reputation as a songwriter, specifically the man who wrote 'Hello Walls', soon made him a well-known face around the Nashville spots. But being a recording artist and a performer in his own right was an entirely different challenge.

Willie Nelson: When I got to Nashville I had to start over again. I had to go back to the songwriting and then come over from there up to the recordings.[3]

The demo recordings he had made for Pamper were impressive calling cards, but the material wasn't particularly commercial. More significant was the fact that he had started to develop his own unique vocal phrasing, singing off the beat and almost talking in places. There is a misconception that Nelson's jazzy vocal inflections and sometimes unusual time signatures were derided in Nashville, that people in high places thought he couldn't sing. This was not the case: people knew he could sing, indeed many of them loved the way he sang. Don Light was the bass player in the house band at the *Grand Ole Opry*, and he recalls the steady buzz that surrounded Nelson in the bars and clubs.

Don Light: I was aware of him. Faron's record of 'Hello Walls' was a big, big record. I remember I met Harlan Howard and we were talking about songs and writers and Harlan said: 'Have you ever heard Willie sing? His demo [of 'Hello Walls'] is as good as Faron's record. You need to hear him.' There was already interest in him at that time.

It is true, however, that there was a caucus of opinion which remained firmly unconvinced that he possessed a voice which could be translated into bumper record sales. In a time of smooth surfaces he had too many sharp angles. It was an age when the broadest of talents were squeezed into the tightest of boxes, and it wasn't at all certain that Nelson would fit. 'Crazy', for instance, had been an unusual smash in that it featured considerably more than the standard three or four chords often used in country music, as well as a slightly unorthodox structure. However, he continued writing hits without compromising his style. Faron Young had cut five of Nelson's songs on his new album, *The Young Approach*, including 'Three Days', which went on to be a Top 10 single. 'Three Days' was a tight, swinging minor key blues-based number, which once again contained a simple but instantly arresting lyric: 'Three days/ Filled with tears and sorrow/ Yesterday, today and tomorrow.'

The obvious creative strengths and commercial returns from Nelson's songs ensured that someone was bound to be seduced into taking a chance on him as an artist in his own right. Hank Cochran had taken his songs to his friend, Joe Allison, another fellow Texan and a producer at Liberty Records. Liberty were based in Los Angeles but had recently branched into country, signing Bob Wills with some success in 1960. The label was on the up, if not quite a major force. Allison twisted the arm of Liberty's money men and Nelson signed. He began his first session late on the night of 22 August, stretching into the early hours of the following morning, recording 'The Part Where I Cry' and 'Touch Me' for later single release. Allison kept things simple but somehow the music never clicked.

The next session was at Liberty's Hollywood studio, conducted while Nelson was on tour in California with Ray Price. He spent the 11 and 12 September working with a band of session musicians under the watchful gaze of Allison, cutting fourteen songs, including 'Crazy', 'Darkness On The Face Of The Earth', 'Three Days', 'Funny How Time Slips Away', 'Mr Record Man' and his own version of 'Hello Walls'. All would be included on his first album, entitled . . . *And Then I Wrote* and issued in September 1962.

They were difficult days in the studio. The experienced musicians and backing singers were utterly baffled by Nelson's off-beat singing, and they kept falling out of time as they attempted to follow him. Eventually, they gave up any attempt to match what he was doing and simply played the song as though he wasn't there. They wouldn't even look at him, in case he put them off. One listen to the gaping pause Nelson leaves between the title phrase in 'How Long Is Forever' (a song recorded at these sessions but not included on the final album) and the following 'this time' illustrates the essential eccentricity of his style. It is dramatic, funny, subtly changing the emphasis in tone and meaning each time. If anyone had needed further indication that they weren't dealing with a standard Nashville act, the sessions in Hollywood were conclusive proof. Only Floyd Tillman had ever

Left Nelson relaxing at the height of his fame in 1978
(© Wally McNamee/ Corbis)

Below Taking his daily medicine on the *Honeysuckle Rose*
(© Getty Images)

Above Aged 17, posing for the Abbott High School yearbook in 1950

Right The shortest basketball player in Texas

Below One of the boys in the school baseball team – note school friend Jack Clements (third left, top row).

Right Playing the game in Nashville: an early, clean-cut publicity shot
(© Getty Images)

Below left Songwriter: working Music Row in the 60s
(© Getty Images)

Below right Recording vocals during the sessions for his debut album *. . . And Then I Wrote* in 1961
(© Getty Images)

Right On stage with Jody
Payne in 1991
(© Getty Images)

Below Backstage in the
70s, when every night was
somebody's Saturday night
(© Wally McNamee/Corbis)

*Bottom Honeysuckle
Rose,* Nelson's old tour bus
(© Graeme Thomson)

Above With Connie, Susie and her boyfriend at Fitzhugh Road in 1973
(Courtesy of Connie Nelson)

Above Nelson and Connie in 1983. They split two years later (© Bettmann/Corbis)

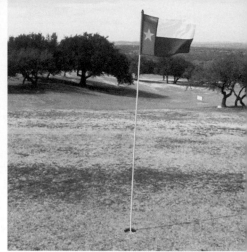

Left On the golf course with Larry Trader
(© Time Life Pictures/Getty Images)

Above Nelson's nine-hole golf course at
Pedernales, complete with Lone Star flags
on each hole
(© Time Life Pictures/Getty Images)

Below One of the many attractions at
Pedernales Country Club – note the
misspelling of the name
(© Time Life Pictures/Getty Images)

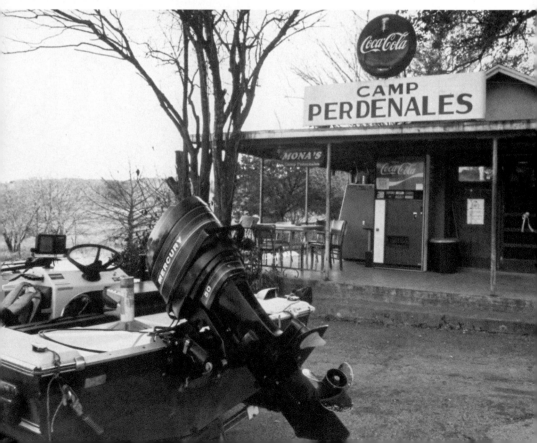

Above The Outlaws: with Waylon Jennings in the early 70s (© Bettmann/Corbis)

Above The Highwaymen: Nelson, Johnny Cash, Waylon Jennings and Kris Kristofferson
(© AP/Empics)

Left On stage with President Jimmy Carter in the late-70s
(© Wally McNamee/Corbis)

Right Keeping fit amidst the madness. Nelson still jogs every day
(© Wally McNamee/Corbis)

sung with such idiosyncratic élan. Nelson was looking towards the likes of Frank Sinatra, singers who expressed the way they were feeling not just by what they sung, but in how – and when, and why – they sung it. Everything was up for grabs.

It was an auspicious trip in other ways as well. While in California, Nelson met his second wife. His marriage to Martha had reached its endgame. She had inflicted a deep cut and permanent scar on Hank Cochran's jaw after throwing a selection of heavy glass ashtrays at her husband from behind the bar of the Wagon Wheel – and missed – and things had continued deteriorating to such an extent that Nelson had effectively moved out of the homestead by the time he was on the road with Ray Price. They were undertaking mammoth tours – sometimes as many as ninety days of one-nighters – and he was coming back only to see the kids, lavishing them with presents, crying as he left again.

One of the new songs he wrote was called 'Home Motel'. Martha's parents came up from Waco to stay and babysit while she went out on the town and began to indulge herself in the kind of escapades her husband had been enjoying for years. She could hardly be blamed, although Nelson reacted to her infidelities with a hypocritical macho rage, despite the fact that he was embarking on his most significant foray to date.

Shirley Collie was tall, dark-haired, glamorous in a brittle kind of way, and a little dangerous-looking in her high heels and fitted dresses. A fellow singer, songwriter, not to mention a yodeller and a far better bass player than Nelson could ever pretend to be, she was also signed to Liberty.

Johnny Bush: She was exceptionally talented. She could sing second [harmony] part to anything Willie could throw at her – you know how he phrases. She was a great songwriter and a terrific bass player. Knew a lot of chords on the guitar. And she was sexy, you know.

Shirley was living in Long Beach with her husband of five years Biff, a well-known local country disc jockey. She was not exactly famous but she had a reasonable profile. Both Hank Cochran and Joe Allison knew her and invited her along to one of Nelson's September recording sessions in Hollywood. Later on the same trip, she watched him perform with Ray Price and the Cherokee Cowboys at a Long Beach dance hall. They talked a little and she was immediately smitten, although nothing happened. Shirley took her marriage vows seriously, even if by this point Nelson did not.

Several weeks later, in November, Shirley was recording in Nashville when Joe Allison invited her to join Nelson on some duets they were working on in the studio. They recorded four in total, including 'Willingly', which became his first chart hit early the following year. That did it. By the time Shirley returned to California a few days later they had fallen in love with each other. It remained an unarticulated and unacknowledged passion until one day he called her at home and simply said: 'I don't have any idea what we're going to do, but I love you.'

The fallout wasn't pretty. Shirley left her husband and hid out on the bus with Nelson and the rest of the Cherokee Cowboys as they slogged around Canada for thirty days. Upon their return, he went home, packed up, and finally left Martha and the kids. It had been coming for a long time, but it was still a desperate wrench. Despite all their madness and unhappiness, he still loved her. He wrote the unbearably poignant 'The Healing Hands Of Time' for her, a song eloquent in the inescapable pain that comes with a break-up and the hope of some peace somewhere down the line. When she eventually re-married soon after he couldn't bring himself to speak to her for a long time, and would use Shirley as an intermediary to deal with the children. For all his years of cheating and the fact that he had precipitated their downfall by finding a new wife, he hadn't expected Martha to get over him that quickly.

It was a nasty, difficult divorce. Nelson and Shirley moved into the Downtowner Motel in central Nashville, and Martha sought confrontation there, phoning up and even checking in on one occasion. When she finally took the kids away from Nashville – dropping them off in Waco with her parents before she headed to Las Vegas alone to begin over again – she initially didn't tell him where they were, despite the fact that he was sending $600 a month in child support via a county court. The figure was calculated from figures based on his recent high royalty earnings, but in all likelihood Shirley was paying some of it. Most of his big money had already been well and truly squandered.

Shirley's husband Biff, meanwhile, tried unsuccessfully to get her sectioned into a psychiatric hospital, presumably on the grounds that anyone would be crazy to leave him. Later, it emerged that she was indeed emotionally fragile and prone to depression, but this time she knew what she was doing. They both worried about how it all looked to the outside world and the country music community in general. Their producer at Liberty, Joe Allison, was a friend of Biff's, and Nelson fretted that the affair might affect his future with the label. Shirley was simply handed the role of the scarlet woman. Guilt, loss and doubt were no strangers, but it finally worked out. Both divorces came through in early 1962, and the couple married almost exactly a year later, in January 1963. Nelson and the band were playing the Golden Nugget in Las Vegas when they decided to tie the knot on the spur of the moment.

Johnny Bush: We went to a wedding chapel and Jimmy Day was the best man, Paul Buskirk was the matron of honour, and I was the flower girl! And that was the wedding.

When Nelson left Martha in early 1962 he also left Ray Price's band. There is a suspicion that he didn't really want to – and Price certainly didn't want him to leave – but he caved into pressure from Shirley, who felt he'd do better alone and didn't really want him trekking around the country anyway. Nevertheless, it made a certain amount of sense for him to come out from under his mentor's shadow. He had a profile of his own and it was the right time to pursue his own ambitions.

The timing was obviously lousy, and he was treading water while domestic matters settled. Shirley went to California to attempt to sort things out with her husband, and he went back to Fort Worth to stay with Bobbie for a while. The fact that Martha's mother had let him know that his children were now living in Waco may have influenced his decision to return to Texas. After a short time, Shirley joined him and they began playing shows with Jimmy Day, capitalising on the success of 'Willingly', which had been released as a single in March 1962 and had done surprisingly well, peaking at No. 10 on the *Billboard* country charts. Written by Hank Cochran, it was an eerily prescient little song – 'If it's fate for us to wait/ Until our love can be/ Then we'll wait/ Willingly' – although in all truth it was an unconvincing mix of voices, while Shirley sings Nelson right off the turntable. His follow-up single, 'Touch Me', came out in May and climbed to No. 7 in the country charts. Despite the success of 'Willingly', and the fact that Patsy Cline's 'Crazy' had now hit big on both the country and pop charts and Jimmy Elledge's version of 'Funny How Time Slips Away' had crossed over to the mainstream Top 30 back in January, 'Touch Me' was Willie Nelson's first ever chart success as a solo artist.

It seemed a good time to think about getting his own band together. They were called, with characteristic swagger and not a little humour, The Offenders, and consisted of Jimmy Day, Johnny Bush, Wade Ray, and a smattering of Shirley on the duets. Bush had caught up with Nelson again when Ray Price and the Cherokee Cowboys had passed through San Antonio in 1961. They talked, and when Price needed a new drummer it was Bush who filled the void and moved to Nashville, from where he later joined The Offenders. Their first major tour was out in Las Vegas in early 1963. It was an eventful trip. Shirley and Nelson finally married, and Nelson also got to spend some time with his children, who had now joined Martha in her cramped apartment in Las Vegas. She was working – with a certain inevitability – as a cocktail waitress. She was still only in her mid-20s, and felt her lucky break in life had just been snatched from under her nose. She was keen to find another one.

The Offenders were playing a two-week residency at the Golden Nugget, one of the longest established casinos on the strip and run by one of the most powerful men in town, Buck Blaine. Although Willie had recently had a big hit with 'Touch Me', he was strictly small fry for Vegas. No one in that most venal of towns cared much about budding songwriters.

Johnny Bush: Vegas was a big deal. It could make or break you as a newcomer coming up. You wanted to show good out there, you wanted to show well. After the second show Buck Blaine sent his henchman down to the motel room where we were staying, and he said, 'Willie, this is coming from Mr Blaine. We want Shirley on the bandstand at all times [Willie was just calling her out for the duets] and we want your guitar player to stand *here*.' In other words, they had some changes they wanted to make to the Willie Nelson show. Willie listened intently until the guy had finished, and then he said, 'Are you through?' The guy said, 'Yeah, that's it,' and Willie said, 'Well, you go back and tell Mr Blaine that I'm not changing a thing. I'm gonna survive with or without the Golden Nugget, now you tell him that.' I nearly fainted. I thought, Oh my God! We had two weeks out there, and I'm adding up the money that I hadn't made yet. But it worked. He called the guy's bluff. Anyone else, myself included, would have conformed to the man's wishes: 'I need Vegas, it's my first time here, I want to make a good impression.' But not Will. Maybe that's why he's the big star he is today. He knew what he wanted, he knew how he wanted it done, and he stuck with it.

There were also the first tangible signs that his debilitating divorce from Martha had made some impact upon the way he observed the world and his place in it. The basic principles that dictate his beliefs today – the omnipotent power of positive thought, allied to a benign acceptance of whatever fate chooses to throw in his face – seemed to have risen slowly, like a thin wisp of smoke, from the embers of his first marriage and the heartbreaking separation from his children. His ideas seemed already to be taking a vaguely philosophical path. He became interested in Eastern thought and began taking lessons in kung fu in Nashville, at which he quickly excelled, interested in channelling his concentration and building self-belief.

He wrote a letter to his ten-year-old daughter Lana, explaining what was happening in their lives, and concluding: 'Happiness does not come from having everything you want, but in understanding and accepting all, and in prayer and the belief that everything always happens for the best.' It was a hard message for any pre-teen to accept from her father, but it is revealing. He has repeated variations of this mantra ever since. It represents either admirable control over his own will and emotional impulses, or else a convenient method by which to abdicate himself from any tiresome responsibilities.

Mickey Raphael: He's definitely not in the real world! We talked about this the other day: we were talking about something in the future that might happen, and I was thinking about all kinds of ways to circumvent the situation, and Willie said: 'I don't worry about it until it happens. We deal with it when it happens.' I wish I could do that. My view is, if I don't worry about it, it will be a problem. It's a choice you make, and he has made the choice not to deal with it. It's a great talent. Almost naïve. Or maybe just that he knows [too] much.

Soon he would write 'One Day At A Time', the first song that explicitly deals with his adjusted world view: 'Don't ask how long I planned to stay/ It never crossed my mind/ I live one day at a time/ See that sparrow fly across the cloudy sky/ Searching for a patch of sunlight, so am I/ Wish I didn't have to follow and perhaps I won't in time/ I live one day at a time/ Yesterday is dead and tomorrow is blind/ I live one day at a time.'

It's a beautiful song, with all the easy, universal reach of an old gospel tune, expressing the kind of true, pure spiritual feeling he would revisit at length on *Yesterday's Wine*. With The Offenders, too, he was anxious that his new, positive outlook would be reciprocated. Johnny Bush was new to the band and to Nashville and he was worried that his drumming wasn't up to scratch among such seasoned pros as Jimmy Day. Bush visited Nelson and told him he felt he was the weakest link in the band and that it would be best for all concerned if he stood down and let someone else come in.

Johnny Bush: I told him: 'Man, this is your big break, and I know that because we're friends I've got this job, but I feel like I'm not hacking it.' He got real mad, and he said: 'You're a negative thinker. You've got to stop it. You're no Gene Krupa but you're a good drummer and you're going to get better, so stop thinking negative. Imagine you're throwing a dart at this target and whatever your goal is – shoot high. Even if you fall below that you're still better off than where you were.' He had a great philosophy. And I said, 'Yes, but you're stronger than I am.' Boy, he went through the roof! He went ballistic. 'No I'm not, Goddamn you!' – he started cussing – 'I am *not* stronger than you are. You've gotta stop thinking negative.'

Negativity and sadness, although it would feature in his songs for some time to come, no longer were his sole means of self-expression. Behind it all was Myrle, who kept in touch through letters and who wrote to him around this time outlining her own philosophy for happiness. Her words were startlingly similar to the way Nelson had endeavoured to live his life ever since: 'I will eliminate hatred, envy, jealousy, selfishness and cynicism by developing love for all humanity, because I know that a negative attitude toward others can never bring me success. I will cause others to believe in me because I will believe in them and in myself.' He must have learned it by heart.

The sessions for his second record for Liberty – the pointedly titled *Here's Willie Nelson*, released in June 1963 – took place in April, and the mood was significantly different from the first album. He recorded hard, swinging, upbeat versions of 'Columbus Stockade Blues' and an old Bob

Wills favourite, 'Roly Poly', but the album as a whole was much lusher than its predecessor, sprinkled with strings, glockenspiels and backing vocals, barely country at all in places. Only four Nelson originals were on show, an indication – along with the title – that he wanted an escape route from the popular perception of him as primarily being a songwriter, and instead wanted to make a splash as a performer. He had also, in hindsight, used up too many of his best songs on his debut.

Willie Nelson: Of course, the name of the first album was . . . *And Then I Wrote*! Quite frankly, I'm sure the people at the record company thought, If his albums don't sell that well, at least we'll have all these songs for other artists. But I had confidence in what I was doing.[4]

For much of the rest of 1963 he was either on the road or in California. He had sold the old family home in Goodlettsville and didn't have a house in Nashville; when in town he would stay with Hank Cochran and his wife. Shirley was still based out West, so Nelson accepted a job running the West Coast office of Pamper Music in order to be near her. He also recorded there. But the job at Pamper was unstimulating and he was pining for Nashville. Royalty money was again growing steadily, and Shirley was a positive influence in the sense that she kept him from spending too much of it.

In late November he returned to Nashville to record what turned out to be his final two sessions for Liberty. Tellingly, these included no Nelson originals whatsoever. The next day, he and Shirley went house hunting and found what amounted to their dream home: a ranch house on Greer Road in Ridgetop, a little town in the hills just under twenty miles north of Nashville. Ridgetop, as the house became generically known, was set in 600 acres of prime farm land and Nelson's serious intention was to become a gentleman farmer: raising hogs and cattle, riding horses, scattering feed for the ducks, geese and chickens all around, living the sweet life.

It became the first truly happy home he had known since childhood, and his absent children – who had never known even one – soon gravitated to it. Billy was the first to come. He was only six and missed his father terribly. Martha's marriage to Chuck Andrews in Las Vegas quickly produced two children, but it was not working out. There was a lot of drink involved, much shouting and physical arguments, and Billy would sit in his room, listening to his father's records and crying. Martha finally allowed him to leave and in the spring of 1964 he went to live at Ridgetop permanently. Shirley, who wasn't able to have children of her own, embraced this new family life. She gave up working on the road and settled into becoming a housewife and surrogate mother.

Shirley Nelson: When Billy came, he was *mine*. We went everywhere together.[5]

By the summer of 1965, all three Nelson children has escaped the chaos of Martha's escalating drinking and screaming in Las Vegas and settled with their father, Shirley and the animals in Ridgetop. He kept sending Martha her $600 each month anyway. He probably felt she had earned it.

His career was stumbling along. His reputation continued to grow as a writer: Ray Price had taken his version of 'Night Life' into the Top 20 in 1963, while Roy Orbison's recording of the Christmas song 'Pretty Paper' reached No. 15 in January 1964 and also became a UK Top 10 single. As a performer, however, things were somewhat different. He was disappointed at his lack of progress. He'd had two Top 10 singles with Liberty, but they had come early on, and subsequent singles had been lacklustre or simply disappeared. Neither of his two albums had set the world on fire or sold especially well. More significantly, neither had really shown him at his best or presented clearly what he wanted to do. It was a time when all the creative decisions lay firmly in the hands of the producer.

Willie Nelson: I thought I'd come in and take over. It didn't take long to see that was not going to happen.[6] You'd walk into the studio and they'd put six guys behind you who'd never seen your music before, and it's impossible to get the feel of it in a three-hour session.[7]

Here's Willie Nelson had been produced by Tommy Allsup following Joe Allison's departure from the label, and it had been overcooked, despite some wonderful performances on the soulful 'Home Motel' and the quintessentially tear-stained ballad 'The Way You See Me'. When the option came for Nelson to re-sign with Liberty in 1964 he spent a few days at their expense in Hollywood, listening to their entreaties, smiling and saying 'OK,' and then decided he would be better off elsewhere.

He eventually signed with Fred Foster's Monument label, despite being courted heavily by RCA. Foster had set up the label in 1958 and had a bona fide star on his books in Roy Orbison, who recorded his classic singles 'Oh, Pretty Woman', 'Only The Lonely' and many others for the label. With its rock 'n' roll and R&B acts, Monument was not an exclusively country label. Nelson had known Foster for a while. The Pamper office in Goodlettsville was near his base in Andersonville, and Nelson would often come over for some lunch, a chat and to play some songs. Foster was a big fan of his writing and had been the man who had rushed to get Orbison to hear 'Pretty Paper' and record it in time for the Christmas market. Significantly, he wasn't in any way scared of Nelson's idiosyncrasies. In fact his definition of a successful artist was someone who could be identified by a listener as soon as the needle hit the groove, and Nelson certainly fell into that category.

Fred Foster: I told him that if he was ever free, I really wanted him. So he came over one day and said, 'I'm free!' I just wanted Willie to be Willie. I thought he was unbelievably great, and I figured: either he's going to make it the way he is – or he won't make it at all. He was not meant to be in a regimented [system]. I figured he was so far ahead of his time, the public would catch up with him sooner or later.

Foster was as good as his word, even if Nelson ultimately wasn't. He only ever recorded two sessions for Monument, and released one single, but as brief as it was, it turned out to be an important moment in his career. Entering the studio with Foster producing on 6 July 1964, the first three-song session was unsuccessful: the material – aside from the marvellous '(There'll Be) Someone Waiting For You' – was uninspired, and Foster's attempt to liven it up with French horns, xylophones and trumpets badly backfired. But he was listening. By the time the next session arrived nearly three weeks later, Foster had learned his lesson, stripping the band right down to guitar, bass, light drums and a little saxophone. The result was 'I Never Cared For You', not only a superb song but also perhaps Nelson's most distinctive and successful recording of the entire 60s.

Beginning with an exhilarating flourish of flamenco guitar and a dramatic, stark vocal proclaiming that 'the sun is filled with ice/ And gives no warmth at all', 'I Never Cared For You' is a true wonder, driven by bongo drums, string bass and rattling acoustic guitars. Lyrically, it's primary trick is to employ a list of almost apocalyptic images, all of which are obviously and dramatically untrue: the sun is filled with ice; the sky was never blue; the stars are searching for a place to fall; and – finally, inevitably – he never cared for you.

As a whole it is unclassifiable, a sparse, rough-around-the-edges Tex-Mex pop song which, viewed from today's perspective and with the comfort of hindsight, sounds unmistakably like classic Willie Nelson: something that might have fitted onto *Red Headed Stranger* or *Spirit*, or indeed a close relation to the haunting title track from *The Great Divide*. But crucially, in 1964 it bore no resemblance to anything he had previously recorded. Along with the excellent, similarly spare B-side 'You Left Me A Long, Long Time Ago', 'I Never Cared For You' was the sound of Nelson finally being allowed to be himself. Although it was not a major hit, it transcended country music and potentially gave him access to a whole new audience.

Rodney Crowell: In 1964, the sounds of Dylan and the Beatles were all around the streets of east Houston where I lived. Willie had a local hit with 'I Never Cared For You'. I didn't listen to country radio then, it was on pop radio in between the Beatles and the Stones. Dylan wasn't on the radio then, but me and a friend shared a copy of *Bringing It All Back Home*. So we were listening to 'Subterranean Homesick Blues', 'I Never Cared For

You' and the Beatles' second album all at the same time. So Willie, for me, was pop music.

Unfortunately, Nelson failed to seize the momentum or see clearly what he had created. It was his last recording for Monument, and the mooted album never came into being. The problems apparently stemmed from a bizarre misunderstanding over advertising. Monument had signed Lloyd Price around the same time as they had Nelson, and Foster planned to run separate full-page adverts in the same issue of *Billboard* welcoming both of them to the label. He told this to Nelson, who loved the idea. Monument's advertising department came up with a regal theme for someone they regarded as musical royalty, planning a purple trim for the advert in a manner which was meant to suggest the hem of a king's robe. But when the advert was printed the colours bled and it looked, according to Foster, horrible.

Fred Foster: I cancelled the ad, and we were going to come up with a better one. The Lloyd Price ad was fine and his ran. I told Willie his was coming, but I think when he picked up *Billboard* and saw that he didn't have an ad and Lloyd did, he figured we didn't believe in him. I don't know what he actually thought. I think he'd had a few drinks, because he called me the next day and said he'd signed for RCA. He said something, the gist was, 'Oh well, I didn't think you wanted me.' I said, 'Well, you really can't do that, you have a contract here. I could cause you a lot of problems, Willie, but I ain't going to do it. I think you're brilliant, I think you're going to be great and have huge success, but I'd rather have your friendship.' So I just gave him a release.

Nelson's rather convoluted side of the story was that he had already told RCA he was going to sign for them before he had signed a contract with Monument, and that he didn't recall telling Fred Foster that he was ever planning on staying with his label long. 'Well, I don't figure how that makes much sense if you've signed a contract,' laughs Foster today. 'It was just a crazy time.' The most likely explanation is that RCA continued their pursuit of Nelson even after he had signed with Monument, and the advert gave him the perfect opportunity to switch sides. After all, he later admitted he regarded RCA as the greatest label in the world. It was a pivotal moment. Within a couple of months of jumping ship from Monument and signing with RCA he was in the studio recording a slushy version of his own Christmas song 'Pretty Paper' and a novelty German tune called 'Whisky Walzer' in abysmal, phonetic German which seemed occasionally to slide into something approaching Japanese. The contrast with 'I Never Cared For You' could not have been greater.

RCA would be his home for the next eight years. It has become shorthand in Nelson's potted biography that after he was signed by RCA he was simply left to wither on the vine, but it's a gross misconception, at least of the early part of the relationship. He had been chased by the label for some time, and his arrival was greeted with great enthusiasm. Chet Atkins, their vice-president and producer, was a gifted musician and recording artist in his own right, a wonderful guitarist and an intelligent man. He was also someone who liked to hold very tightly onto the reins. What he wanted to do was take the essential qualities that made Nelson unique – his songs and his voice – and apply the standard RCA house sound to them in an attempt to sugar the more obtuse parts of his music to appeal to a mass country music audience. Roger Miller – another eccentric songwriter, although he leaned more towards novelty – had just started having hits for Smash Records, and Atkins envisaged Nelson filling a similar role for RCA.

Don Light: Chet believed in Willie Nelson really early. He loved his songs, he loved his phrasings, he loved the way he sang. They weren't close friends but they *were* friends and they had huge mutual respect.

His initial recordings for RCA were a mixed bag. 'She's Not For You' and 'Permanently Lonely' were recorded in January 1965, for single release in May. 'She's Not For You' was the A-side and a fine song that he has often revisited, but the B-side was the real classic. Even through the Eddy Arnold style over-production, Nelson sounds like a man singing softly to the face in the mirror. For a man who has made a habit of departing, Nelson has written a lot of songs about being abandoned. Without underestimating the impact of his childhood trauma, it is nevertheless an interesting exercise to listen to many of Nelson's songs and imagine him singing softly to himself. 'You'll always be running and wondering/ What has happened to hearts that you've broken and left all alone.' It only made No. 43.

The first of the two albums he recorded for RCA in 1965 was called *Country Willie: His Own Songs*, taped over three days in April. It was largely an attempt to remind people who he was – a second introduction. Once again it emphasised his prowess as a songwriter, from its title on down, but many of the songs had initially been recorded for his Liberty debut and they did not generally benefit from being revisited. Atkins' production ideas on *Country Willie* were somewhat bizarre. Where he should have kept things simple – on 'Hello Walls' and 'So Much To Do', for example – he opted instead for a fussy approach littered with annoying little touches, such as Pete Drake's 'talking' steel guitar and over-elaborate lead guitar. Conversely, where a song called for a little more punch and pizzazz – re-recordings of 'Night Life' and 'Mr Record Man', for instance – he switched to a bare acoustic approach which sapped all the energy from the performances.

Nelson frequently sounded on the verge of sleep. It was generally a sympathetic record, however, and 'One Day At A Time' and 'It Should Be

Easier Now' were simply triumphant, whether thanks to luck or design. In December he recorded *Country Favourites: Willie Nelson Style*, which contained no Nelson originals whatsoever. Backed by the Texas Troubadours, it was designed as a tip of the hat to his roots in the dance halls of his home state and worked well to fulfil that premise.

Both of his first two RCA albums emphasised that he was not enjoying a particularly purple patch in terms of his songwriting. For all his open-mindedness, Nelson has never been a man who has had the luxury of calling upon a particularly wide palette of musical textures or a broad lyrical lexicon. His subject matter in the early and mid-60s was limited and, as such, the success of his early songs depended on a certain alchemy taking place between simple, spare words and a basic melody: when it worked it was mesmerising, but when it was off it could be ordinary. Having covered his elemental themes so exceptionally in the likes of 'Night Life' and 'Crazy', he was often left raking over the same ground.

Merle Haggard: Once you've filled a void, you can't go back and re-write 'Crazy' or 'Night Life'. That void is already filled. He's already done that. He's probably like me, in that he probably ends up re-writing each one of those great ideas over and over. Obviously, they're written, they're gone, archived and past, and it's pretty hard to satisfy himself and continue on with thoughts worthy of writing.

Nelson had signed a contract with the *Grand Ole Opry* on 28 November, 1964, soon after signing with RCA. It was the cherry on the cake. He was settled into Ridgetop with his new wife, he was contracted to one of the most established and respected record companies in town, and now he had become a member of the most famous country music institution that had ever been. And the songwriting royalties were still pouring in. For the first time in his life, he had reached the point where he could simply slow up, roll down the window and enjoy the view. Accordingly, 1965 became something of a lost year for Willie Nelson the road traveller. He acceded to severe pressure from Shirley to quit the road and settle down on the farm with her. He would play some dates during this period, but nothing like the intensive touring he had previously undertaken.

Johnny Bush: Shirley was as good as she could be, but she was very domineering and wanted him isolated from all of us. She figured that we were the bad influence, not knowing that it was him! But when they were at home she wanted Willie to be with her. She wanted him off the road, and she wanted him home.

There was no financial imperative to tour. The BMI royalties for radio, television and live performances of his big hits like 'Crazy' were, at a conservative estimate, bringing in $100,000 a year, and that wasn't including the royalties from sales. He was aware his songwriting needed attention and felt a break would do no harm. He was comfortable, his children were heading back home to live with him, and he had his farm to occupy his time. In a little over a year, he put on 30 lbs in weight and began to look almost plump.

Ridgetop was important to him. He installed a farm manager called George Hughes, who ran the place with his wife Ruby on a day-to-day basis. They started off with one pig, which soon expanded to two hundred Angus cattle, eight hundred hogs, nine horses, three ponies, numerous fowl, dogs and cats. He would sell his hogs at market, eat fresh eggs, trade horses, and cheerfully watch some of his money disappear. He had grown up among real farming stock and he knew the difference between serious farming and a rich man's hobby. He didn't look upon it as a serious business, which was just as well.

Johnny Bush: He thought he was going to be a hog farmer. That was another trip! His feed bills were three times what he sold the hogs for – he was not a successful hog farmer. That went down the tube. I was in on that. I was just out helping to build fences.

His other main achievement as a gentleman farmer was shooting Ray Price's prizefighting rooster, a story which gives as clear a picture of both the cultural climate of Nashville in the mid-60s and the kind of environment Nelson thrived in as anything can. Price had sent his rooster to Ridgetop to 'get some exercise' before a fight, but it began killing some of the hens, who were regarded as pets by Shirley. When Price dragged his heels taking the rooster away, Nelson went into the barn with a double-barrelled shotgun and blew its brains out. 'It was the end of everything between us,' he later recalled.[8] It took Price literally years to forgive him.

But it was not all hog-raising and cock-killing. As well as the occasional session for his two RCA albums, he also had two reasonably high profile projects in Nashville to keep things ticking over. His membership of the *Grand Ole Opry* obliged him to perform at the Ryman Auditorium around thirty times a year, usually on a Saturday night, so most weekends he had to be home. It was all about prestige: he would play three songs at intervals throughout the evening, and would pick up only $35 a show, which was scale. At least he was near Tootsie's.

He also became a regular face on Ernest Tubb's TV show, which was syndicated nationally and ran for half an hour every Saturday afternoon. Tubb was a veteran Texan performer and, of course, an old childhood idol of Nelson's; his backing band was the Texas Troubadours, whom Nelson had recorded with on *Country Favourites*. It was a pleasant gig. He was a frequent guest host and performer, appearing as many as one hundred times in total, and it did his profile no harm. He was firmly part of the establishment, and his image was tailored to match: $300 suits, always with a tie, Stacey Adams shoes, clean-shaven, a neat haircut, a slick repartee with the audience and a ready grin. From a certain angle he was a dead ringer for Joe Pesci in *Goodfellas*.

He might have looked every inch the country superstar, but he was really no such thing. He hadn't had a hit record since 'Touch Me' in 1962, and although *Country Favourites* was poised to make it to No. 9 in the *Billboard* country album charts and stay in the run-down for seventeen weeks, it was having hit singles that really mattered. It was all getting a little too cosy. And he had a familiar itch that had to be scratched.

Johnny Bush: Well, you can't cage Willie Nelson! That year he took off, I think to him it was like being in jail.

The road was calling.

SMOKING POT MADE IT BETTER

Willie Nelson is talking about drugs.

On cue, the figure lying on his sofa suddenly rises from his stupor and staggers to his feet in the centre of the room.

'Are you all right?' Nelson asks.

'No,' the man replies. He isn't all right. He rushes out of the room. Nelson smiles and continues sucking on his joint. 'I guess he had a little too much pot with the wine.'

He is almost as famous for his dope-smoking as he is for his music. It is a well-deserved reputation. His room in the hotel could be smelt before it was seen. One of his band members, Mickey Raphael, describes his weed as the Dope That Killed Elvis. Whatever that means.

Nelson calls it his medicine. It grows naturally and should be legalised. He hates cigarettes, though he used to smoke them. And alcohol is just no good for him.

'I switched from whisky to marijuana,' he says slowly. He makes it sounds like it happened overnight or even during the course of an evening, but it was a long, gradual process of realisation. 'Whisky made me very negative and pot sort of calmed me down a little bit. I don't want to give either one of those too much power, but the facts are the facts. I was drinking too much and smoking a little pot made it better.'

He still drinks a little alcohol, but nothing compared to the amount he imbibed in the past. Now he prefers water. Fruit. Natural highs.

'I still drink now but I know that when I do my thinking is not going to be as clear,' he admits. 'You can just as well be a happy drunk if you want to be, and sing happy songs and have a good time, but a lot of the time there's that negative thing that leaks in there. So I quit drinking a lot, and I found out that my thinking was a little bit clearer.'

Marijuana is almost like a sedative for him. Some may wonder whether he uses it to escape his true personality. That one day every unique character trait might become buried under a cloud of dope dust. That he'll forget who he really is.

'No,' he says softly. 'I haven't really worried about that, because I know that there would be some part of me that would demand to be remembered.' He smiles and looks serene. 'That's not something I really can or would want to have any control over. It's just a matter, I guess, of whatever energy we have in us that will make us individuals.' He takes his medicine every day. He will occasionally have a lay off, although not usually through choice. Doctor's orders.

'My throat went out and I did three weeks of silence: no smoking. It wasn't hard, but one of the problems for me not smoking is sleeping and the dreams that you have. Then you remember why you started smoking, to stop all them crazy fucking dreams. Those crazy dreams that you never really get used to.'

He looks down at the joint in his hand, lights its cold tip, and puts the other end in his mouth. There will be no crazy dreams tonight.

5. 1966–1970

He started out again, almost alone. Nelson had been off the road for the best part of a year and, though his spell of domesticity had been fun while it lasted, it was ultimately unfulfilling. He was longing to get back out there again. In doing so he was going directly against his wife's wishes, but he felt he had no choice. Although his marriage to Shirley gave the appearance of being a reasonably happy one up until this point, in reality he was feeling trapped and had resorted to familiar ways; he had already, for instance, started running around with other women.

Willie Nelson: Shirley loved farming as long as I was there with her. But then when it came time for me to go back on the road, she had to stay home. I knew that was probably the wrong thing to do, I should have taken her out with me again. She got restless, and the marriage started going downhill after that.[1]

Mostly he played Texas. He had a new booking agent in Hayes Jones, who could get him plenty of work, particularly back home. Aside from Wade Ray on bass, who travelled with him, he would work with the house band at each venue, which caused problems. With his unusual rhythms and improvisory singing style, other musicians – particularly drummers – had trouble keeping in time, so he put the call out to Johnny Bush. Bush had been living in Nashville, helping out occasionally with general farm work at Ridgetop when he wasn't trying to make his way as a session drummer for the studios, but despite the fact he was only charging $10 per side for his talents it was slow work – most of the session jobs in Nashville were well and truly sown up. He was, however, reluctant to go out on the road because he had ambitions as a singer and a songwriter. Nelson cut him a deal: if he promised to stay with him for a year, at the end of that period he would produce a session for Bush and pay for the studio time out of his own pocket.

Practically the trio's first gig together was at Panther Hall Ballroom in Fort Worth on 9 July 1966, part of a string of one-night stands in Texas. The performance was recorded for release as *Live Country Music Concert*, produced by Felton Jarvis, Chet Atkins' assistant and the man would later inject some life into Elvis Presley's comatose career in the late-60s. The live album remains Nelson's most successful RCA release, precisely because it is free of any studio fuss and elaboration. Instead, it is an electrically charged document of Nelson, Bush and Ray performing in front of a rowdy and loudly appreciative Texas audience (Nashville session man Chip Young added rhythm guitar later in the studio, but it is almost inaudible), with the vocals way up front and more of Nelson's distinctive, clambering guitar runs than would normally have survived on record. It really isn't so different – aside from the fact it is a much shorter set and his voice is far richer – than the kind of show he plays today. Among the fourteen songs aired, most were Nelson classics like 'Hello Walls', 'Touch Me' and 'One Day At A Time', but the most interesting selection was a version of the Beatles' 'Yesterday', which had been out for about a year. The Beatles weren't exactly popular in country music circles, but Nelson loved the song as soon as he heard it. It was all just music to him. He would never be swayed by petty prejudice or, God forbid, collar-length hair.

The rest of the touring band came together shortly after the Panther Hall record. Loyal on–off sidekick and force of nature Jimmy Day joined the fold on steel guitar, while David Zettner, a young bass player whom Bush had discovered playing in San Antonio, came in soon after. Collectively, they called themselves the Record Men, a rather ironic choice given that they almost never made it into the studio.

And then there was Paul English. Manager, bouncer, drummer, good-luck charm and stone bad news all rolled into one, English was a cartoon character, or at the very least a creature who had swaggered off the pages of a Damon Runyon novel. His speaking voice was a low-frequency nasal mumble, his clothes habitually dark, topped off with a black cowboy hat. His sculpted beard was 'pirate black' and – as the song that was written in his honour would later run – he looked like the devil. He has never drunk alcohol but gained his kicks in numerous other ways, very few of which were legal. He was both a gentleman and a gangster, a fighter and a diplomat, a redneck cowboy and a romantic fool.

English had grown up in Fort Worth and was the genuine article, working as a pimp for many of the local hotels – and the local police – organising girls for the guests. He prided himself on his professionalism. The motto was: 'Girls come and go but pimps are here to stay.' Running prostitutes was his main source of income, but he did a little of everything. He wore a gun in his belt and a gold medal around his neck depicting St Dismas, the Good Thief who died on the cross next to Jesus. The inference was clear: honour amongst thieves.

Paul English: I was a police character, a guy who is in the underworld but not connected with anyone. Just an outlaw. We were the Ten Most Unwanted. We'd get barred from entire towns. But I had a good name, a name that was solid. I didn't do anybody wrong, I never had it in me. We had a lot of good rules: you don't mess with somebody else's wife; you don't go into somebody's house unless you're invited; you don't carry a weapon in people's houses – if you got a weapon you give it to them when you walk in the door; you don't ever call a guy a friend and then do him wrong – that's just against the rules; you don't rob Mom and Pop. We had a lot of character. We had more morals than the square guy on the corner.

English had first run into Willie Nelson back in the wild lands of Fort Worth in the mid-50s, when Nelson was working as a disc jockey at KCNC. Their initial connection came from Paul's brother Oliver playing guitar with Nelson during the half-hour live spot on his radio show. One day they found they were a drummer short. Despite the fact that English had never played drums before in his life – he was, he claims, a trumpet player – Oliver called him up. All he did was keep time tapping on a snare, but that was all they needed. When Nelson got a steady job at one of the Fort Worth clubs, he asked English to join the band.

They worked together as a three-piece with a long-forgotten front man for about six weeks, until Nelson got a better job on the Jacksonboro Highway. But they stayed friends and remained in contact. It's likely that a few favours passed back and forth along the way. Later, English moved to Houston and continued working on the wrong side of the tracks, and whenever Nelson passed through he and the band would stay with him and his wife Carlene. In 1966, Nelson and the Record Men came to town, and he mentioned he was trying to get hold of Skeeter Davis's drummer, whom they both knew from Fort Worth. English said, 'Hell, I play drums better than him!' and Nelson replied: 'Well, you wouldn't work for $30 a day, would you?' So he did. And he's been there ever since.

Paul English: I was not a very nice person when I went to work for Willie. I was pretty roustabout – if a fight came along I was gonna be in there. I've never lied about that. I never did wear that badge [of respectability]. Whatever you saw with me was what I was, and Willie knew that when he hired me. When Willie came along I gave it up. If I hadn't met him I'd be doing time.

English didn't automatically turn into a saint. Initially, his job in the entourage was to play behind Johnny Bush in the section of the show where Bush sang a few of his own songs. The Record Men would play two two-hour shows each night and eventually, when Bush felt English was sufficiently equipped to follow Nelson's wayward muse, he allowed him to play drums on the first Record Men set. He finally took over drums completely in 1968 when Bush left to pursue his own very successful solo career, but being a musician has always been perhaps the least notable of English's attributes. He has rather unkindly been called the worst drummer in the world, and anybody who has heard his snare shuffling up a tempo and then slowing down again during the same song might have some sympathy with that judgment.

He has played with Nelson for approaching forty years and has known him for fifty, which leads to the inevitable conclusion that English was not brought on board simply for his musical prowess. Although he is now into his 70s and times have changed, in the old days his role was untitled but well-defined: he was there to take care of business, whether that meant paying hotel bills, or simply pulling a gun when the promoter proved reluctant to pay, or keeping the band and crew in line. He was brought in to give the band a bit of swagger and muscle and danger, and he did it admirably. Above all, he was there to look out for his boss.

This was the first real band of Nelson's career, and it contained trace elements of the general ethos which eventually transferred itself to his famous Family Band, the one that's still on the seemingly eternal road with him today. During the next three years they not only evolved into an extraordinarily tight musical unit, but also became fast and loyal friends, a true gang in thought and word and deed. It *was* like a family. When David Zettner – by far the youngest member – was drafted in 1970, Nelson paid for him to fly home and then talked around his contacts to try and get him off the hook. When Zettner was later discharged on medical grounds, the band picked him up from the army base in a limousine and instantly created a role for him back in the band, despite the fact they now had a new bass player. 'It was,' he recalls, 'like I'd just been in the bathroom for a long time.'

It was a communal philosophy that also worked its way down into his home life. Between 1965 and 1970, Ridgetop became the base for an extended family of Nelson acolytes. After she divorced her second husband, Martha re-married and came to live nearby so she could be near the children. Ira and Myrle came – separately, of course – with their spouses and their other children and settled. Nelson may have noted ruefully that there was nothing like money and success for bringing a family back together, but he never provided anything other than love and support for his parents. His sister Bobbie moved with her third husband Jack and her three children. David Zettner took a room. Paul English and his family came and moved to Madison, about ten miles away. Wade Ray was across the road. It became a little rebel county, an independent annex of Texas in the Tennessee mountains.

RCA were running out of ideas. Felton Jarvis's first session in 1966 had been a disaster. He had tried to update Nelson's sound by throwing strings, cheesy trumpets, scratchy funk guitar and a truly awful swinging rock beat to 'San Antonio Rose' and 'Columbus Stockade Blues', of all things, and it had been – inevitably – a spectacular failure. Nelson tried to sing with a cheerful swing but merely sounded rightfully embarrassed. Even the most significant new song that he had recently written – 'The Party's Over', a classic 4 a.m. ballad in its rawest form – was scrubbed and sanitised by the production sheen. The single reached No. 24 in March 1967, following on from the minor success of 'One In A Row', which had climbed to No. 19 in late 1966. It was a reasonable showing, but not good enough. The label was tiring of Nelson's inability to make a major breakthrough and had no solution to offer other than to keep throwing different styles at him in the hope that something might stick. Nelson thought the solution should have been simple: let him do what he wanted – which was to recreate in the studio the natural, slightly rough music he was making on the road with the band – and then get the label to push it as hard as they could. Their failure to do so told him they didn't really believe in him.

Willie Nelson: With that name RCA they should be able to do anything they want to do with an artist. If an artist has any talent at all they should have enough money and promotional work and experience to at least get that artist's material out somewhere and get it exposed. I was an artist on RCA but there was no money being spent promotion-wise on Willie Nelson and it seemed like I was only cutting my albums there like dub sessions. They would release them and see if anyone [else] wanted to record them. I just didn't feel the promotional department were behind me. In fact, I knew they weren't.[2]

It was not an uncommon problem. The RCA roster back in the mid to late 60s was full of successful songwriters. It was a definite and conscious policy of the time to sign a top writer like, say, Justin Tubb, and at least ensure that you had access to his best songs for your major artists. In many ways, Nelson was becoming a victim of his own early, spectacular success as a songwriter, but he was also at fault for choosing the wrong label when he stood at the crossroads between RCA and Monument back in 1964. Strangely, he didn't really fight his corner. There were no stand-up fights over artistic freedom. He just did what he was told and went away and brooded.

He was also a victim of timing: there wasn't a general public appetite for raw country music at this time, and there's no indication that, even if he had been allowed to do what he wanted and it had been promoted to the hilt, he would necessarily have broken through. He would, however, have relished the opportunity to find out. The two sessions in Nashville for *The Party's Over* album in June 1967 summed up the whole problem. It was a rare session in that both Johnny Bush and Jimmy Day were part of the studio band, which they thought augured well for the outcome. However, the ideas they had worked up together night after night on tour were dismissed out of hand by Chet Atkins.

Johnny Bush: Willie would write these things and we would want to play them the way we were doing them on the road. I knew what he wanted. When we got to the studio, Chet would take over: 'Well, we're going to do it this way.' It would be completely different from what we were doing on the road. The day we cut [this] session, Jimmy Day and Paul English and I drove from Texas to Nashville. Chet had rode my ass unmercifully, kept saying the drums weren't very good. I was playing a bolero beat the way I knew Willie liked it, and he really embarrassed me. Jerry Reed was on that session, and [later] he turned and said: 'Why don't you go over there and tell Chet Atkins to kiss your ass!' I thought that was a great compliment.

Bush would soon be free to pursue his own interests. As promised, Nelson did produce his first session – taping Bush's 'Sound Of A Heartache' and his own 'A Moment Isn't Very Long' in June 1967 – and by the time Bush left in 1968 he was making $2,500 a night as opposed to the Record Men's $800. They gave him a rowdy send-off nonetheless.

As a songwriter, Nelson was still capable of fitful genius, but life on the road sapped time and energy. He usually wrote alone in the seclusion of his hotel room, but 'pre-production' tended not to be a quiet, contemplative process, but rather a chaotic immersion in bits and pieces of half-ideas which somehow came together at the last minute. He literally picked up scraps of inspiration wherever he could.

David Zettner: The way he would go about writing a tune was just extraordinary to me. My first job in the band was to help Johnny Bush take care of Willie's clothes. I kind of took over that job. John told me, 'Make sure you always go through all the pockets, especially in the coats.' And sure enough, I'd find little pieces of newspapers with something written on it, napkins – a lot of napkins – with stuff written on it. I'd always fold it up and put it in a cigar box, and after one of the shows we'd present Willie with what we'd found. He'd go, 'Oh yeah, this is a cool tune!' He was writing these tunes in little bits and pieces, and he'd sit there and play them. I remember asking him, 'How can you remember all of this?' We were all pretty wasted, you know. He said, 'I never worry about it. My rule of thumb is: if it comes back a second time and I remember it, it's worth looking at. It's a good 'un.'

It was 1967. *Pet Sounds* had been and gone and the Beatles' *Sergeant Pepper's Lonely Hearts Club Band* was just around the corner, but the vibrant primary colours and LSD-influenced carnivalism of prime psyche-delia seemed a long way away from Nashville and the conservative enclave of country music. Johnny Cash and Bob Dylan were close friends but, by and large, any attempts to emulate the counter-culture were generally hopelessly misguided, uncomprehending and 'square', amounting to little more than a cynical effort in taking a popular song of the time, castrating it and then selling it to a country audience. However, shifts in society ensured that small changes were taking place at a personal level. Marijuana had now become a drug of choice for many artists, including The Record Men, although by no means exclusively. Nelson would occasionally take amphetamine on the road to keep awake, and although he had already had lots of experience with pot, for a long time he could take or leave it.

Johnny Bush: I was smoking this shit before he was. I remember one night in south Texas, at a place called Schroeder Hall. Wade Ray and Jimmy Day and I were out under this tree and we were burning one. Willie walked by and we said, 'Want some?' and he said, 'Nah, that stuff gives me a headache,' and just kept walking. Can you imagine that!

Alcohol was still his primary means of escape – and his downfall. 'Aw, I never drank half as much as people thought I did,' he said later. '[But] once I did pull a bender everybody in the world heard about it.'[3] Indeed, he was by all accounts a horrible drunk, violent and prone to blackouts, and the endless routine of the road exacerbated it: they would play the gig, then afterwards pile into the station wagon and head off to wherever the good times might reasonably be expected to be. When Nelson later claimed that he 'knew all the bartenders and waitresses by their first names [in Texas]',[4] he really wasn't kidding. Often he would shout from the back of the car, 'Y'all pull down to this club, I've got some old friends there.' They would stay up all night entertaining and then head on up the road in the morning, usually with Paul English cracking the whip.

It got so bad that in a hotel in Waco the band engineered his arrest. Nelson had been up partying for days, playing shows then getting everyone back to the hotel for some more fun, then doing it all over again. He was exhausted, but genetically simply incapable of calling it quits. Paul slipped some cash to the man at the reception desk and told him: 'Could you go up there and just arrest him? Just say, "Y'all been making too much noise, Mr Nelson, will you come with us?" Then we're going to get him another

room down the hall and we'll put him in there. Nobody will be the wiser.'
Nelson was thus manoeuvred two doors down to a new room, and the
party was broken up. Except nobody seemed to have told him.

David Zettner: We started hearing this crash! boom! bang! two doors
down in Willie's [new] room. It was 1 a.m. So we called Paul. He went in
there and when he came out, he said, 'It's OK. We're going to have to pay
for that room though!' Willie was practising karate and had kicked out all
the lights in the ceiling. Poor guy, I don't think he even remembered doing
it.

English simply lit up a joint for Nelson and they smoked 'until his head
was literally under the table'. He was put to bed and the next day woke
up in a ransacked room, asking innocently, 'What happened?' Alcohol
unleashed a depressive rage that worried his friends, but marijuana seemed
to tame him. Both he and his closest friends have commented how it acts
like medicine, how it calms him and makes him see clearly. He is 'hostile'
without it, claims Johnny Bush, and long ago reached the stage where he
struggles to function without it.

Paul English: When Willie drank he was a terrible drunk. He knows it, he
really does. Willie's not [a happy drunk]. He was the kind of drunk who
doesn't know anything that happened. He'd always want to drive,
somehow I'd have to catch him and get his feet on the ground so he can't
run away from me. I remember this one thing very vividly: he had a new
Lincoln – this was in Nashville – and he kicked the door then he tried to
get in. I finally got the keys off him and said, 'I'm driving.' I pulled him
by the belt into the car and said, 'You don't want to hurt my friends. You
don't want to get arrested or anything?' 'Awww no, I wouldn't do that.'
Then he tried to jump out! That's the kind of drunk he is. He started
kicking the window, and he kicked that window about three inches out.
It's better for him to smoke that marijuana. He don't get out of it. He says
he smokes to get normal. He don't get high, he gets normal. And I believe
him.

It was a symptom of unhappiness, and by the late-60s Nelson was actively
feeling around and asking some serious spiritual questions, and there is
little doubt that his escalating use of marijuana was a factor in some of the
answers he would later come up with. Having Paul English on the road
made access to drugs easier all round. He could arrange safe and regular
supplies through his contacts, paying $15–20 for a can – or a lid as they
called it – and spread it around. Other drug use was limited. The band had
all been slipped a Mickey Finn containing some kind of horse tranquilliser
before a show in Fort Worth which caused them to have a nightmarish
onstage experience, shaking and sweating through gritted teeth. Although

Nelson experimented with hallucinogens for a short time, he found that his psyche wasn't cut out for it. He had one too many bad trips and quit.

Willie Nelson: I was thinking I was going to have to go out into the mountains and face down the devil, and I finally figured out that I don't need to worry about that shit.[5]

The other most obvious secession to the spirit of the times occurred when the band went to play on the West Coast. They rented a place in Hollywood on Sunset Strip and Nelson handed out $100 each for them all to buy some new clothes. Until then they had been wearing brocade jackets, frilly shirts and bulldog ties, pretty standard uniform for a country outfit. This time they decided to cut loose. English bought his famous black cape for $29, and added a sash, trousers and a shirt – the whole thing coming off like a cross between Count Dracula and a low-rent magician. Day bought a pirate-style outfit, Zettner chose a Davy Crockett costume, and Nelson bought some kind of fishnet shirt and a poncho. Of course, they were able to walk down the Strip in the late-60s wearing whatever they wanted and nobody batted an eyelid, but when they got back to Texas the reaction was somewhat different. It might have been that Nelson was already thinking that he could attract a hippie audience to country music and thus bring the redneck and the long-hair closer together, as he eventually was credited with doing in 1973, but it was still too early for Texas. More likely he was just trying to cause a bit of a stir. A fraught night in Fort Worth was enough to make them all think twice.

David Zettner: About the first twenty minutes of that show it was normal, then all of a sudden they turned on us. We noticed how they were coming closer to the bandstand: 'Hey, what's the matter with you? You queer or something? What's that thing you're wearing? What happened to you?' And it starts spreading. They didn't like us, because we looked like these hippies. It kinda scared me. Paul told me, 'I wouldn't go out there in that crowd. Just stay back here.' It was fashion. We thought we were hip, man, but Texas was not ready for this West Coast, hippie thing, where men and women were both wearing the same clothes. We had to watch ourselves after that. We thought: Let's go buy our cowboy clothes and get blue jeans again, and in Texas we'll just dress like street guys. Save the other stuff.

Paul English could always get away with a little more than the others because he gave off the kind of vibe which strongly suggested it would require either a brave or foolish man to take him on. He was obviously packing something. He became a kind of protector for all the guys in the band, and several times he had to approach an unfriendly face and quietly ask, 'What's your problem?' He couldn't have been further removed from the hippie mentality if he had tried, but he liked the theatrical aspect of it all, as well as the fact that it wound people up and put them on edge. Nelson has always been an arch-antagonist in his own sweet way, and English could relate to that. Besides, the new look worked for him. Before a show at Panther Hall, most bands would appear on the *Panther Hall Ballroom TV Show* on KTVY Channel 11, hosted by Texas DJ Bill Mack. The show was taped at six o'clock and then broadcast at eight. English had worn his cape on the show and when he came off the bandstand there were thirteen girls waiting for his autograph. And he thought to himself: the cape, it stays.

None of this frenetic, electric last-gang-in-town interplay was making it onto record. Nelson released two albums in 1968, *Texas In My Soul* and *Good Times*. The former had been an easy sell, recorded back in August 1967 in two quick sessions. Nelson needed no bidding to sing the songs that eulogised his home state, while Chet Atkins believed it would at least have a ready-made audience: the clubs and honky-tonks of Texas remained Nelson's primary hunting ground as a live act. He was back in the studio in December 1967 and March 1968, cutting the tracks for *Good Times*. It was an odd record, with some of the songs culled from sessions as far back as 1965. While attractively sparse in places – with just guitar, bass and vocals – elsewhere its two producers (Jarvis and Atkins) and three arrangers administered overdubs of varying quality and styles, ensuring it was ultimately a patchy, disjointed piece of work. One thing Nelson became brilliantly adept at when he finally gained control over his own recordings was creating a strong single mood throughout an entire record, but too many of his RCA albums were simply collections of disparate songs rather than proper albums.

Paul English: He wasn't doing anything with RCA. We were doing pretty well on the road, but our records weren't doing it. They didn't sound like us and we couldn't sound like them. They were slick and polished, and we weren't, by far, anywhere near slick and polished! Sometimes slick and polished don't go with the common people – they like something real.

Having a photograph of the artist on the cover teaching a woman in shorts how to grip a golf club didn't really help sell him as a serious artist: in taking him out of his suits and ties, they succeeded only in making him look cheesy. The stand-outs on *Good Times* were the laid-back, tongue-in-cheek pop of the title track, which reached the nursery slopes of the country charts but was later taken to greater mainstream success by Jack Jones, and the jazzy, melancholy 'December Day', later worked over for *Yesterday's Wine* and hinting a little at the more philosophical side of Nelson's current predilections.

The record also featured a trio of songs co-written with Shirley: 'Pages', 'She's Still Gone' and 'Little Things', each one an essay in escalating mawkish despair. The latter in particular is almost a textbook study of knee-jerk country ticks: abandoned children with outstanding school grades, a broken-down marriage, even houses torn down to make way for freeways. If this was what life was like for Nelson and his wife in Ridgetop, then God help them. In fact, the marriage was in worse shape than even the songs which described it. 'We were in a very bad period,' Nelson later admitted. 'Having terrible fights, breaking up and getting back together again then breaking up again.'[6]

Having long ago failed in her attempts to keep her husband off the road, Shirley now looked on as he continued with his career and hers disappeared as she stayed at home and raised the children – *his* children. Who knows what private pacts were broken. There was certainly a little old-fashioned chauvinism going on: he asked her to stop writing songs, perhaps wary of the competition, or not caring to hear whatever home truths they contained.

All in all, she was both professionally and emotionally frustrated, drinking as hard if not harder than Nelson, popping pills and generally running out of control. She was in and out of hospital, if not for her drinking or drug-taking then for her annual bouts of pneumonia. She wrecked numerous cars, once skidding for 200 metres as she mowed down post-boxes, fences and hedges. She threw her husband through a glass door – 'He taught me just enough karate to make me dangerous,' she said – during one of their almost endless arguments. When Nelson was home, he would often camp out in the hollow behind the house. She slapped the children, who – under Shirley's wayward jurisdiction – looked upon school as a mere option. Susie once went 28 days without attending, while Lana, at 14, was dating a 27-year-old called Mickey Newbury and planning to run away with him until Nelson pulled a gun on Newbury and told him to disappear. Newbury was a Nashville songwriter who would later write 'Sweet Memories' and '(I Just Dropped In) To See What Condition My Condition Was In', both of which have since been recorded by Nelson. Circles and cycles, indeed. Lana had other admirers, too.

David Zettner: I was living in the house when all that occurred. I was 23 and Willie had this gorgeous daughter named Lana. Oh shit! We became two peas in a pod, which worried Shirley. She very nicely asked, 'Don't you think y'all getting a little heavy here in the house?' So I thought maybe I'd better find an apartment to make it easier on the family. Willie didn't really want that to happen: 'I don't see anything wrong with it, I enjoy having you around.' I think him and Shirley were having problems. They were good about keeping it from all of us, but we just knew they were having a problem.

All in all, his marriage to Shirley was a story with only one possible ending. In his autobiography, which is largely free of great emotional insight, Nelson recounts the truly horrendous moment when Shirley discovered that another women had borne him a child. It was November 1969, and baby Paula Carlene had been born in Houston on 27 October. The hospital bill had been sent to his home address, and Shirley had opened the mail to read the blunt, mechanical facts which confirmed that her husband had not merely been unfaithful (in broad terms at least, she must surely have known that was already a likelihood) but had now also fathered an illegitimate child; the one thing, of course, she could never give him. Perhaps the deepest cut of all was that the faceless woman who had finally destroyed her marriage was registered as Mrs Connie Nelson. She had not only stolen her man, thought Shirley, she had also stolen her name.

It would have been scant consolation to know that, back in Texas, the so-called Mrs Connie Nelson wasn't feeling much better about the whole thing. Like so many young women before her, Constance Koepke had fallen in love with the song first, and the singer second. Born on 6 June 1944, Connie was a Texas girl. Smart, tall, beautiful and inherently nice, she was raised as a Catholic in the roughhouse suburbs of Federal Road, east Houston, described by Rodney Crowell, who also grew up there, as a 'hellhole'. At the age of twenty she was still living at home with her parents, working in Anchor Hocking Glass factory in Jacinto City just east of Houston, bingeing on British rock 'n' roll and dismissing the country music that buzzed all around her as 'twangy' and headache inducing. Then she heard Willie Nelson's 'I Never Cared For You' in late 1964.

Connie Nelson: Oh my God, it was just haunting – the melody, the words, the voice. I just absolutely loved it. I knew when I heard that song that there was nothing like him. I would listen to the [pop] radio all the time trying to hear that song as much as I could, and one day the DJ mentioned that it was a crossover hit by a country singer, Willie Nelson. So I started listening to the country stations just to hear that song more.

When she heard one country station announce that Nelson was coming to play at the 21 Club in the tiny town of Cut 'n' Shoot, near Conroe, about forty miles north of Houston, she couldn't resist. She and a girlfriend were booked to work the 3 p.m.–11 p.m. shift at the factory, but they both skipped work and headed up to Conroe at the last minute. They made no reservations. Connie and her friend were sitting at the back until Jimmy Day spotted them and motioned them to sit right at the front. This wasn't fate, merely tactics. Connie was exceptionally pretty, blonde, blue-eyed, and Nelson wasn't the first – nor indeed the hundredth – musician to have a piece of eye candy manoeuvred into his eye line. On the contrary, he was very good at it.

Johnny Bush: Where do wives come from? They come from the third row at a concert. It's the tender trap. Willie once said, 'If they're gonna bait the trap with pussy, they're going to catch me every time!'

For her part, Connie had arrived with no expectations. She wasn't going to see Willie Nelson, she was going to hear 'I Never Cared For You'. Or at least that's what she told herself until she saw him.

Connie Nelson: Willie got up to sing, we were right in front of him, and he kept looking down and smiling, you know. And I thought, Oooh, he's even cute! Oh God, it was ridiculous.

According to David Zettner, who wasn't there but obviously heard the story passed down through the band, 'Willie spotted Connie out on the dance floor – and it was all over. I mean, Jimmy Day went out there during the break and told this beautiful girl, "Willie would sure like to meet you if that's possible." She just jumped right up – "Sure" – and walked back there and, man, they were rocking and rolling from that time on.'

Nelson invited Connie and her friend back to his hotel room after the show. It was an innocent and entirely routine occasion: around twenty people, including the band, friends and various hangers-on, spent the night passing a guitar around, drinking and singing and playing songs until the sun rose. Connie listened to Nelson talking a little and singing a lot and became smitten. He took her phone number, and every time he passed through town – which was a lot in those days, Texas being their main source of live income – she would go and see him. And one thing led to another. She became his Houston Girl. It was 1965.

Though they continued seeing each other throughout that year and into 1966, they weren't really an item. If she had even thought or indeed cared about it, Connie must have been aware that she was not holding exclusive world rights to the Willie Nelson franchise. Far from it. Even so, she claims she had no idea that Nelson was a married man with children. He didn't wear a ring, he didn't mention a wife and, anyway, she didn't really want to know. She was, she confesses, in 'denial, denial, denial', about it all. By the time Paul English confirmed her unarticulated suspicions and told her about Shirley, it barely measured as a shock.

Even then, English tried to twist her arm. The band liked her, thought she was fun and good for their friend. 'It's a *bad* marriage,' English told Connie. 'She's in and out of the hospital, she's sick, and Willie's scared if he divorces her that something bad will happen.' This was obviously a reference to suicide, underlining the extent to which Shirley's drinking, depressions, drug dependency and spells in detox were laying her low. Desperate to believe there was some justification for continuing their relationship despite the fact that she instinctively balked at the idea of dating a married man, Connie felt sympathetic for Nelson. In truth, she had fallen for him with a passion beyond that which a mere fling demanded. She recalls an evening in one of the Houston clubs where she and Nelson and some of the band were sitting at a table having drinks after the show.

Connie Nelson: This falling-down-on-you drunk guy off the street kept falling over me, and the table, and into Willie, and saying, Oh man, I love you so much, I love this song and that. And I was thinking to myself, 'Oh God, will you just please *leave*,' but Willie is talking to him like he's an old friend that he hadn't seen in years, as nice to him as he was to anybody. And I sat there long enough to just start watching the way Willie was, and there was something so gentle and sweet about it. This guy was drunk, so what? He was a nice guy, and he was a fan, and he liked Willie's music. It made me look at the whole situation different, and at Willie different. That was exactly the moment when I knew I was in love with him.

It was this easy quality which generally seemed to hold the key to Nelson's allure for women. He was kind yet mischievous; the ultimate what-you-see-is-what-you-get person. Fundamentally rather shy, certainly not loud, he would never walk into a room and announce his presence. Then again, everyone would know that he was there, and they would also pick up on his vibe, which essentially said: 'I know who I am and I'm comfortable with it.' And it would also state: 'I don't really care who you are, just sit down and we'll see how it goes.' It was a slightly mysterious aura, essentially benevolent, somehow wise. And very attractive. There was no fakery in him, which is not the same thing as saying he was without a dishonest streak. He was capable of grave deceits, but it was all done with a take-it-or-leave-it insouciance. He would almost always give the lasting impression that being true and honest to his own heart was the best way forwards for everyone. It would have been a neat trick, except it didn't seem to be a trick at all. As Connie would one day find out, it allowed him to get away with some unbelievably bad behaviour over the years without severing bonds of friendship or trust.

After a while spent chewing over Nelson's marital status, Connie's conscience got the better of her. She resolved to back off sometime in 1967 and they stopped seeing each other for about a year. She embarked on a relationship with another man who, she discovered after many months, was also married. 'He just flat lied, said that he wasn't. So that was over.' She split up with her married man in February 1968, and the very same night she heard that Nelson was coming into Houston. She went to see him, thinking – hoping – that perhaps he would now be available.

Connie Nelson: His marriage wasn't over, but it was still bad. And anyway, when I went back to see him that was just that. I was with him from then on.

This time, she became more than his Houston Girl. The two were hardly a conventional couple, but they had known each other for almost three years, and Nelson was now 'stone in love' with her. In contrast to his marriage, every day they were together was like going on honeymoon. She would travel a little with him and he wrote the wonderful 'Local Memory' about her, describing how he would lie unhappily in bed – presumably with his wife – and be haunted in his dreams by 'the hardest working memory in this town'. He first recorded the song in November of 1968, and at this point it sounds like he is documenting a doomed affair, a love that can never be properly fulfilled. Or more likely, that was still the only kind of love song he knew how to write.

Connie fell pregnant in January 1969 and the goalposts instantly moved. Nelson seemed to see a way out of his predicament with Shirley. He 'honestly just happened' to be in Houston on the day she went into labour and so drove her to hospital, went off to do the gig at night, and then returned after the show to find he had a new baby daughter. The rest of the band stopped by in the morning with flowers. Then he returned to Nashville, and all hell broke loose. He had given the hospital his home address so that he could arrange to pay the bill, and despite Connie's frantic last-minute efforts to get it stopped when she found out what he had done, it was too late. It was clearly a calculated and deliberate move. As he later admitted, 'I ain't stupid. I must have been tired of the secrecy.'[7] He would have known that Shirley would read the letter – addressed as it was to Mrs Nelson, not to mention the fact that he was away from home much of the time – and that the information it contained would at long last have forced her beyond the point of no return; what's more, he wouldn't even have to go through the trauma of a confession. It was textbook passive aggressive and unbearably cruel, especially on a woman whose mentality was as fragile as Shirley's.

Connie Nelson: Maybe he was [subconsciously trying to force the issue]. Probably, when you really think about it. I can't imagine any other reason he would have had it sent to the house. It was probably easier than telling her. Maybe it wasn't subconscious, either! I never wanted to break up a marriage, ever, although consequently that's what happened. I sure never intended it.

A few screaming rows later and Shirley was gone. Nelson shuttled the kids off to live in an apartment complex next to Paul and Carlene English in Madison, where they were looked after for a spell by a topless dancer from Atlanta called Helen, who would leave them on their own as she ducked out to watch Tom Jones concerts. Shirley apparently made efforts to see the children, but she wasn't allowed through. Nobody even spoke her name. 'It was,' recalled Susie Nelson, 'like she had died.'[8] In fact, she very nearly had. Stricken with pneumonia and alcoholism, she returned to her parents in Chillicothe, Missouri and fell apart. Nelson wouldn't see her again for ten years, and even then she somehow found the good grace not to kill him.

Shirley Nelson: I just couldn't handle it. I thought it was my fault. Maybe I wasn't a good enough mother. I never did think that Willie did anything wrong.[9]

Within a month of her leaving, Connie was installed in Ridgetop. If the freeze-out had been harsh on Shirley, it was also utterly alienating to the children. Lana, Billy and Susie had a new maternal figure to deal with, the third in their short lifetimes, and a new half-sister in Paula Carlene. Nelson introduced Connie to his children with the immortal words: 'Here's your new mother.'

It was Christmas time 1969, and Connie could have had absolutely no idea what she was walking into. She entered a household that bore comparison with few others. There were visitors and guests of all sorts at all hours, Zettner was still bunking down in the basement, and then there were the kids: Lana was 16 and already pregnant (she would, with almost comical mawkishness, christen the baby 'Nelson'), having replaced Mickey Newbury with another 27-year-old ne'er-do-well called Steve Warren, who was beating her up. Susie was almost thirteen, and frequently strung out on pot or tripping on acid; her father's idea of bonding with her was to join her in her walk-in double wardrobe and smoke a joint with her while she played Jimi Hendrix or Doors records.

Then there was Billy, who had already had enough. Barely out of short trousers, the off-kilter lifestyle that was raging around him was to cause him eternal insecurity and do him permanent damage. He had a father he rarely saw and a seemingly endless succession of mother figures in his life, from Martha and Shirley to Lana and now Connie. He had been old enough to realise that things had been going downhill between his father and Shirley, with whom he was especially close, and he used to ask her to take him with her when she eventually left Ridgetop. When she did go, of course, he had been left behind. When Connie arrived at Ridgetop, Billy shut himself in his room and refused to speak to her. She tried but never got through. It's debatable whether anyone ever would.

Connie Nelson: Billy was a tortured little soul, God bless him. He was [eleven] when I moved in with Willie, and he was *always* a tortured little soul. That was a tough time. I met their mom, Martha, and she and I became really good friends, so I never really tried to take over being the mom. I was more of a supervisor while Willie was away. That's how I viewed it.

The new woman at Ridgetop tried to impose some sort of order on this chaos. Cook proper meals, get the kids to school more regularly, give them some kind of stability. It was altogether a losing battle, and though the girls quite liked her they were wary of getting too close. Connie was more successful in supporting Nelson. She tried to get him organised by gathering all his phone contacts together and calling the likes of Roger Miller and Hank Cochran to invite them over to write and play. Shirley had not been keen on that side of things.

David Zettner, too, had become an indispensable ally, a kind of in-house jack of all trades. It was he who had found Nelson his legendary guitar, 'Trigger'. Nelson had previously played a red Fender Melody Master, until he signed a deal with Baldwin Piano Company who wanted to outfit him with their own equipment. The guitar they sent him wasn't working out for him – 'It had all these knobs and shit and he couldn't keep it together,' says Zettner – and so he and Jimmy Day went down to Sho-buds guitar store on Broadway in Nashville and spent $400 on a little gut-string Martin guitar. Then, armed with a fifth of Crown Royal Scotch, they bribed the owner Shot Jackson into gutting the guitar and putting the Baldwin pick-up inside – highly improper practice. 'Trigger' is therefore a true one-off, an irreplaceable mongrel beast. And the Smithsonian Institute have recently deemed it to be officially priceless.

At Ridgetop, Zettner also built a little makeshift studio in the basement, with an old Walhamsack reel-to-reel tape recorder and three or four microphones, and his job was to change the tapes every half-hour or so as the guys got down to it. It was serious but hardly studious work.

David Zettner: Once Roger [Miller] pulled up and asked me if I'd mind getting some stuff out of the back of his truck. Of course, I opened the truck and there was a case of Scotch – and a couple of little notebooks. That was it! I could tell they were getting all wound up in there. In the next two days I ended up cutting about thirteen of those big tapes. These guys would just write and write and write and write. Then go down and cut a hit record.

Nelson was indeed still cutting records, but in reality there were no hits being had. *My Own Peculiar Way* had been released early in 1969, and just a few days after he had reaped the full force of Hurricane Shirley, he was back in the studio for the first time in a year, recording tracks for what became the *Both Sides Now* album. It was the only time at RCA that he was ever allowed in with his touring band (although for reasons that aren't clear Paul English's younger brother Billy took his place on the drums. English may not have been up to the task), thanks to Felton Jarvis twisting some arms. They had become a fearsomely tight little foursome: Nelson leading from the front on vocals, with a guitar style which could switch between rhythm, lead and all points in between; Jimmy Day weaving wonderful pedal steel, finding hooks and swoops in the songs that weren't even there to begin with; and a solid rhythm section in David Zettner and English, although no one would claim English could ever match Johnny

Bush. On stage, they would wait for the house lights to dim and – bang! Jimmy Day would watch the curtain man's hand: as soon as he hit that rope and began pulling, Day would start playing. Everyone had to be right on top of their game, and they generally were.

David Zettner: God, it was a hot band. It would blow your mind away. We used to love to show off with it, our music was so together. Everybody was saying, 'God, why don't y'all record this?' We couldn't. [RCA] wouldn't let us. But Willie talked to a guy named Felton Jarvis, and he set up some sessions where we could go in and just kind of do our thing. We could tell by those little recordings that, God Almighty, if we were just allowed to get in there it could be good. But it never happened [again]. It was a tragedy.

Half of *Both Sides Now* is a brilliant document of a band at their peak. Alongside the wonderful, deceptively chipper 'I Gotta Get Drunk', a classic slice of drinker's dread at the inevitability of his fate, Nelson also recorded Shirley's own 'Once More With Feeling', perhaps intended as a round-about, backhanded sort of goodbye. The other half of the record grasped a little too hard for some kind of contemporary relevance with the inclusion of a rather sickly version of Joni Mitchell's title track – which showcased Nelson's lithe acoustic guitar – and a melancholy reading of Fred Neil's 'Everybody's Talkin' ', but the performances were uniformly excellent, hot off the road, unadorned and all the better for it. The original 'Bloody Mary Morning' – bizarrely called 'Bloody Merry Morning' – was also among the eleven sides cut, and would go on to be re-recorded for *Phases And Stages* in 1974 and finally become a classic. It could have been a classic in 1969, but nobody at RCA was listening. The song would seem to suggest that as well as Shirley and Connie, Nelson had also been keeping himself characteristically busy with at least one other squeeze somewhere out there on the endless road; in California, perhaps?

Connie Nelson: 'Bloody Mary Morning', the line about flying back to Houston – that was *kinda* about me. I'm not real sure who he was leaving [in LA], that was never made clear! I never went into it. It was like, OK, fine. But the flying back to Houston was coming back to me.

Around the same time, Nelson and the Record Men made a trip to Europe – Scandinavia in particular had always been a hot country music spot – on an RCA package tour. It was a big deal, a holiday for the company CEOs and their wives, with a climactic concert at the prestigious London Palladium. Nelson, however, wasn't really playing the game. He was uncomfortable overseas, partly because he was out of his comfort zone and it disrupted the steady supply of pot he was now smoking, and partly because he was genuinely sick and tired with what he was doing.

Jessi Colter: I first met Willie playing some dates in London. I worried about him because he seemed like he was on autopilot. At that point, he had been somehow pretty hurt and lived pretty hard already. It took a lot to keep him going and press him toward the future and wait for some good people to come into his life. I always had a sense that he had given up somewhere.

He was not in the best of moods. He clashed with Jimmy Day backstage at the Palladium and stormed off, leaving Day to perform a solo set. Of all the band, Jimmy Day had the greatest claim to being a true artist in his own right; he could be difficult and demanding, with a robust ego which matched his employer's. In London, Nelson watched from the side of the stage as Day performed a rendition of 'Londonderry Air' which brought the house down. Later backstage they bumped into Ringo Starr, who was just about to head to Nashville to make his own country record, *Beaucoup Of Blues*. Starr invited Day to play steel on the album, but eventually chose Nashville's other great player Pete Drake, who had recently worked with George Harrison. Day wasn't too upset, mainly because he had absolutely no idea who Starr was.

David Zettner: Jimmy looked up and said, 'Come on in, bud!' He didn't know who he was. Old Ringo was like The Fonz. He'd stacked his hair and had this little pretty girl with him. She handed him this big bag, he opened it up and hauled out this quart of Smirnoff vodka. He said, 'Awright luvs, let's party.' After that incident, [Jimmy and Willie] didn't seem to be on each other's nerves any more.

Upon returning to the States, the band undertook another package slog with the Harry 'Hap' Peebles Agency, perhaps the king of country music bookers. It was a tour of the north-east of the country and the bill included Faron Young, Kitty Wells, Marty Robbins, Charley Pride and Johnny Wright. Nelson was fourth on the bill, but he wasn't happy. Other acts kept cutting into his time every night, to the point where he and the band would barely have time to set up and play a couple of songs before one of the headline acts would be scheduled to go on. He regarded it as a further slight, and in Buffalo he took matters into his own hands.

David Zettner: Willie called us in the hotel and said, 'I want to meet you all downstairs at eleven o'clock.' In the bar. In the morning. Oops, something has happened. So all of us were down there, Paul was with Willie already. They were working on a Bloody Mary. I'd never seen Paul English drink any liquor – ever. That morning he was. He was mumbling, and Willie was just staring at the wall. What's going on? After about three or four Bloody Marys, Willie said, 'Too much juice. Gimme the jug.' Drinking vodka straight up.

When they got to the show, a drunk Nelson ran onto the stage and grabbed the microphone from the DJ's hands and started into the kind of spiel he had woven back at KCNC fifteen years earlier. 'How did you like that, ladies and gentlemen! Now, the next king of country music – the one and only Mr Charley Pride!' Instead of Pride, Paul English walked on with his guitar, banging into the microphone and slurring 'Hello Walls' to a bewildered audience. It was a light-hearted way of confronting a serious issue, but before the second show English and Nelson had it out properly with Peebles. For some reason, English had bought a wig made out of his real hair. Part of his shtick with the crowd on stage was standing up in his cape and tipping his wig in thanks, as though it were a hat. That was just part of his personality. That night backstage, the argument ended with English taking off his wig, slapping it onto 'Hap' Peebles's bald head and commanding: 'Now you go up there and you introduce Willie.' He did. Nelson duly walked on stage with the band in tow, went up to the mike, said, 'It's been nice seeing you,' and just kept walking until he reached the other side.

David Zettner: Woah! I looked at Jimmy and he said: 'Pack 'em up. Let's go!' That was Willie's way of saying, 'I don't need this.' He knew how to handle it without making anybody say anything. The audience thought it was part of the show but we never reappeared. We took off for California and never came back.

The verse in the classic 'Me And Paul' referencing the package show in Buffalo catches the essence of that night: 'We came to play and not just for the ride.' It was funny, but it also concealed the bitterness he felt deep down. In essence, that line summed up the futility he felt with much of his work over the previous decade. He had come to Nashville to play his music, not just for the ride, and now he was burning bridges, finally losing patience with what he was being asked to do and also what he wasn't being allowed to do. He had recently written and recorded a demo called 'What Can They Do To Me Now?' in his basement in Ridgetop, which he had recorded at one of six sessions he had undertaken for RCA in 1970 that would make up the *Laying My Burdens Down* and *Willie Nelson & Family* albums. It was not a happy song, even by his standards. He was 37 and his career was going nowhere fast.

Then came the fire, and that would finally change everything.

WHERE WAS I GOING TO GO?

Willie Nelson is talking about his house burning down.

'I had a fireplace and I had stove pipes that were kind of going across the ceiling, and they got hot one night and those stove pipes caught the house on fire,' he says, smiling. 'And burned the house down.'

He smiles. He has turned this story into a party piece. Everyone knows how it goes.

'I was down at a Christmas party and they called me and told me that my house was on fire. I think I told them: "Pull the car in the garage and get the hell out!" By the time I got out there it was full of smoke and fire and everything.'

He is still smiling. 'So I did go in there and I knew what I was going in there for. I got my guitar out and I got some dope out and hid everything down in the hollow down there. And then I got out myself.'

He stops suddenly.

'My house was burning,' he says, as though the ramifications had just occurred to him. 'Where was I going to go?'

6. 1970–1972

T he Ridgetop fire has become a legendary chapter in a life hardly
    lacking in natural disasters. It has taken on the significance of a
terrible omen, a sign in the sky, an almost biblical event. Like many of the
misfortunes which have befallen Nelson through the years, it has also
become little more than a comic anecdote, another box to be ticked in his
potted biography, but at the time it was a shock, a heavy setback to him
and his family, and one which had far-reaching consequences on his life
and career.

Like most legends the facts have become twisted over time and tangled
up in folklore. Even the date has slipped its leash: in his loose-limbed
autobiography, Nelson had it down as Christmas Eve 1969. Other sources
swear it was 1971. In fact, it happened on 23 December 1970. Nelson was
attending Lucky Moeller's Christmas party at the King Of The Road club
in downtown Nashville when the fire struck. He had recently taken on
'Crash' Stewart as his – for want of a better title – manager. The
ex-football player from San Antonio had specialised for some time in
booking country acts into venues in Texas, and the fact that Nelson had
taken him on hinted that he was already looking towards home for the
next stage of his career. But he was less a manager and more of a regional
booker. The Moeller Talent Agency still booked most of his gigs and
although they were firmly part of the establishment that was strangling

Nelson's creativity, they were also friends. Their Christmas bash was one of those occasions where the leading lights of the Nashville scene would sit around, picking guitars and singing their songs long into the night.

Back at Ridgetop, things were quiet. David Zettner had gone home to his parents for the holidays, as usual the kids were doing their own thing, Paula Carlene – only one year old – was asleep in the back bedroom, and Connie was napping on the couch. She was awoken by Bobbie's eldest son Randy ringing the doorbell, announcing his arrival from Austin to spend Christmas. Connie went into the bedroom to get Paula Carlene so that Randy could say hello to her, and when she did so she knew that something was terribly wrong.

Connie Nelson: I could hear her talking in the back bedroom, so she was up. We went back and there was smoke just going straight up the wall. 'What could that be?' So I picked Paula Carlene up out of bed, walked down the hall and opened the basement door, and as soon as I did it just flooded the house with smoke, to the point that we had to get [straight] out. As I'm walking by to go outside I picked up the telephone and it was dead. It had been going in the basement for God only knows how long.

It was already consuming the house. There are conflicting theories about the cause of the blaze. Nelson's stepfather had undertaken some work in the basement a few years before. He had installed a wooden stove with pipes that ran across the ceiling beneath the ground floor, and Nelson claims that they overheated and caught alight. Connie Nelson also points the finger at the stepfather, who seems to have been the handyman from Hell whichever way you look at it, but cites a different source. 'Willie's stepdad had done the wiring in the house before I lived there, down in the basement, and it had started somewhere in the wiring. Insurance paid for it, because there was a defect somewhere.'

Connie, Randy and the kids quickly made it out of the house to safety and went over to Myrle's house a few miles away, from where they called Nelson at the King Of The Road. Again, there are several versions recounting his reaction: some at the party remember him taking a call and then sitting calmly, waiting patiently and politely for the next song to finish before he got up to leave: 'Excuse me, I have to go,' he said quietly. 'My house is burning down.' Others claim he went off to play a show that night before going home. The most reliable and sober witnesses remember him as being more shaken, as one might expect, and rushing out immediately to get home. He may be laid-back, but the news that his home was burning down was almost guaranteed to make an impact.

The most enduring part of the legend of the Ridgetop fire is that Nelson hot-footed it home and ran into the burning house to rescue his beloved 'Trigger' and a prime stash of Colombian marijuana as the flames crackled around him, like a scene from *Towering Inferno* crossed with *The*

Waltons. It's a tale that has its basis in truth but has been distorted over the years, not least by Nelson's own love of a good hero story. In actual fact, 'Trigger' was taken out almost immediately, long before Nelson arrived on the scene from the King Of The Road. Susie had also rescued David Zettner's Goya guitar and some clothes. Nobody thought to rescue any drugs. The fire had spread up the walls of the house and the ranch was collapsing from the top downwards; there was very little time to do anything other than escape before the whole thing caved in.

The losses were devastating: most of the song charts and the myriad recordings that had been made down in the basement over the past year went up in smoke, although some did survive and were eventually restored. Numerous personal effects and irreplaceable items were destroyed. Only later, when the site had settled and it became safe to re-enter, did Nelson and others start rooting around to assess the full scale of the damage. Zettner had come straight back up from San Antonio and recalls the scavenging process, which did involve pulling some dope out of the remains of the house: the penalties for possession were still incredibly harsh even then.

David Zettner: It was just charcoal and slabs and junk everywhere. All these guns were in there with all the barrels bent over. 'What are we looking for, Willie?' 'Oh, it's a box.' Well we found a jar full of old [grass] seeds. We went through that house and we [tried to] figure out what happened.

Everything changed immediately after the fire. Nelson had loved Ridgetop, it had been a true home to him and his kids and he had built a community around it. He was genuinely upset by the fire and immediately had to work out what to do. At first the family lived in a trailer behind the house through Christmas, which the children rather enjoyed, and then Nelson took Connie and the kids to stay next to Paul and his family in an apartment in Madison until he came up with a viable solution. In general terms, he had to provide a roof for his family. In career terms, he had to consider whether Nashville was really the best place for him to be.

This is the first time that anyone recalls the friendship between Nelson and Waylon Jennings becoming really tight. Jennings and his drummer Richie Albright would come up to visit Nelson in Madison in their old black bus and 'talk, talk, talk for days about something'.[1] It is far too convenient to view this as a cowboy council of war, the inaugural meeting of the Outlaw Society, but it was a significant crossroads in both their careers nonetheless.

Jessi Colter: Waylon was very concerned about Willie just going around in circles. His house had burned down and he was very burned out about Nashville, and Waylon was very concerned about that.

95

Nelson and Jennings had been good but not close friends for years. Jennings was a fellow Texan, born in Littlefield in 1937, who had played bass with Buddy Holly's backing band in the late-50s following the demise of the Crickets. They had first crossed paths back in 1964, when Jennings was playing a residency at JDs in Phoenix, Arizona. Jennings also had a Saturday afternoon TV show, and when Nelson came into town to play at the Riverside Ballroom, he was invited on. Later, Jennings asked advice about whether he should go to Nashville as RCA were showing interest. Nelson asked what kind of money he was making in Phoenix and – already disillusioned with the way things were working out for himself – when he heard the reply he said: 'Stay right where you're at!' Of course, the lure of Nashville proved too strong. Jennings moved there in 1965 and he and Nelson became friends, without getting really close. There was a mutual respect and understanding which grew, fuelled by a sense of injustice at the way they had been treated by their label and a natural tendency to stir up trouble.

In Madison they talked and a decision was finally reached. One afternoon in the spring of 1971, Nelson announced to his family and his band that 'Crash' Stewart had arranged for them to go and stay for free at the Lost Valley Ranch in Bandera, about fifty miles north-west of San Antonio. The ranch was closed, apparently in receivership, and consisted of a main lodge with a group of smaller cabins scattered over its many acres. The scenery was beautiful, and there were tennis courts, a swimming pool and a nine-hole golf course at their disposal. It was at Bandera that the golfing bug really hit him. With little to do and lots of time to do it in, he played obsessively and has been virtually addicted to it ever since.

There was no sudden epiphany. He had been toying with the idea of going back to live in Texas for some time, but Bandera was only a temporary solution: he loved Ridgetop and planned to return after the fire. He, Connie and the children took the lodge house at the ranch, and all the band and their families came to gather around them. There was a new face: an eighteen-year-old friend of David Zettner who had been hanging out with the group for a while on the road, Dan 'Bee' Spears had arrived recently to take over bass duties when Zettner got drafted. Spears was the baby of the band. Zettner later returned to play second guitar behind Nelson for a short while.

Bee Spears: They talked it over and they just decided on me. I was just there. I hadn't been playing very long, only about a year and a half, but that was one reason why they hired me. They discussed it and said, 'Well, he learns fast, and we can teach him what we want him to play.' It was a good deal for them, I guess, and a great deal for me.

Despite the tranquil nature of the setting, they were long, hard, slow months in Bandera. The records weren't selling and the royalties had stopped flowing quite so freely. More importantly, the band weren't playing many shows. John T. Floores Country Store club in Helotes was nearby and they would play there once or twice a month, but it would only bring in $700 or $800 and Nelson had to provide for his entire entourage until things started ticking over again. Many times Connie and Carlene would sit at the kitchen table and count out pennies, hoping to scrape enough money together to buy groceries. It became like a redneck version of a hippie commune, with cowboy boots and guns replacing beads and joss sticks. This kind of coming together was already common in rock music: there were already 'family' bands in San Francisco and The Band had come together in Woodstock, but it was unheard of in country music. The experience helped to fully cement the familial bond which had been forged on the road. The strength of the loyalties formed at Bandera have been severely tested over the years but have never been breached.

Paul English: We sure weren't hippies! We were just there hanging out, but we weren't making any money. One evening we'd all have a big dinner at Willie's house, and Connie would fix up a stew or a Hungarian goulash, and that would be great. Another night we'd have a barbecue up at Bee's, another night Carlene would fix something up at my house. We all lived within forty feet of each other and we just sort of pooled everything we had, our cars or whatever.

During their time at Bandera, Nelson and Connie married in Las Vegas, on 30 April 1971, Nelson's 38th birthday. The date became something of a joke over the years. He has always been a keen marker of his birthday, and during the 70s the celebrations grew bigger and bigger until one year they both forgot it was their anniversary at all, so they decided to re-marry on 10 June 1978, in Nevada. There was another reason, as it turned out, why this was a wise move. When he originally married Connie in 1971, Nelson was still married to Shirley. They wouldn't be officially divorced until November, so for six months he was technically a bigamist. Connie didn't discover the truth until the late-80s.

Connie Nelson: I had no idea! You know how I found out? I saw it at a convenience store on the front of the *National Enquirer*, because he had written his book: 'One thing Connie never knew, I never told her, was that I was still married to Shirley.' I had no idea. God! It's just unbelievable.

Nelson later claimed that getting married was the beginning of the end for he and Connie, that it added stress and took the fun and spontaneity out of their relationship. However, he thought it was an important commitment to make at the time, and it is one he has been prepared to make again. He has been a serial husband since his teens. It seems he can hardly bear to be alone, and yet can't embrace or conform to the reality of what being married actually means. Which is where the Family Band comes in: a mobile family with him at the head, no conventional moral boundaries, no judgments, no expectations other than to go on the road and keep the show moving. Most families – his own included – crumble under the weight of constant flight, so he managed to create a family that couldn't exist without movement, whose entire *raison d'etre* was to be in motion.

Connie Nelson: When he and I got married, he said the one thing he'd always wanted but had never had was a family. Those were his exact words to me. And I thought, Well, I can my gosh give you that! And I did, for a lot of years. I honestly think [the Family Band] is all a big part of that. I think family is *extremely* important to Willie, it was something that was always missing from his life.

The shock of the fire and life at Bandera brought a lot of these deep, raw feelings to the surface. Things had been getting interesting around Nelson for a while, and one way of life going up in flames to be replaced by communal life on the ranch simply seemed to unify and clarify matters in his head, culminating finally in the creation of a truly marvellous work of art. The people who held the reins in country music seemed to want the genre to exist in a vacuum, but it was like trying to put a finger in the dyke as all around them the plains flooded with fresh ideas, social shifts and unlikely unions. In the last few years, Bob Dylan and Johnny Cash had been forming a mutual admiration which led to Dylan's *Nashville Skyline* and Cash becoming an icon of American music, way beyond country music boundaries. On the West Coast, the Byrds had cross-pollinated old-time country with their psychedelic pop sensibility, recording their landmark *Sweetheart Of The Rodeo* record, made with Gram Parsons, in 1968, which featured songs by the Louvin Brothers, Merle Haggard and several other country greats. They played the *Grand Ole Opry* the same year, to almost universal disdain from the country community: DJ Ralph Emery even publicly vilified them on his radio show. Later Parsons would form the Flying Burrito Brothers and delve even deeper into country roots on *The Gilded Palace Of Sin* album and beyond into his remarkable solo records.

'Going country' was not really a commercially successful move. *Sweetheart Of The Radio* bombed, but it was culturally significant. Where once there had been rock music and country music and a whole ocean of deep water in between, things were beginning to close up a little, although there was still much resistance from both sides. By 1970 the Grateful Dead were revisiting old-time country on their two records, *American Beauty* and *Workingman's Dead*, laced with pedal steel and harmony and garnering great acclaim. On the East Coast The Band were recording 'Long Black Veil'. Even the Rolling Stones were in on the act, recording

'Country Honk' on *Let It Bleed*. Country was moving out of the ghetto and into the slipstream of what Parsons would later define as 'Cosmic American Music', although it was generally one-way traffic: pop and rock were embracing and absorbing country, but country would always be a little slower in returning the favour. Nelson was perhaps a little ahead of the game: he had played Beatles songs in concert, and was aware of the influence of Jimi Hendrix, the Doors and Leon Russell through his children's musical tastes. He had observed Woodstock in 1969 with interest and admiration. And although at this stage he was very much on the outside looking in, a peripheral figure without any power within the industry, he was aware that things were in the process of change: musically, culturally, politically.

And yet it would be difficult to pin any explicitly political badges on him around this time. Admittedly, he did perform a song at a benefit in support of Democratic US senator Ralph Yarborough's re-election campaign in 1970, and had written and recorded 'Jimmy's Road' back in the summer of 1968, his most explicit and unnerving protest song. 'Jimmy's Road' had originally been called 'David's Road' and was based on a letter that Nelson had written to David Zettner when it looked like the bass player was going to be drafted. The name was changed, either because Jimmy scanned better or – as Zettner believes – because Jimmy Day undertook some pretty intensive lobbying. It was an eerie little anti-war song, but hardly political. More like metaphysical. He cut a zippy 'Bring Me Sunshine' at the same session just for balance, a bizarre juxtaposition of moods which pretty much sums up his later RCA years.

But he remained a conundrum, or more likely a product of his upbringing and background colliding head-on with the times. He would always take each man as he came and had done his bit for race relations by kissing the black country singer Charley Pride on stage in front of a hostile cowboy crowd at the Longhorn Ballroom in Dallas, but would still use the term 'nigger' – non-ironically – in conversation and indeed even in print well into the 70s. He was living in a commune, beginning to grow his hair longer and sporting an earring, yet he was still spending most of his time with the kind of people many would dismiss as gun-carrying rednecks, the type of folk most hippies would cross the road to avoid. He later claimed that the gradual change in his appearance was primarily for mischief and effect: no one was playing country music looking like this, and it is tempting to view it as less a sincere engagement with the counter-culture than simply an easy way of mixing things up a little. He wasn't a hippie so much as a pirate. He wanted to know, he said, what it felt like to be a nigger.

Willie Nelson: I like to piss people off. I'd go around to truck stops hoping people would say something to me about my hair. Back before I was really trying to take care of myself.[2]

He was getting more and more into smoking pot, seeing it as one of many avenues towards finding a way of squeezing some kind of happiness and significance out of his existence. His interest in kung fu and the power of positive thought had led him to investigate Buddhism and other more mystically spiritual avenues such as the Astarian principles of Dr Earlyne Chaney, Rosicruciansim, the writings of Edgar Cayce and the poems of Kahlil Gibran, which advocated the idea that life on earth is a continual quest to return to God. Nelson's strong belief in reincarnation and his interest in psychic power and mysticism can be traced back to these sources. It naturally wasn't long until the mood of the times and his own beliefs started to find their way into his music, albeit in the most esoteric and unusual of ways. He had something more profound than protest songs in mind, something on a grander scale. During the latter days of the Record Men, he sought a kind of ESP-based understanding between himself and boys. They would be the first telepathic country band.

Willie Nelson: As you get more into it, you realise, hey, this is kind of like [a] universal thing. The universal mind and your own mind is the same thing. We're all thinking basically the same thing, we're all basically the same person, and once you realise that everything is kinda simplified.[3]

It says something for Nelson's charisma and gentle powers of persuasion that he got away with this kind of half-baked stoner talk amongst a bunch of hard-nosed country shit-kickers. Of course, they were all smoking a lot of dope. For months on the road the band would get in the dressing room and lock the door. Usually the door would have been left open and everyone from stage crew to members of other groups would mill in and out. Now it was locked. Everybody would take a little pillow and they would stand on their heads in a circle – Jimmy Day never quite managed to stand on his head so he learned to lean against a wall – and they would begin deep breathing exercises. Then Nelson would say: 'I'll start sending now,' and the band would close their eyes and attempt to receive. This was pure Cayce-ism, adopting a meditative state of self-induced sleep and attempting to take 'readings'.

David Zettner: Willie had all these books about everything from Buddhism to the correct way to breathe. He started training us about mind over matter stuff. We discussed it: where does this all get to? And he said, 'In the end I should be able to send messages to you guys and y'all would pick them up instantaneously, and you'd be able to replicate it.' Wow! OK! I never could get any revelation until one night we went out on stage. I'll never forget this as long as I live. Big old show. Willie walked out there and started, and in the middle of 'Night Life' he just flipped into another song we'd never heard. Everybody went right with him. Another key, another beat. *Everybody*, just like that. After that show we sat back and said, 'Man, it's true! You can reach people like that.' We all got into this thing real heavy for a while.

Zettner still believes he and Nelson and Bush have a telepathic understanding. Naturally, this kind of behaviour didn't go unnoticed among the other musicians on the circuit. There was plenty of ribbing. Other bands would watch them meditating on the bus and yell, 'Man, you're all a sect. Help!' Faron Young looked at his drummer Jerry 'Cootie' Hunley one night and barked: 'The only [telepathic] message I've got for you, Cootie, is that when you die I'm going to have you stuffed and made into a couch.' But what is astonishing is that it seemed to gain Nelson respect. Primarily, this was down to the fact that he treated his group like equals, and they therefore seemed like a proper band rather than the star and a bunch of menials. They liked being with each other. Ernest Tubbs' band would try and hide from Tubbs because he discouraged any kind of fun, and soon half of the other bands on a package tour would want to ride on the Nelson bus. It was fun, but it was also interesting. He was not merely trying to use his music to bring people together, but to explore the concept of psychic unity among his fellow musicians and by extension, the audience. It is still the key to what he does as a performer.

All of these loose strands first found a crucible on the *Yesterday's Wine* record, which he cut in Nashville in May 1971. He would go on to record six more sessions for RCA before he left the label, but *Yesterday's Wine* was effectively his farewell. It remains an astonishing album, and for all the alienating nonsense in the opening intonation about 'Perfect Man' and 'Imperfect Man' and his later talk about it being a concept album documenting a man attending his own funeral, it is in reality a very stark and clear cry from the heart. Nelson revisits the religious imagery of his childhood, rustles up old characters and reclaims old places, until finally the simple, beautiful universality of his writing cuts through to a calm, spiritual understanding you can physically *hear* on the closing 'Goin' Home'.

The album as a whole denotes nothing less than a man giving himself up to God. 'I'm born,' he sings. 'Can you use me?' Looking back at his life, Nelson sounds like he is both giving up and starting again at the very same time, which is not very far from the truth. It is, almost literally, a rebirth. He was saying goodbye to something and would never be quite the same again: 'Remember the good times/ They're smaller in number and easier to recall/ Don't spend too much time on the bad times/ Their staggering number will be heavy as lead on your mind.'

Musically, the title track and 'In God's Eyes' look forward to the stark, hard, old country of *Red Headed Stranger*, while 'Summer Of Roses' and 'December Day' nodded their heads to the standards he would later re-visit on *Stardust*. *Yesterday's Wine* is all the more incredible for the fact that it was written by a man with his back up against the wall. Apart from

'Family Bible' and 'December Day', all the rest of the songs were new and at least seven of them were written on the night before he was due in the studio.

David Zettner: He said, 'I've *got* to turn in another record. I'm on a contract, but I haven't written shit.' I went with him [to Nashville] for some reason. Lucky Moeller had a son named Larry, and he came over to the Holiday Inn, it was about four in the afternoon, and Willie told us both, 'Man, if you don't mind, could y'all just get lost! I've got to do some work. I've got to try to get something down.' We came back about 4 a.m. and we opened up Willie's room and there were pieces of paper all over the fucking floor – on tables and chairs, some had pins in them. He was laying on the bed, and we just closed the door. 'Jesus, what has he done?!' Later we called up: 'Yeah, I'm ready. Y'all come on up.' He had all these pieces of paper and he said, 'OK, I'm ready to go cut.' [It was a 10 a.m. start at the studio]. His eyes were all bloodshot, he put on these old sunglasses, got into the car and, boy, just started off. 'Me And Paul', all those songs, he wrote them in one night. I'd never seen anything like it.

Sometime during the long night of writing, a wired Nelson had called Paul English and told him he was writing a song about him. 'Me And Paul' was a true classic, a slice of real road life made heroic, each verse detailing an on-the-edge escapade which only serves to mythologise the two buddies as the Butch Cassidy and the Sundance Kid of country music. 'It really got me,' admits English. And the coy mention of being 'busted' in Laredo was pretty daring in country music, even in 1971.

Sadly, the album went over everybody's head. The eccentric religious overtones on the liner notes and the bizarre introduction instantly put listeners on the back foot, but look beyond that and it is perhaps the most true and pure country album he has ever made. It was a new start creatively, and would act as an escape route from the hole he was in and lead him towards the green pastures of *Shotgun Willie* and *Phases And Stages*. But commercially it plummeted, and when Nelson returned to the redecorated Ridgetop in October 1971 his career was in no better shape than it had been a year ago. He was depressed. Legend has it that one night before Christmas, in a drunken moment of melodrama, he lay down outside Tootsie's in the snow and waited for a car to come along and run him over.

Pat Croslin: Poor ole little Willie. He'd just got down and out. He just went out in the middle of the street, got down on the road and begged people to run him over.

If it even happened at all, it was hardly a serious suicide attempt. It's not hard to picture a few old regulars standing on the icy pavement laughing at his antics. After a while he found he was still alive, so he picked himself up and walked away.

The most important figure to enter Nelson's life at this time was Neil Reshen. Reshen was a hard-nosed East Coaster who had – through friends of friends – started filing tax returns for executives at CBS Records in New York back in the 60s. This led him, circuitously yet rapidly, to handling the affairs of jazz drummer and notorious heroin addict Art Blakey. Reshen would dole out Blakey's dough like it was a child's pocket money, trying to ensure it didn't all disappear overnight into his veins. He would later manage Miles Davis and Frank Zappa. For all his stoned outlaw vibe, looking after Willie Nelson seemed like a walk in the park.

Improbably, Reshen claims to have been a genuine country music fan, fascinated by Jimmie Rodgers and Hank Williams as a child. It was exotic fare for a Jewish boy growing up in New Jersey, and he listened religiously to the one local station which played country music. Its appeal had never left him, but as a man utterly obsessed with the market value of each and every thing, in adulthood he must also have been aware of its commercial potential. As he built up an impressive raft of rock and jazz clients in the 60s, he trained his sights on one artist in particular.

Neil Reshen: Sometime in the 60s, Waylon Jennings played the Taft Hotel. I went to see him and there were only 100 people in the room. I went backstage and I talked to him, and basically he said, 'I'm sorta happy with Nashville. I don't like it but I don't think I could use a northerner.' Later on, when I was managing him, he told me that he didn't want to bring in a Jewish guy. Well, Nashville was a very parochial place. Waylon was not prejudiced at all, but he knew that he would have all this trouble.

Reshen dropped the idea of managing Jennings. Or rather, he put it to one side. By 1971 he was based in leafy Connecticut, looking after the likes of Zappa, Linda Ronstadt and Goose Creek Symphony, the band who had the original record of 'Mercedes Benz'. His whole ethos as a manager was to sign up acts who – no matter what your personal tastes, whether you liked them or not – you couldn't possibly state that they weren't good at what they did. Out of the blue, he got a call summoning him to Nashville. Jennings was sick with hepatitis and RCA were trying to exploit his weakness by getting him to re-sign to the label for a paltry $5,000. His drummer, Richie Albright, had worked with Goose Creek Symphony and knew Reshen a little, which meant he already knew he was unpleasant, uncouth, untrustworthy and almost entirely devoid of compassion. He recommended that Jennings at least talk with him.

Richie Albright: I said to Waylon, 'You're probably not going to like this guy, he's pretty ruthless. But he knows where all the bodies are buried, you know.'

Jennings could see the beauty in that, and reasoned that he couldn't be ripped off any more than he was being already. Reshen took the next plane down, to find Jennings lying in bed 'dying'. Outside, the swimming pool was covered in algae. None of it signified an artist in his prime.

Neil Reshen: It was the most horrendous place you'd ever seen. Waylon was sick and RCA wouldn't give him any money. I said to Waylon, 'Let me manage you. Let me do it for a year, I can't do any worse than this. I'll go to RCA and get you the money.' So I went to RCA and I met with Chet and [RCA President] Jerry Bradley and they gave me $20,000. So I came back with the money, and Waylon said OK. He didn't sign that day, but he [eventually] signed up. In the meantime, I read through his contract and I found out that RCA had neglected to pick up his option. That was the way I finally got Waylon free.

Richie Albright also called Willie Nelson to tell him about Reshen. On the day he was leaving Nashville to return to Connecticut, Reshen met Nelson, Paul English and Bee Spears at the airport before they caught a flight back to Texas. It was late April 1972. The trio had just attempted what would be their final sessions for RCA; cutting embryonic versions of the material that would end up on the *Phases And Stages* record two years later. They had managed to cut nine tracks over two sessions, including 'Phases, Stages, Circles, Cycles And Scenes' and 'Mountain Dew', the songs which would fill both sides on his last 45 for RCA. It was the first time since November 1969 that Willie had been allowed to use his own musicians in the studio, and he had blown it. They had been kicked out of the studio for smoking dope. It was the final straw for both sides.

At the airport, Reshen and Nelson talked. He outlined his growing contempt and frustrations with his situation: 'I can't take it any more, I'm going back to Texas,' he said. 'If we want to play we can always play in Texas and get in the car and drive from place to place. I'll keep writing songs and one day I'll get a hit record.' Reshen nodded his sympathies. At the end of the conversation he offered to embark on a quest: if he could extricate Nelson from his RCA contract, would he sign a management deal with him? Nelson agreed.

Neil Reshen: So I called Jerry Bradley and said, 'Listen, I'm going to manage Willie, how do you want to handle it?' He said, 'Willie can't record any more for us. We caught him smoking pot in the studio, we can't have that. I won't give you a release because we cancelled the session and

I think Willie owes us about $1,250.' I said, 'If I give you the money can I have Willie?' He said, 'Yeah, you give us the money, you got him.'

Thus Nelson was sold as a going concern for a little over a $1,000. RCA would go on to make millions from his back catalogue once he became a star, but it stills stands as a shoddy piece of business and a creative own-goal of enormous proportions. But then the top brass at the company had misrepresented him through the full eight years of his contract, and it would have been astonishing had they recognised his true worth now. In retrospect, he never really had a chance. An employee at RCA later told Willie they usually only pressed 2,500 copies of his albums.

The period he spent at RCA – prime years in most artists' careers, those between 30 and 39 – are pivotal in understanding what has made him tick ever since. Soon after he became hugely famous in the mid-70s, he confided to a friend that: 'I played the same songs [tonight] and I wrote most of those songs ten or twenty years ago, but nobody gave a shit about me then. And now I'm twenty years older and I can get every girl because my name is Willie Nelson, but sometimes I wish I could have gotten the same girls twenty years ago.' He also discussed his use of drugs in reference to the way he felt about how he had been treated by RCA. It was around this time that Nelson switched from drinking a lot of whisky to smoking more. It calmed him down, curbed his blackest moods. 'I take it because there are some days that I get so mad at Chet Atkins and Jerry Bradley, that if I wasn't smoking dope I'd go in and shoot them.'

Chet Atkins: I was just about the worst at promotion and sales. I didn't care anything about that part of the business. It hurt Willie a lot to have a guy with my attitude as the one who was supposed to push his product. I guess the timing just wasn't right.[4]

In fact, Atkins was really just a musician. He can certainly be held responsible for some dubious musical decisions made on Nelson's records, but the really big commercial calls were made at company headquarters in New York, and once Nelson had been around for a few years and done nothing major they gave up interest. He was far from immune from blame himself. There is a case to be made for saying that he should never have left Monument so readily, given the quality of what he was doing there. Too single-minded to really play the RCA game fully once he arrived there, he was nonetheless unhappy and not a little bitter that he couldn't participate in the game to the extent that he would have wished. He was too stubborn to want a proper manager, but there is no doubt that if he had had better representation earlier on he would have got further ahead.

It is one of the interesting and unanswerable questions posed by his 60s career: if he had become successful and really broken through adhering to the RCA script, would he have been satisfied? After all, he had not failed because he was too radical. He had not failed on his own terms. Atkins once recalled that Nelson never once complained, that he seemed happy with the music he was making. For all the later media talk of him as an outlaw who had taken on Nashville and won, Nelson did no such thing: rather, he was a passive co-conspirator in his own downfall. He had cut his hair, worn the suits, smiled the smile, let Grady Martin and Chet Atkins play guitar on his songs because he felt they knew best, and none of it had really worked. He had changed tack when asked, made records of contemporary pop songs, and been overdubbed virtually out of existence. Like many others before and after him, he had been cajoled and connived into toeing the company line, even though the company had much bigger fish to fry. He had tried his best to conform and it hadn't worked. It was humiliating.

Don Light: I know [journalists] always try and make out these guys were being suppressed or restrained in some way; but they were just trying to make the same kinds of records everyone else was making. Then one day they decided they didn't want to make those kinds of records any more. It evolved, that's all.

He didn't have the force of personality of a Johnny Cash or even a Roger Miller, someone who could break through no matter how extenuating the circumstances. Things were changing by the late-60s, but Nelson had been churning around the system for so long he had no platform on which to perform. By then he was barely a country act at all, certainly not in the studio. With the exception of *Both Sides Now* and *Yesterday's Wine*, his records were all over the place; they lacked personality and unity, and he had become detached from what he really wanted to do. He walked away from confrontation and held it in, but it had made him depressed and angry.

Willie Nelson: There's nothing wrong with [working within the system] unless you're being restricted on what you can do. If a guy says, 'OK, I'm going to put up the money and then leave it up to you, you come in and play your music,' then that's perfect. But if a guy says, 'OK, I'm going to put up the money but you're going to do *these* songs, and you're gonna do them in *this* key, and *this* tempo,' then that's not good. I knew how it was, and I knew that one way to do it was to do it their way to get inside. Which I did. I did it their way and I got inside and I started trying to change it to my way. It took a while to do it, you know, but I did it.

It's a typically optimistic reading of the situation, suggesting that he somehow subverted the Nashville system and eventually won people over, but he never did quite 'do it' that way, at least not at RCA. It would take companies such as Atlantic and finally Columbia to grant him – and somewhat reluctantly at that – his full creative freedom. He was working for a giant conglomerate, one which had all the angles covered. Control was not going to be handed over willy-nilly. It's not too hard to see why most of the people who had real creative freedom in country music didn't record in Nashville: Merle Haggard and Buck Owens recorded for Capitol – the Beatles' label, based in Hollywood – a company who understood that the artist often knew best, or at least should sometimes be allowed the chance to fall flat on their faces on their own terms. In Nashville, they wanted their artists tied to their studios because they could make their profit that way. It was, claims Reshen, like 'a fucking real estate company'.

The fact that Reshen was an outsider was crucial. He wasn't in the country business and had no interest in or respect for the hierarchical structures of Nashville. He regarded the people with disdain and saw the system for the anachronistic, backward-looking control-freakery that it was. He came from the rock 'n' roll industry, where artists were used to demanding promotion, tour money, a bit of leeway, basic support, and where managers could be as obnoxious as they liked.

Jessi Colter: I loved Neil Reshen because he was the first man who had the knowledge and the guts to bring something back when he would go to the companies. Neil knew how they operated. When he came in to find out what was going on, he did, and he came home with [the] money. I will forever appreciate him; he avenged a lot that had been done to Waylon unjustly. He showed their tactics could be exposed and that gave us confidence and strength. And Waylon – as he often did – wanted to share this with Willie.

Reshen discovered that even the booking agencies in Nashville were a closed shop. Nelson – like many other Nashville acts, including Waylon Jennings – was tied to the Moeller Talent Agency, run by Lucky Moeller. That too was afflicted by stasis and a complete ignorance of what their clients were worth, despite the fact that the bookers themselves were making money hand over fist. One night not long after he had taken over the reins, Reshen was working late in his New York office when he received a call from a major bar owner in west Texas who wanted to book Willie and Waylon.

Neil Reshen: I'm desperately looking through the bookings, and I see the guy has been paying about $1,900 for two separate nights. The promoters were always smarter than the [booking] agents, they found out how much you could go for the cheapest and they'd pay that. So every date was for gas money. I said to the guy: 'Y'know, new management team. I need $2,500 a night.' The guy said, 'OK, you got it.' I asked him why he gave in so easy, and he said, 'Well, let me tell you what we did with Waylon and Willie. We'd call Moeller Talent about this time of the night and we'd get their [answering] machine. We'd tell them what night we wanted and we gave them the same price as always, and the secretary types up the contract in the morning and sends it. We've been waiting about four years for someone to tell us we're charging too little, but nobody ever does. So I'll be happy to pay you that and I'll probably pay you $3,500 next time. Waylon sells out every night.' I knew right there we were going to win!

Reshen thrived on such victories; they were his fuel. He didn't care too much about the niceties of life. Nobody was ever working under the illusion that he was a particularly pleasant guy. He was a rock manager in the classic tradition: blunt, not overly well groomed, too interested in the hustle to be socially easy, not even a little bit trustworthy. All these traits would eventually come back to haunt Nelson, but at the time they seemed to be precisely what was needed. He had enough friends. What was required was a bully who was on his side.

Willie Nelson: He's probably the most hated and the most effective manager I know of. He's so sadistic. He enjoys going up to those big corporations and going over their figures. It's a challenge to like Neil.[5]

To Waylon Jennings he was a 'mad dog on a leash'. To Connie he was a 'bulldog' who could be trusted only slightly further than he could be thrown. It was Reshen who presented her with her first ever diamonds, a pair of beautiful earrings. He watched in delight, proud as could be, as she cried with joy and thanked him. Years later she got them valued and they turned out be fake, worth only $50: 'That's Neil in a nutshell,' she says. However, he undeniably did the job that was asked of him. After barking at Bradley, Reshen called Nelson and informed him that 'he had just bought him' from RCA. He was free for the first time in eight years. Having seen Reshen prove his mettle, Nelson told him to send the management contract down and he signed it. A deal was a deal, after all.

TEXAS WAS ALWAYS THERE

W illie Nelson is talking about home.
        He speaks about Texas as though it were a living, breathing entity. A friend. Over and over again when times have turned tough he has found solace there. Personally. Creatively. Spiritually. He used to say that no matter what time it was on the bus, whether he was asleep or awake, he would always sense the precise moment when they crossed the state line and were back home.

'Texas was always there; it was an easy place to go back to,' he says. 'It's a good place to live. I still live there.' He sounds oddly like a very laid-back travel agent. His pitch is simple. 'Anybody who doesn't live there should come there and see what it's all about.'

He leans forwards a little. 'You been to Abbott?' he says, almost animated. He is sitting on the edge of the sofa. Hands clasped together. Elbows on his knees. Water drum between his feet. 'Well, Abbott is still home.'

He falls into something of a reverie as old names and memories from six decades ago come spilling out. He has a ramshackle old house in Abbott, no different to the ones on either side of it, but he doesn't spend much time there these days.

The Austin area has been his home for three decades. It holds a special energy. It is where he finally found an audience big enough to embrace his music; to link arms and encircle it in its entirety.

'I think they were way ahead in Austin,' he says. 'I realised that this is a place it can happen. It makes sense. It just means that these guys know what's going on and they're not afraid to say it. And it's still there. Oh yeah, it's still there. Ain't nothing changed about Austin. In fact, it's so good that a lot of people are coming there to experience it, but it doesn't make it any less great.'

He beams, and when he does his eyes almost close and his head tilts slightly upwards, like a shaggy dog seeking approval. His enormous ranch outside Austin has a mocked-up Wild West town in its grounds and real deer prints scattered on the red earth. At its entrance, the black wrought iron gate spells out T-E-X-A-S. As if he would forget. There is a pair of old sunglasses hidden in the wall that can only be seen when the security code is punched in and the gate swings open.

It is about two hours and a whole world away from Abbott. But they both hold him.

7. 1972–1973

A ustin had been waiting for Willie Nelson. All he really had to do was to go and claim it. It was almost as though he were living two separate lives. He couldn't get arrested in Nashville but in Texas, and especially in Austin, he was fast on his way to becoming a star. This was way beyond the popularity he had enjoyed in his home state since the early-60s, the simple comfort of knowing that he could always come home and play to a packed house, charge up his confidence and earn some decent money. Something more profound was brewing.

He finally moved back to Texas for good in 1972. The return to Ridgetop from Bandera in the autumn of 1971 had left nobody happy. He had 'Texas fever'. The house had changed physically, of course, and with his recording career stuttering to a halt, increasingly there seemed little point in being in Nashville. Nelson spent most of his time driving to shows and then turning around and contemplating the long haul back to Tennessee. His parents were at Ridgetop, but Myrle would shortly move back to Washington state on the north-west coast and Ira would return to Texas. Connie especially missed home and her own parents in Houston. Indeed, when they first moved back to their home state it was Houston they picked. Connie put down a deposit on a nice new apartment, but her husband took one look at its cold concrete and glass and shuddered. It would be Austin.

Willie Nelson: I literally picked up, left and went back to Texas. I thought maybe I'm going about this the wrong way, maybe I'm spinning my wheels, maybe I should go back home and not try to travel in such a great circle. Maybe I should just work Texas, Oklahoma and New Mexico, places where I was known and where I could draw good crowds. Where I could make a living.[1]

Such modest ambitions were to grow as he saw what was achievable thanks to the unique configuration of the times, but initially he planned a quiet semi-retirement as a working musician playing around his homeland, ticking over financially. He was, after all, almost forty years old and had little cause for believing that his best years would be ahead of him. The advantages of Austin were manifest. It was a physically appealing location, nestled among the gentle slopes of Hill Country and built on the banks of the Colorado river. Its population was a shade over 200,000, just a third of the size it is today, and it really felt more like a good-sized town. It was manageable; knowable. It was also, as Nelson acknowledges, a 'little oasis in the middle of the desert', culturally rather than literally. It still is. In the 2004 US elections, Austin came in as the only Democratic part of Texas. The white-washed mansion that stands just across the street from the impressive State Capitol building at the top of Congress Avenue is the official governor's residence, the place where George W. Bush called home when he was Governor of Texas, but most of Austin's residents take pride in the fact that this part of the state didn't vote him in.

Music has always been an integral part of the landscape. Nowadays Austin hosts the South By Southwest festival in March and you have to book a hotel room half a year in advance, but back in the 60s it was very much the poor country cousin to the larger south Texas cities of Houston and San Antonio. Things were less hectic but still interesting. It was mainly blues and country, but Austin also found room for the psychedelia of Roky Erikson's Thirteenth Floor Elevators and later spawned a vital alternative rock scene. There has always been room for a little weirdness here. Home to the University of Texas, the biggest in the country, it has forever swarmed with young people. Year after year students graduated but refused to leave the town, creating an ever-expanding educated, culturally enlightened core which began to rub up against the traditional old-time Texan caucus. Nowadays, the liberals, new media kids and musicians have practically taken over, but 35 years ago the balance between the two was pretty evenly split and shifting yearly. By the late-60s, this rumbling tectonic activity began to alter the landscape and ultimately came to define the place.

In 1970, when Nelson and the band would visit Austin, they would play the Broken Spoke or the Alliance Wagon Yard or Big G's in Round Rock. These were cowboy outposts. The Broken Spoke is a traditional roadside honky-tonk on the outskirts of the town, and though its once pastoral location has since been subsumed by the city's rapid expansion, the surroundings are about all that have changed. It remains an authentic period piece: the back room is still decked out with a dance floor and a small stage, the tables are dressed in red-checked cloths, chicken-fried steak is on the menu. Owner James White is resplendent in his Stetson and leather waistcoat, and his welcome is large and genuine, but you can imagine that it would take an extremely brave hippie to venture inside these doors 35 years ago. It was a hard-core country establishment, and the lines of social delineation were very strictly drawn and often violently preserved. Even members of Nelson's own band didn't always feel safe.

Paul English: We had Bee and he had long hair. Oh, they didn't like his long hair. I told Bee at the time: 'When we're in beer joints and you go to the bathroom and people stick their foot out [to trip you up], just step over their foot and say, 'Thank you very much!' with a big smile and just keep on going. I'll watch your back, don't worry about it. I'll watch your back.'

It would be hard to over-emphasise how conservative country audiences were. They were predominantly middle-aged or older, and working class. Country music was the preserve of either the genteel old-timer in the sticks or the beer-drinking truck driver at the bar, who liked cars, beer and women, maybe guns too, and had very little truck with liberal politics, drugs, or anything as obviously effeminate as long hair. Merle Haggard's 1969 hit 'Okie From Muskogee' was a hippie-baiting, redneck republican anthem, released at the height of the Vietnam War. Its lyrics ('We don't smoke marijuana in Muskogee/ We don't take our trips on LSD/ We don't burn our draft cards down on Main Street/ Cause we like living right and bein' free') were a hymn to the enduring values of short hair, manly footwear, respect for your elders and waving Old Glory down at the county courthouse. Haggard later claimed he had at least part of his tongue buried in his cheek when he wrote the song and that it didn't necessarily reflect his inner feelings, but he knew what would hit the spot with a country audience. 'Okie From Muskogee' became a country No. 1 and won Single of the Year at the 1970 CMA Awards.

From the other side of the fence, country music had traditionally been regarded with disdain by most teenagers and hippies: an out-of-date institution which said little to them about their own circumstances. It was backward, insular, conservative, and musically behind the times, but perceptions were changing. Everything was open to re-examination. Richard Nixon was in power and the Vietnam War was still rumbling disastrously on, inflicting deeper wounds upon the nation's psyche and killing young men from college and cowboy backgrounds alike. Death didn't discriminate, and the experiences of war bred unity across all kinds of social borders: black soul music, for instance, became politicised, reaching its apogee with Marvin Gaye's *What's Goin' On* in 1971. In country music, the grimness of the age invited a dip into nostalgia, a refresher course in simplicity and enduring values. Joe Gracey became a DJ at the local rebel radio station KOKE-FM in Austin, and he began playing Bob Wills and Lightnin' Hopkins next to Willie Nelson, the Allman Brothers and the Rolling Stones. Country music was being reclaimed as just *music* – removed from its ghetto. Astute listeners were bypassing the schlocky Nashville product of the 60s and making a connection straight back to the elemental raw country of the 40s and the 50s. Sociologists have a name for what was happening: Hansen's Law of the Third Generation, the theory that the grandson wants to remember all the things the son wanted to forget.

Joe Gracey: The first generation does things a certain way, maybe they are immigrants or new arrivals to an area, and things get done a sort of basic and soulful way. The next generation wants to distance itself from the old ways and generally screws everything up and you have stuff like frozen dinners and Melmac and all that awful 50s and early-60s nonsense. The third generation realises that something precious has been lost and tries to revive and preserve and renovate the positive things in the first generation's lives. We truly believed that we were on a kind of holy mission to save and protect and revive Texan culture. Or at least I did.

Slowly, a merging of the battle-lines began. As late as it was, Texas was still catching the slipstream of the whole hippie movement just as it was disappearing over the horizon practically everywhere else. As David Zettner later recalled – and it had earlier been proven when Nelson and the band tried to wear their West Coast clothes in Fort Worth – if something happened in California, it usually took five years to get to the Lone Star State. Austin was, however, already perhaps the capital of the US in terms of psychedelic drug use. Long before acid became *de rigueur*, mescaline and peyote were in constant supply. Texas may have been a conservative state by nature but it was not immune to the ripple effects of the civil rights movement, anti-war feeling, drugs, music and general cultural change, and it followed that Austin – the university town – would be the epicentre of what was going on. Added to that potent brew, musicians of the calibre of Jerry Jeff Walker, Michael Murphey, Doug Sahm, Townes Van Zandt and Billy Joe Shaver could be seen almost every night in Austin in one club or another. Threadgills had been a favourite college hangout during the 60s and had always played country music. Janis Joplin started out there. Now it was jammed every night and some tentative cross-fertilisation was going on; it took really brave hippies and really tolerant rednecks, but it was happening. A psychedelic club called the Vulcan Gas Company opened in 1967, and among its mainly white, collegiate clientele were a few blacks who came to dance and a few airmen who came to check out the hippie girls. And all the time more and more players piled into the city, attracted by its easy lifestyle.

Jerry Jeff Walker: In the early-70s Austin was one of the cheapest cities to live in, so that gave [musicians] a chance. You could play three or four gigs a month and pay the rent and live around. You had a small town and a big college with 50,000 students, which put bodies in the bars to pay for beer and stuff to support the bands, which made it an ideal musical source to draw from. It was a good hotchpotch. You had country bands, rock bands, the songwriters were mostly folky kind of guys who had grown up with singer-songwriters, and you had all these musicians who would say, 'Yeah, I'd love to play on that song.'

There was a need for this burgeoning movement to find a place to call home. The Armadillo World Headquarters looked an unlikely candidate, housed in a plug-ugly former National Guard Armoury on Riverside Drive. Founded by Eddie Wilson – a music-loving, university drop-out who was managing local psychedelic group Shiva's Headband – an artist called Jim Franklin and a lawyer, Mike Polleson, the 2,000-capacity Armadillo opened for business in 1970 and was intended to provide an outlet for rock bands coming in from the East and West Coasts and any other act that couldn't be accommodated in town. It started slowly but soon picked up pace, with the likes of Frank Zappa, Captain Beefheart, Freddie King, Leon Russell and Commander Cody all passing through. In time, Bill and Hilary Clinton came, and Laura Bush illicitly watched Bruce Springsteen there. It became a legendary venue.

Eddie Wilson: We were space cadet hippies. We thought of Armadillo as an experimental Arts Lab. Gradually it all came to pass. The Armadillo was where it came together like a clap of thunder, and that was where we had these great crowds, with people either growing their hair or wearing a hat! It was like a huge costume party.

All of this was already in the air when Nelson arrived in Austin: social foment, a blurring of cultural boundaries and stereotypes, scores of great musicians, all playing night after night, sitting in with each other, mixing up a brew of country and rock, folk and blues, then keeping on after closing time; a venue which was becoming a focus for a new consciousness; marijuana and LSD were everywhere. In March 1972 the Dripping Springs Reunion concert was held, a huge open-air gathering in the tiny town of Dripping Springs, about twenty miles outside Austin. It was essentially a Nashville show: Kris Kristofferson, Rita Coolidge, Charlie Rich and Waylon Jennings played. And so did Willie Nelson. Although it was a shambolic disaster in many ways, haemorrhaging money and terribly organised, it was significant in that, scattered among the usual country crowd, a smattering of long-hairs showed up and got stoned in the sun. Nelson had been aware of Woodstock and had visited the Atlanta Pop Festival in July 1970 and been impressed by the concept, but the combination of hippie and cowboy 'out in the pasture' in Texas was so unusual and so striking it gave him the idea of organising his own grand event: the Fourth of July picnics would begin the following year. He could see things changing in front of his eyes, all it needed was someone to bring it all together. Within a matter of weeks he had moved to Austin.

Rodney Crowell: In country music culture, it was the 70s before the sub-culture of the 60s, the counter-culture, the so-called mind-expanding culture, drifted over and found a focal artist, and that was Willie. In the same way that Dylan, Hendrix and other artists were the focus of that in pop culture, Willie was the first to really focus it in the culture that country music took its livelihood from. If Gram Parsons had lived he may have done it, but Willie Nelson was more salt of the earth. He captured that imagination more simply than another artist might have done.

Willie Nelson emerged as the undisputed king of Texas by covering all the angles: he befriended the most powerful, conservative members of Austin society and got them on side for life, while at the same time connecting with the hippies and the counter-culture's leading lights. It was a cunning smoke-and-mirrors trick and proof positive that he could, in fact, be all things to all people if people wanted him to be badly enough. Nelson had been well connected in Texas for a long time. In the 60s he'd receive visits from old redneck lawmen who would give him presents. In Houston, the head of narcotics in the city would come backstage after every show he attended, take Nelson out to his car and open the trunk and tell him to choose a gun to take away with him as a gift. That's not all he would get.

Willie Nelson: Some of the best marijuana I ever got came from narcotics agents. They'll bust somebody then come by and share it. That's why I'm not necessarily hassled. Course, as long as it's illegal I'm subject to getting popped one of these days. Some local guy that didn't get the word.[2]

While attending the Dripping Springs concert, he hadn't bunked down with the masses. Instead, he had stayed at the extremely well-heeled Austin abode of Darrell Royal, the coach of the University of Texas football team and a highly influential local figure. Royal was a conservative – he hated the Armadillo, because his daughter went there to hang out with the debauched hippies – but he was instrumental in Nelson's rise in Texas. He had been coach since 1957 and, although his reputation was tarnished by persistent allegations that he refused to pick black footballers for his team, he had a lot of people on his side.

He was also a die-hard country music fan. Royal had first met Nelson when they were both staying at the same Holiday Inn. They talked and got to know each other and became firm allies, to the extent that Nelson was guided almost step by step by Royal. He would take him golfing with his millionaire friends, or set up numerous impromptu private showcases for Nelson in hotels in Austin. He would invite the governor and other important people: businessmen, policemen, politicians, union leaders. He performed at local benefits for major used-car dealers who were feeling the pinch of escalating oil prices. These were men who often sailed a little close to the wind, but they were influential.

David Zettner: Whatever they pulled off, they really did pull it off. It is extraordinary. I've never seen another 'star' actually make himself like Willie did. They just kind of grabbed him and said, 'This is our guy.'

They would come to hear him pick and sing and bask in a little reflected glamour, while Nelson went away with some powerful new friends in his pocket, whose collective clout came in extremely handy much further down the line. He would throw a little money into their schemes, invest here and there. Always a man who liked to cut a deal rather than sit on his money, he enjoyed playing the cowboy businessman with his corporate friends.

With a local power base established, Nelson set about assessing the music scene. Or, as Eddie Wilson puts it, 'Willie was the guy who had the big, rich powerful redneck elite in his pocket, and then he rounded up all those little flower children too!' He was always astute enough not to align himself too clearly with one crowd. Each artist had a favourite bar and a group they would hang out with. Nelson would show up at gigs by local bands like Frida and the Firehogs and sit in for a while, then disappear and turn up at a Doug Sahm show with someone else. 'He was,' recalls Joe Gracey, 'unobtrusively obtrusive.' He gave the impression of sitting back and letting things happen around him, but he knew what he was doing. He had a powerful, indeed spiritual belief that music could unite. And he knew enough about both whisky and marijuana to understand both points of view.

He was living just down the road from the Armadillo. The Nelsons had moved into a rented second floor apartment on East Riverside Drive, a stone's throw from the banks of the Colorado river. As was the way of these things, Paul English moved his family next door, and soon the gang was all there. It was fine for a temporary home, but it was really too small for them all. Home life was strained. Billy and Susie felt increasingly alienated from Connie, as well as their father and Paula Carlene. Susie would soon be following the example of her sister, mother and aunt by marrying, aged just sixteen. There was little discipline, and it didn't necessarily help that Connie was pregnant again. She would give birth to Amy on 6 July 1973, by which point the family had moved to a sprawling split-level ranch in 44 acres of land out in the woods of south Austin, off Fitzhugh Road.

But for now he was still living in town amidst the thick of it, and he would often walk along Riverside and pop in for a beer at the Armadillo and a chat with Wilson, checking out whoever was on stage and, crucially, taking the temperature of the crowd. Wilson had been a fan since the mid-60s when he had heard Nelson cover 'Yesterday' on the *Live Country Music Concert* in California, and together they talked about bringing things together. Nelson soon got the feeling that this would be the perfect place to try and explore just how far things had moved – or could be moved – in a social sense. His immediate problem was that none of the new, young audience that was ready to be converted would come near most of the places he played, like Big G's in Round Rock. It physically wasn't safe. If he wanted them to hear his music, he would have to go into their territory, and that meant the Armadillo.

Willie Nelson: Eddie Wilson was the manager there and he and I got to be good buddies, and I knew this would be a good place to experiment with what I was trying to do, which was bring the hippies and the cowboys together. At the time I said I wanted to do it I really didn't know how it could be done, but when the Armadillo came along I realised that this is a place it can happen. You've already got the long-haired cowboys, and you've got your short-haired cowboys, and if you put me and Waylon and Jerry Jeff and all these different people in there, then you're going to bring them all together. That was just an idea that I had.[3]

Nelson first played at the Armadillo World Headquarters in August 1972. Cover charge that night was $2 but even then it was far from a full house. When Wilson announced he was about to come on about fifteen people clapped, and he shouted out: 'He's only the Bob Dylan of country music, you hippie assholes!' About forty people clapped this time. It looked inauspicious, but Nelson won them over immediately. That wild guitar playing, which was not only unusual in the context of a country band but indeed *any* band, the shaggy hair, earring and beard. He looked like one of their own. And with Paul English's cape, Jimmy Day's wild-eyed look and Bee Spears sporting a rooster which would perch on the head of his bass as he played, even the most stoned hippies at the Armadillo had never seen anything like it. And that was before they heard the songs. They worshipped him right off the bat. He was by no means a universally well-known name, but as the biggest and most successful – not to mention the oldest – artist around at the time, he was clearly important. And so he became the figurehead for a scene he had effectively gatecrashed.

Eddie Wilson: He just saw a bunch of people heading in this direction and managed to get in front of them. He was the very best example I've ever seen of someone not just being in the right place at the right time, but having the right consciousness and the right motivation. And, of course, the right network. I was impressed and moved to write that it reminded me of the story about the young bull and the old bull. The young bull says,

'Let's run down there and tap one of those heifers,' and the old bull, and this is Willie, says, 'No, let's *walk* down there and tap *all* of them!'

He only played the Armadillo perhaps half a dozen times over a twelve month period between the summers of 1972 and 1973, but it was hugely symbolic. He brought Waylon Jennings down to play, who couldn't believe his eyes at the crowd: young, and loud, and stoned! This was no country audience, and it took many people aback, but they adapted. Previously conservative songwriters like Tom T. Hall would pick joints up from the stage and smoke them. This new audience re-energised the performers, raised them to new heights. Alliances were made. Dennis Hopper was making a film called *Kid Blue* in Texas and he and writers Bud Shrake and Gary Cartwright would hang out at the Armadillo, calling themselves the Mad Dogs, emphasising it as the centre of a certain collective rebelliousness. They were high times, and Nelson somehow seemed to be at the epicentre.

Dennis Hopper: He was leading the way, no question. Around the time of the picnics, the whole feeling made Austin one of the greatest places I've ever been.

Nelson and Leon Russell, the rocker who had led the band on Joe Cocker's *Mad Dogs And Englishmen* live album and written 'Delta Lady' and 'A Song For You', became good friends. Each introduced the other to their audience, and Russell in particular was pivotal in shaping Nelson's image. Until now he was just a little shaggy and scruffy looking, but when he saw Russell who sported waist-length silver hair and silver beard, like some futuristic and slightly malevolent version of Merlin – he decided to take his image to its farthest extreme. He understood the instant head start an outlandish and unique visual image would give him to a wider audience. There would never be any confusion over his identity.

Nevertheless, it took a little while to really catch alight. Just as Nelson had been required to keep shrinking his circle, returning to Texas, then to Austin, and then finally to the Armadillo World HQ in order to find the connection he had been seeking for so long, so the ripples took time to slowly spread back out from the source through 1973 and 1974. Firstly, they hit Austin itself, with all social stripes claiming him as their own; then through south Texas, with new fans travelling deep into redneck country to watch him at places like John T. Floores' country store in Helotes. It was an ad hoc and primitive means of mutual education: the younger, hipper fans pressing against the stage, staring up as Nelson played; the old cowboys just wanted to drink and dance. And fight.

Mickey Raphael: There were a few fights – there were some great fights, actually! Willie had long hair, so it kinda defused it a little bit. When you had hippies drinking, *they'd* want to fight too, but they were mostly on drugs and the cowboys were drinking. When we were really playing the funky joints, I wouldn't wander too far, because I was a little intimidated by it. I was this little hippie kid, with an Afro, and there was no way I could walk into some of these beer joints by myself. I'd just stand close by Willie. He's [unbreachable], they're not going to threaten him.

It was the picnics that really cemented the union. Nelson's inaugural Fourth of July Picnic in Dripping Springs attracted 50,000 people in July 1973, but it was a bit of a mess, financially disastrous and badly organised. The path to the venue was a single road and many stalled cars were left in ditches as people walked. Trees were sawn down to clear the way. They ran out of food, water and the toilet facilities were utterly inadequate. The heat was almost unbearable. But there was non-stop music from noon past midnight and it caught and shaped the mood of the times. Texan musician Steve Earle recalls being badly beaten up on his way home from school because he had long hair, 'and that didn't really change until Willie Nelson moved back to Texas and started having the Fourth of July Picnics. All of a sudden Texas, at least on that level, became more tolerant.'[4] The same year, Jerry Jeff Walker released *Viva Terlingua*, Doug Sahm put out two albums, Michael Murphey released *Michael Murphey* and – right at the head of the pack – Willie Nelson made *Shotgun Willie*. All those faces and many more turned up again at the second Fourth of July Picnic in 1974, alongside the likes of Leon Russell from outside of country music circles. It was here that Nelson was truly anointed a Texas legend, unifying a second summer of love and sealing the coming of age of the Austin scene.

Joe Gracey: For a while there a Willie Nelson Picnic was like Fear and Loathing in Texas. Whatever it was you were looking for, you were gonna find there, I assure you. There was nothing that did not get smoked, ingested, made love to, or done at some point at one of those picnics. It was glorious. Everybody was into free sex and good cheap Mexican weed and cold Pearl Beer and Shiner and swimming naked together.

In many ways the reality was less important than the concept which had taken hold. In truth, the idyll of Nelson's time at the Armadillo was largely a mirage that by late 1973 had already vanished. The meeting of minds between the redneck and the hippie was never seamless, and was often uneasy. There were several bomb scares at the Armadillo, and tear gas was thrown in on one occasion. The loose collection of ne'er-do-wells who made up Nelson's entourage were never going to have their heads turned by flower power, and things began to get a little hairy. There were all sorts of affiliations being made and agendas being pursued behind the scenes. Aside from the likes of Paul English and Billy Cooper – a former used-car salesman whom Nelson had appointed driver and *de facto* bodyguard a few years earlier – who were basically decent but had what one local rather quaintly describes as 'old habits', in the sense that they packed a piece and would not shirk from violence, there were other less savoury characters on the scene. There was Arlon Walter, a sleazy-looking piece of work with a pencil-thin moustache and a fedora, who would tell people that his job was to go to every Johnny Bush gig and collect a little something towards a 'Willie debt'. Who knows whether he was telling the truth? He was from the Dixie Mafia and ended up getting shot in a card game.

Austinite Tim O'Connor became another member of the gang, one of several general dogsbodies who hung around and helped out and got close to Nelson. He left town for a while after shooting someone in the leg. Then there was Larry Trader, who had started working with Nelson before the fire in Ridgetop and who had also decamped to Austin. It wasn't that difficult to become a member of the inner circle – you didn't need any qualifications, your face just had to fit somehow. Trader had worked for Ray Price when he met Nelson.

Larry Trader: Willie sent me on a chore. I did what I had to do and came back, and he said if you ever need a job come along. And that was that. 1969. I got in my Vauxhall and drove to Ridgetop.

He has been with Nelson ever since. However, Trader was unpopular among certain members of the Armadillo staff for regularly failing to pay bands in San Antonio. Nelson was all too aware of this, but was unrepentant. He would tell people: 'Larry's done stuff for me that can never be repaid. Now y'all shake hands and be friends.' It was the kind of blind loyalty that inspired devotion in return.

After the first picnic there had been rumblings throughout the Austin scene. Money, success, personal jealousies and ambition reared their heads, and nobody seemed to be satisfied. Eddie Wilson had put capital into the festival when it looked like it was sinking, and there were accusations and counter-claims about who had taken what. Cocaine, too, moved in quickly. Tensions grew between Nelson and the Armadillo, and finally there was a falling out over some of 'his people' carrying arms around the hippies; guns were flashed in the beer garden, carloads of guys would roar by and intimidate the bouncers. Shortly afterwards, Nelson came to the office to talk about playing more shows at the Armadillo, keen to keep the momentum going, and he was told it was unacceptable for his guys to be behaving in this way. Could he rein them in a little? Never keen on direct confrontation, he flashed the famous Nelson grin and said, 'Aw, they don't *all* carry guns.' A couple of days later a more direct message was passed from Neil Reshen back to the Armadillo: 'Willie says go fuck yourself.'

Eddie Wilson: They were the antithesis of all the [hippie] stuff we were about. There wasn't a lot of loyalty on anybody's part back then. Everyone was looking for a gig, everyone was looking to make a buck. But great art is often produced in camps of smugglers, thugs and thieves.

In truth, Nelson didn't need them any more. Having finally escaped Nashville and RCA, he had managed to find his audience and his time. He was yet only a local hero, but soon the ripple effect would be spreading out of Austin and Texas and across the mountains, plains, lakes and valleys of the United States. Within a year of his first picnic he would be playing to an audience consisting mainly of transvestites – and Bob Dylan – at Max's Kansas City in New York, the club where the Velvet Underground used to perform. Within two years he would be a superstar. He had waited and waited, seemingly standing still, and the times had finally turned to face him.

Neil Reshen's first task in the latter part of 1972 had been to get Nelson signed to another label. He may never have struck gold within the Nashville system, at least not as a performer, but there were plenty of record companies outside the straight country labels who were progressive enough to realise that he had something. Leon Russell had wanted to sign him to his Shelter label, but in the end Nelson went with Atlantic. The New York label was famed principally for its classic R&B recordings of the likes of Aretha Franklin and Ray Charles, but in the autumn of 1972 it was all geared up to establish a country branch in Nashville. This was really Jerry Wexler's baby. The legendary producer co-owned the company with Ahmet Ertegun but his idea for a country venture didn't receive much support from head office, a setback which would eventually kill it. Wexler had dispatched Rick Sanjek down to Nashville as general manager of Atlantic Country. The first artist signed was Troy Seals. And then there was Willie Nelson.

Jerry Wexler: I wanted to have a well-rounded record company, to operate in all the current areas. I was at this party for Harlan Howard [in Nashville] and there was Willie Nelson, among other people. I was very 'on top' of Willie Nelson. I'd been a big fan for a long, long time. So when we met, I said, 'Willie, this is a great occasion, I've been waiting for a long time to meet you.' And he said, 'Well, it's great to meet you.' He was free of contract. There were a lot of reasons for that. The Pooh-Bahs in Nashville regarded him as an outlaw – in heavy quotation marks: he had an earring and long hair – and they thought that these were the stigmata of an outcast. It's one of the most hypocritical, stupid, spurious attitudes in the history of music. And I was the gainer from that, because he was free of contract and I signed him up.

The plan was to bring both Nelson and Waylon Jennings in as a package deal but, ironically, although Atlantic was a much more creatively stimulating home than RCA, some of the same old problems still got in the way. Wexler was an auteur record-maker; he loved music and musicians and knew his stuff inside out. He was also full of piss and vinegar – and remains so – and would not bow to bullying or bluster. He and Waylon locked horns and neither really got what they wanted. Jennings had agreed to come to Atlantic and had agreed on the money, but Wexler refused to allow him to produce himself. It was a deal breaker and Jennings went back to RCA.

It has been said many times over that Jennings was the true renegade in the partnership with Nelson; the one who always stood up for himself with the dramatic gesture. Prior to him meeting Neil Reshen, the only time Waylon had ever got away with using his own musicians in the studio was by coming in with a gun and threatening to shoot the session musicians unless he could use his own. They thought he was serious. Of course, those were the kind of rebellions that, ultimately, didn't get you anywhere. Nelson, on the other hand, was cannier, and had quietly engineered something unique at the Armadillo. With Atlantic, he was happy enough to accept a minor compromise. He was in the hands of a company he trusted and which would let him get on with business. He could play whatever songs he wanted and choose his own musicians. Jennings seemed to be intent on the sprint, keen to win every victory immediately and simultaneously, but Nelson had his eye on the marathon.

When he entered Atlantic's studio B in New York in early February 1973 to record, he had more freedom than he'd ever had before. The band all came: Jimmy Day, Bee Spears, Paul English, as well as local Austinites Doug Sahm and fiddle maestro Johnny Gimble. Bobbie was now also part of the Family Band, coming in on the piano. She had been living in Austin with her third husband Jack Fletcher for the past few years, raising her three kids, playing in hotel bars and working for Hammond demonstrating the organs at 'every carny and every stock show. It was the nearest I could get to performing.'[5] Now that Nelson was going places she was one of the gang.

In New York, two months shy of his fortieth birthday, Nelson was ready to grasp the nettle. The recording was a genuine event. There was talk of Bob Dylan, newly back in New York after a tortuous spell filming *Pat Garrett And Billy The Kid* in Mexico, coming along. He never did show, and neither did George Jones or Kris Kristofferson, also rumoured to be coming, but it was still a packed studio: Doug Sahm was there, Larry Gatlin, David Bromberg. *Rolling Stone* magazine sent a reporter, an indication that what had been happening down in Texas recently was starting to reach a national audience. One man who wasn't around much was Wexler, who was undergoing seismic changes in his personal life.

Nick Hunter: Jerry fell in love with a younger woman and pretty much by the beginning of *Shotgun Willie* he disappeared for a year and really had nothing to do with it. I believe the actual producer of that first record was Arif Mardin, not Jerry.

Nelson already had most of the *Phases And Stages* songs in his back pocket, but there were problems with clearing them for recording because he had originally cut them for RCA back in April 1972. In any case, he seemed not to want to make a conventional country record at this point. In the end he came away with not one but two albums, and neither was like anything he had ever made before. They cut 33 songs in 5 days – 'It's a record, even for Atlantic!' shouted Arif Mardin happily,[6] little realising that this was slow by Nashville standards. Working twelve-hour shifts, the musicians still found time for carousing and what *Rolling Stone* postulated may have been 'coupling' in the darkest corners of the studio. In the first two days he recorded the tracks for a gospel record, or rather a record of traditional gospel songs filtered through a country sensibility, with Bobbie's piano well to the fore. It had been a project he'd been trying to get going for years.

Willie Nelson: RCA wouldn't let me do one. They thought I needed to be a more established country artist before I could do a gospel album. They didn't think gospel songs were commercial themselves and I knew they were because I knew that we were singing 'Will The Circle Be Unbroken' and 'Amazing Grace' every night and everyone was singing along.[7]

The one contemporary song was 'The Troublemaker', written by doowop singers Bruce Belland and David Somerville, which drew an explicit analogy between the hippie dissenters of the time and Jesus. Indeed, it would have been impossible for Nelson not to have recognised more than a passing resemblance to his own recent situation with RCA and the country music establishment in the opening stanzas: 'He was nothing but the troublemaking kind/ His hair was much too long and his motley group of friends/ Had nothing but rebellion on their minds.' Indeed, music business politics were never far from the surface. There is no doubt that the gospel record was close to Nelson's – and his sister's – heart, but as Reshen points out, it was also a firm statement of intent.

Neil Reshen: Willie was astounded when we took him to Atlantic and he sat down with Jerry Wexler. The first albums we did, *Shotgun Willie* and the gospel album, he did basically to see how far he could push Atlantic. He would test everything.

In this case, Atlantic played a canny game with Nelson: they allowed him to record the gospel record but made no promises about when it would come out. Having exhausted his favourite standards from the book of Sacred Service Hymns, he then turned from the holy to the profane. The remainder of the sessions were devoted to making what would become *Shotgun Willie*, the album proper. He had no new songs when he arrived in New York. The title track came to him in the bathroom of the Holiday Inn where he was staying during the recording of the record, and its light-hearted shuffle masks the deeper panic of writer's block as he prepared to throw himself into his new record for a new label. 'You can't make a record/ If you ain't got nothin' to say,' he sang, and it is indeed a litany of non-sequiturs, unconnected images and scenes of creative stasis. It seemed to do the trick.

Willie Nelson: [It] assured me once again that when I was under pressure to write songs in a hurry, I could still do it. I wrote . . . that whole album in about a week.

In fact, there were only four new originals on the record. 'Shotgun Willie' kicked off side one with a soulful swagger, its drunken horns and easy blues announcing it as one for the kids at the Armadillo rather than the good ole boys in the Broken Spoke, but 'Sad Songs And Waltzes' was pure blue country, both a broken-hearted love song and a pointed dig at how out of step he had been in the music industry through the years: 'It's a good thing that I'm not a star/ You don't know how lucky you are/ My record may say it/ But no one will play it/ Sad songs and waltzes aren't selling this year.' The syncopated rock of 'Devil In The Sleeping Bag' was an ode to Paul, hunkered down in the van as the band travelled back to – inevitably – Texas. The record ended with Willie alone with his guitar on 'A Song For You', Leon Russell's minor-key marvel, and in-between Nelson nailed some classics to the mast: he cut Johnny Bush's 'Whiskey River', although those familiar with the versions he has since played – what is it, about a million times? – in concert will find its relaxed pace a shock. He revisited 'Local Memory', 'She's Not For You' and 'So Much To Do' from his RCA days and revved up versions of Bob Wills' peerless 'Stay All Night (Stay A Little Longer)' and Cindy Walker's 'Bubbles In My Beer', both of which had been recorded in Nashville.

Satisfied, after five days he called a cab from the studio, headed for the airport, and was playing at Big G's in Round Rock by the following night. The album was launched at the Armadillo in April 1973 and the end result sounded like a man set free, the horns and strings adding texture as he gleefully skidded all over the vast expanses of American music. There is little sense – aside perhaps from the closing 'A Song For You' – that *Shotgun Willie* was made against the backdrop of real personal tragedy. Paul English's wife Carlene killed herself on 3 January, just a month before recording began, and Nelson had been at the scene when it had happened at the apartment complex on Riverside Drive.

Connie Nelson: I was four months pregnant with Amy, and I was fixing breakfast. I'd just gotten the kids up for school, Billy and Susie, and Paula was there. I heard screaming from somewhere but I didn't know what it was. I didn't hear it again, and went back to fixing breakfast. Then I heard a banging on our glass door, and it was Carlene's son. I opened it up and he said, 'It's Mom, it's Mom, come quick, come on!' I ran over in my pyjamas, Willie was in his underwear, ran next door and she was gone. It was horrible. Just disbelief.

Paul English, by his own admission, went even further off the rails than he was already. He couldn't part with Carlene's clothes, he went from 180 lbs to 130 lbs in 'the press of a button', he began living life with a death wish. For the next five years he became the eye of the hurricane as the band went through their wildest times on the road. After the suicide, Nelson had told him, 'We'll go to work whenever you're ready to go to work,' and he had showed up for the *Shotgun Willie* sessions less than two months later. But he wasn't really there.

Paul English: I don't remember much. I didn't want to live, I wanted to die, I didn't care what happened. Tried to make myself die and I couldn't even do it. Willie put up with me and I don't know how. Just a solid kind of person. I appreciate him for that because I look back and think: Well I did that and I did that. That was terrible. I scared myself. I'd look in the mirror and I didn't know who the guy was. I was taking a lot of pills. I'd just go to the drugstore and get what I wanted. Didn't pay for them or anything – I'd just take them.

Connie arranged for Nelson to take Paul to Mexico in his old Mercedes to meet up with Kris Kristofferson, who was filming *Pat Garrett And Billy The Kid* down in Durango with Bob Dylan and Sam Peckinpah. While they were gone, she went over to the English apartment and got rid of all Carlene's old clothes, which were still hanging in the closet. Later, Nelson wrote 'I Still Can't Believe That You're Gone' about English's wife. His daughter Paula Carlene had been named in her honour, and she had been a close friend over the years. He waited nearly a year before playing it to English, unsure of what his reaction might be.

Paul English: I didn't know he wrote it, as a matter of fact we were over at Darrell Royal's house, and the Coach asked me, 'Have you heard this song that Willie wrote about Carlene?' I said, 'No, I haven't.' Of course he did it for me then, and it brought me to tears, I tell you that.

'I Still Can't Believe That You're Gone' would end up on Nelson's next Atlantic album, *Phases And Stages*. That *Shotgun Willie* had sold far better than anything he had ever done was hardly an achievement in itself, but it had taken him firmly out of the country camp and into the endless waters of contemporary music. Far from seeing Nelson's image as a disadvantage, Atlantic were happy to emphasise it. This was 1973, after all, and the Rolling Stones had just made *Exile On Main Street*, David Bowie was miming fellatio upon his guitarist on stage, and punk was no more than three years away. A beard, an earring and a little pot were hardly going to hurt. The *Shotgun Willie* album cover showed him cheerfully dishevelled, staring out of the twin barrels of what was supposed to be a shotgun, but actually looked like a pair of aviator shades turned upside down. Even the choice of the first single, released in July 1973, was tactical. Common sense dictated that 'Stay All Night (Stay A Little Longer)' would be the obvious choice – it was a familiar song and perhaps the most straightforward and upbeat country song on the record – but it was felt that might be too safe an option.

Nick Hunter: I remember Neil [Reshen] wanted to put out 'Shotgun Willie' as the first single. I asked why and he said, 'Well, it's not a hit, but the image will last with Willie Nelson for a long time.' I didn't quite get that at the time, but he was correct. The record wasn't a hit, but you'll still see Willie referred to in some quarters still as 'Shotgun Willie'.

'Stay All Night (Stay A Little Longer)' became the second single and was more successful, reaching No. 22 in the *Billboard* country charts in October. The same month Nelson was voted into the Nashville Songwriter's Association Hall Of Fame, which must have struck him as a rich irony. At the presentation dinner he picked up his guitar and got up to sing all his best songs, one coming relentlessly after the other. It was a show of defiance; a thank you; and above all, a final farewell.

THE OUTLAW

What does it mean to be an Outlaw?

Willie Nelson talks about Waylon Jennings.

'He was an ornery son-of-a-bitch and I could relate to that. I seemed to be a little more laid-back, but I could definitely relate to where he was because I was also there at one time. That's why I could laugh and say, "Waylon, go for it." We were doing the same thing, basically.'

He talks about the convenience of the label.

'It was definitely necessary,' he says. 'Otherwise, everybody would have thought it was OK to do it the way it was being done. So that's where I was, and Waylon and Kris and John. A whole lot of guys who were doing it the way they felt it.'

But what does it mean to be an Outlaw?

He thinks for a while. Somewhere down below some music is playing.

'I think I'm most interested in pleasing myself.'

8. 1974–1976

There is an extremely persuasive argument which states that the first half of the 70s, the period immediately prior to mainstream exposure, marks the creative pinnacle of Nelson's entire career. There were several factors in his favour: he had escaped from the Nashville system and was now working with a rock label – albeit in their stuttering country division – with people who understood what he was and what he needed, and the effect on his output was audible. In the years between 1971 and 1975 his records became more focused than they had ever been previously and – with a few notable exceptions – would ever be again. Rather than simply laying down a series of unconnected tracks, he thought deeply about what he was doing in the studio and found unifying themes and emotions linking the songs. While he remained an enthusiast of the one-or-two-takes-and-move-on ethos, his writing, his sound and his ideas all came together with a cohesion and a confidence – and an intensity – which he would later find hard to match. Crucially, he was untethered by any artistic restrictions and could write freely in the knowledge that he would hear his ideas reach fruition on record, but on the other hand he was not yet at the stage where he could release anything he wanted – and thus not have to write at all. This sheltered cusp between cult status and superstardom created both a necessity and an outlet which made it a gloriously fertile time to create.

His songwriting and recording also benefited from the fact that he was touring less heavily and within a smaller radius than he had previously. Texas had become a base, a haven, and one he was reluctant to leave. He recorded the pilot episode for the landmark *Austin City Limits* TV show in October 1974. Originally it was going to feature both Nelson and Doug Sahm, until he came back and said: 'My manager said I can't do it with Doug. I've got to do it by myself or I don't do it.' It was a smart tactical manoeuvre by the leader of the Texas pack: don't share it. He knew he was building something important and solid there, and felt little inclination to go slogging around the country trying to break every last market.

Nick Hunter: When we were at Atlantic he didn't want to go on the road, it was just something he didn't really want to do. Part of it was he didn't feel he was really accomplishing anything out there.

He had a vibrant epicentre in his annual showpiece picnics and he believed that the aftershock would spread, at which point it would be time to go and proclaim the word in person. But it was records which would really get him noticed. After the *Shotgun Willie* album he was increasingly picked up on the wider radar. The Rolling Stones came knocking but the timing was all wrong. The band – most specifically Keith Richards, who had been close friends with Gram Parsons – were all country fans, and in 1974 they asked Nelson to open for them on their 1975 US tour. He turned them down.

Mickey Raphael: You know, that stuff didn't mean anything to him. I was 20, 21, and to me they were the biggest band in the world. They were my idols, and I was like, 'What are we doing? [Turning down the Stones] to stay in Texas?!' Willie was like, 'Oh, here I can go home every night and we play sold out audiences. Why go around the world with them when I can play to my fans here? What's the point?' Why go from number one to an opening act, which is what he would have been on that tour. He was King of the Hill in Texas.

His time at Atlantic was to prove short-lived but it left a significant legacy. Rather like his spell with Monument a decade earlier, some of his best work was created at a label which – with the benefit of hindsight – was not all that much more than a stepping stone. Following on from the considered success of *Shotgun Willie*, Nelson went back into the studio to make *Phases And Stages* for Atlantic, a record which had been almost complete in his mind for at least two years. He had originally recorded most of the songs in his final sessions for RCA in April 1972, and had had to utilise all of Neil Reshen's hard-headed legal trickery to get the songs back. He had loved *Yesterday's Wine*, his concept album about life and death. The idea of a cycle of songs appealed to his world view, the circular, karmic notion of endless life, as well as to his view of music as a unifying force.

Willie Nelson: I was just tired of albums with twelve separate moods and twelve separate ideas and with nothing to connect them, no thought following through the album. If you're sitting in a living room and you're listening to an album and you have a certain mood going, you don't want that trip broken.[1]

He now planned a thematic album looking at the end of a relationship, first from the perspective of the man on side one, and then from the perspective of the woman on side two. Obviously it was territory he knew well, by heart you might say, but it was a flimsy concept which soon expanded to find room for 'I Still Can't Believe That You're Gone', Nelson's heartfelt farewell to Carlene English; 'It's Not Supposed To Be This Way' – a new song written for his daughter Susie as they drove to Colorado together and tried to work out how to get close to the heart of the matter – and the closing 'Pick Up The Tempo', which was both a defiant cry of belief in what he was doing and a rallying call to his fellow musical rebels: 'People are saying that time will take care of people like me/ And that I'm living too fast and they say I can't last for much longer/ But little they see that their thoughts of me is my saviour/ And little they know that the beat ought to go just a little faster.' In other words: you ain't seen nothin' yet.

This time Wexler was on board as producer and he pushed hard to bring Nelson down to Muscle Shoals in Alabama to work with his elite team of studio musicians, who had played on fistfuls of classic recordings by Aretha Franklin, Otis Redding, Ray Charles *et al.* The band were used to working primarily within the boundaries of R&B and rock music but could turn their hand to virtually anything. Wexler liked to keep them fresh and had said very little about what was expected, with the result that only a few of them really had any idea who Nelson was; they knew that if Wexler was a fan then he must have something going for him and were excited by the prospect of the experience, but they also found Nelson's working methods a little incongruous. He arrived alone in his old Mercedes, having driven himself from Texas. There were no advance tapes of the material, and yet he expected them to simply play the whole album through from start to finish.

David Hood: He walks in with that guitar that has the hole in it, and he's ready to go. That's what was so funny for us: him wanting to sit down and play straight through – 'But we don't know the songs!' Normally you learn a song, record it, learn another song, record it, but he just wanted to go through the whole thing. He just thought we could pick 'em up and do it. We had to talk him into more or less doing it our way.

It went very fast. The record came together quickly, virtually live. Most of the tracks were first or second takes. The Muscle Shoals men had worked together for an age and were experts at divining the heart and soul of a song quicker than most. They were businesslike, on time and ready to go any time of day or night. Perfect for Nelson. He would play the songs to the band on his guitar, they would make a chord chart, it would be recorded, and they would move on. Barry Beckett, playing keyboards, regarded it as a meeting of country and blues, and Wexler's role was no more complicated than making sure everyone was happy, pulling in the same direction, and ensuring that the tapes were rolling.

It was Nelson who quietly commanded the sessions. In the studio, he works in a singular way: without necessarily explaining in words what he wants, and without troubling the musicians with anything so airy-fairy as a concept, he will guide the musicians through sheer serendipity, letting them discover what it is he is looking for in a song by the way he plays, the way he sings, the way he smiles and moves. If it's not coming out the way he wants he might return to guitar and vocal, willing them to really *listen*. Rarely will he say – 'do this, don't do that'. It's music-making based on trust and belief. That old ESP thing again.

Barry Beckett: In the studio, he lets it happen. If it doesn't happen it doesn't happen. He won't force it. He works with people he respects and who respect him. Nobody is going to interrupt him, not only because it's Willie, but just because of what is happening. Nobody is going to interrupt his train of thought.

The Family Band were nowhere to be seen on *Phases And Stages*, although there were some fine country musicians on hand: Johnny Gimble and his fiddle showed up, as did Fred Carter Jr, a superb Nashville guitarist, and steel player John Hughey. Wexler was certainly intrigued by the possibilities of cutting a country record with an R&B band, but – like many producers before and since – he also wasn't entirely convinced that Nelson's live band wasn't a one-trick pony, and wondered whether they could cut the mustard in the studio. It was a rather interesting echo of the problems Nelson had encountered with RCA in the 60s, and there is evidence that he may not have been entirely happy with this scenario.

Willie Nelson: Jerry Wexler had a brainstorm that he wanted me to go to Muscle Shoals. Since he'd let me do the first one my way, I decided to let him do the second one his way.[2]

Although Wexler was *simpatico* and Nelson felt duty bound to listen to his ideas, he had not come this far to be pushed into tit-for-tat artistic compromises, however superb the final outcome. He wanted, indeed expected, to record with his band. Perhaps Waylon Jennings had been right after all. He returned to Nashville and listened to the final tapes of the album and thought he could do better himself. Instead of confronting Wexler directly with his thoughts, he went into Fred Carter's studio in Nashville and tinkered with the master tapes.

Nick Hunter: Willie's a great con man. He does it nicely, but he's a con man. He and Fred came walking in one day to the [Atlantic] office and they decided they could cut a better version of *Phases And Stages* than Jerry did. So they went and did it. Rick Sanjek was involved, because they had to convince Rick it was a good idea. I remember going to New York with Rick and walking into Jerry's office. The only thing I remember about Wexler's office was that it was very long – at the very back wall by the door there was a couch, and I remember sitting on the couch figuring: when the shooting starts I probably wouldn't get shot. Rick told them that they'd cut a better version of *Phases And Stages* than Jerry had. That didn't sit very well. Of course [Jerry won].

Wexler, typically, remembers the incident slightly differently.

Jerry Wexler: I permitted the man in charge of our country music department – I'm not even going to mention his name [Rick Sanjek] – to mix the record, because he assured me it had to have a country mix, whatever the hell that was. So he sent me this mix: it was horrible. Horrible. We buried it. There's no such thing as a country mix. So I just had Tom Dowd remix it, and that's the record that came out. To my spec. To *my* satisfaction.

It was the last time – bar none – that Nelson would cede control; he would work many more times without his band or with a producer in the studio, but the final call would be his. However, there could be little complaint about the final product, released in May 1974. Despite the 'Phases And Stages Theme' which kept interrupting the flow of the record and became an escalating irritant, it was a magical piece of work and perhaps, as Wexler concedes, 'his best. *Sotto voce*, but a lot of Willie's people say that.' 'I Still Can't Believe That You're Gone' is the emotional peak – the music is so lovely, so perfect and overwhelming that it takes a few listens to realise that Nelson isn't singing his own sad farewell to his friend's wife, but is instead singing *as* Paul English. It's a brilliant insight into his art as a songwriter: not content merely to empathise with a friend's grief, but instead to inhabit it, claim it as his own and use it to create a work of universal depth. When he explains that his songwriting is based on the belief that everybody thinks and feels the same basic things the world over, 'I Still Can't Believe That You're Gone' is Exhibit A. It is the sound of him singing from deep within another man's soul.

Phases And Stages was a triumph, but the weight of expectation on the record was too heavy. Problems were brewing at the Nashville branch of Atlantic, which was already several thousands of dollars in the red, mainly due to start-up expenses and the fact that they had signed nobody of comparable calibre to Nelson. It was a stable with only one real thoroughbred, and although *Phases And Stages* would go on to sell around 400,000 copies, he wasn't yet a big enough act to sustain an entire country music department. The re-recording of the classic 'Bloody Mary Morning' became a moderate country hit, but there was no Top 10 success or crossover single to make the leap to the mainstream.

The main problem, however, had been there from the beginning and was fundamentally insurmountable: the lack of enthusiasm and support for the Nashville operation from head office in New York. It was a crude sketch in imitation of what had afflicted Nelson at RCA, except this time it wasn't simply a misunderstood artist, it was a whole misunderstood genre. Wexler claims he was the only staff member at Atlantic Records at any level – 'administrator, boss, worker, toiler in the field' – who had any interest in or feel for country music. This is a characteristic Wexler exaggeration, but only just. Everyone had their pet projects and – as the most recent – the country music offshoot quickly became the fall guy for the whole label. Everything that was failing commercially was dumped into the Nashville department, ensuring that there was no economic viability for the project. On 6 September 1974, only twenty months after it opened, the Nashville office was closed down and all staff laid off, including Nick Hunter. Initially, the idea was that Nelson was going to stay on the label and report to the New York executives.

Jerry Wexler: Lemme tell you what happened. My associates said, 'We're going to close the Nashville office because we're in the red.' I said they couldn't do that, because they've got Willie Nelson and he's going to be tremendous. If they insisted on closing it, I said we had to give Willie his release, because we couldn't have a performer like Willie without a Nashville base. They said, 'Go ahead.' So I called up Willie and said, 'I'm turning you loose.' He understood and was very grateful. It was one of those egregious mistakes on the part of my associates.

Nelson was released with immediate effect from the remainder of his contract and became a free agent. It was a good time for him to be negotiating a deal. *Phases And Stages* had been well received. It was reviewed well in the *New York Times*, a sure sign of growing stature, and was selling well. At the same time, he was in the Top 20 country charts with an unlikely duet of 'After The Fire Has Gone' sung with Tracey Nelson, a fellow Atlantic artist who had been the lead singer with Mother

Earth and who leaned more to the rock side. The duet had been a spur-of-the-moment thing. Nashville producer Bob Johnston, who had cut Dylan's *Blonde On Blonde* in Nashville in 1966, was in love with Conway Twitty and Loretta Lynn's current version of 'After The Fire Is Gone'. He was producing Tracey Nelson and bumped into Nick Hunter one night outside the Exit Inn, slightly inebriated, and the idea for a duet came up. Even back in those days, Nelson would sing on just about anything. They threw Tracey's vocal onto 'Whiskey River' for the B-side and that was that – a medium-sized hit single, as well as a Grammy nomination for Best Country Vocal Performance for 1974.

It was also in his favour that he had walked away from Atlantic with a valuable goodwill gesture in the form of the master tapes for his two already completed albums, which he now owned and could bring to a new label: his gospel album *The Troublemaker* and a superb live album recorded on 29 and 30 June 1974 in Austin, called *Willie Nelson Live At The Texas Opry House*, both of which were virtually ready for the shelves when Atlantic shut down. The live record has never been released in its entirety, but it is a magnificent document of a band storming through instrumentals, gospel tunes, improvised snippets, Nelson originals, classic old songs, and covers of everything from Bob Wills' 'Take Me Back To Tulsa' and Hank Williams' 'Jambalaya' to Merle Haggard's 'Okie From Muskogee'. It is the sound of a whole world of music being blown wide open and is still the template for the kind of show he puts on today. The sound of his mind.

One night early in 1975 Nelson and Connie were driving home from Steamboat Springs in Colorado, where Connie had a three-storey Swiss chalet as a holiday home. They had been on a skiing vacation, but now it was time for the familiar pre-album panic.

Connie Nelson: We were driving back, just the two of us, and Willie said, 'You know, as soon as I get back I've got to go into the studio and do an album and I don't have *any* idea what I'm doing! Not even one song, nothing. Help me think of some songs I could do.' And so I got out a pad and a pen while he's driving, and I said, 'Why don't you do the "Red Headed Stranger" song?' He used to sing that song to the girls when they were getting ready to go to sleep at night, just as he had done to his [older] kids before. I said, 'It's a whole story right there, you can just fill in songs around it and it's done.' So we did. He would say songs like 'Blue Eyes Crying In The Rain' that he wanted to do, and as he's driving I'm writing, and he's filling in the whole story of the 'Red Headed Stranger', this preacher, he's telling it to me and I'm writing it all down. By the time we got to Texas it was pretty much done. He just put it on a tape recorder the way he had it, just with a guitar. Then he filled in the story, and then they just went in the studio and did it.

He had recently signed with Columbia, home of Bob Dylan, Bruce Springsteen, Johnny Cash and a whole host of other A-listers. Neil Reshen had many old contacts at the label from his days filing tax returns for its executives and from managing Miles Davis, and had called CBS President Bruce Lundvall in New York to see if he was interested in Nelson. He was, but Lundvall came up against stiff opposition from the Nashville office. Billy Sherill, the hugely successful staff producer and director of A&R at CBS in Nashville, didn't think he would sell any records. It was the old story: 'Great songs, but . . .' However, Lundvall had loved 'Bloody Mary Morning' and wasn't necessarily burdened with the baggage of Nelson's perceived Nashville failures, and after some consideration he overruled Sherill and signed Nelson up. It was an interesting and significant reversal of the norm: the New York execs trumping the Nashville crowd, and one which ensured he would have the support of the head office when the crunch came. The deal was in the region of $40,000 per album initially (it was renegotiated for far greater sums in 1980 and 1983) plus Columbia agreed to buy the rights to *The Troublemaker* and the *Live At The Opry House* albums – both of which Nelson had been given *gratis* by Atlantic – for $17,000 each. It was a canny piece of business, but he was still a small fish in a very big pond, and Columbia's welcome party for him at Toot Shors restaurant on New York's 52nd Street was sparsely attended.

Nelson went away and nobody heard anything for a few weeks. Executives were slowly preparing to get the wheels in motion for the new record – locations, producers, songs – when Reshen called in mid-February to say the album was ready. 'How could you have the finished album?' asked Lundvall. 'I've only just signed him. The ink on the contract isn't even dry yet!' The album – which took its inspiration from the title track, a children's song that Nelson used to play on his radio shows and sing to his kids at bedtime – jumped hot from the page on the drive from Colorado and leapt into the studio in Dallas, taking three days in all: day one for playing, day two for any small overdubs, day three for mixing. Nelson would arrive in the afternoon, loosen up a bit then record through the night. It cost $5,000.

This time he was using his own band. The line-up had changed a little. Shortly after recording *Shotgun Willie* Jimmy Day had left the group. Instead of replacing him with another steel guitar player, Nelson had drafted in Mickey Raphael on the harmonica to add melody lines. Raphael was a 21-year-old middle-class son of Jewish immigrants who had been spotted by Darrell Royal and plucked out of Dallas into one of those little picking parties Royal was famed for. Raphael was really a fan of folk and rock – he knew next to nothing about country music, but Nelson invited him to sit in with the band and he has stayed ever since, his distinctive harmonica playing becoming one of the defining elements of the Family Band's sound. Jody Payne, the husband of country singer Sammi Smith, also fell in with the band on the road and became the second guitar player in the line up, letting Nelson embark on more experimental forays with 'Trigger'.

In the studio, the band were initially a little confused by what he wanted, and they charged in much as they would have on stage. Nelson stripped things down to just guitar and vocals and then added only the most necessary instrumentation, sketching in detail but keeping it finely drawn. It was the difference between a black and white etching and a full-blown watercolour.

Bee Spears: He'd been talking about doing the album, but he didn't really explain in great detail what it was going to be. We got to the studio and he cut it all out of sequence. We'd be doing something and he'd just decide to play one of the little interludes or something – so it took about half the album [session] to figure out where it was going. Of course, we were excited about doing it because we got to play with Will on the record.

Red Headed Stranger has been called Nelson's masterpiece; if so, it's a masterpiece of narrative structure, cinematic imagery, spare atmospherics and an all-encompassing vision. It's emphatically not a masterpiece of songwriting. In many ways, it is a lesson in how to make wonderful art from the most basic of material: the only truly great original song on the record is 'Time Of The Preacher', which appears three times in various incarnations. But if his glory years as a writer were largely to be behind him, the record secured his iconic status. The album's mood and imagery was so persuasive and enduring that the only real comparison was with one of Sinatra's classic themed Capitol albums from the 50s.

Through the extended story-in-song of a vengeful preacher who rides out in search of the man who has stolen his wife, eventually killing them both and a woman who tries to steal his horse, Nelson got to live out his own fantasy of the lone drifter – emotionally unreachable – cutting through the harshness of the old West on his trusty stallion, chasing down a terrible and inevitable fate. But there was more going on. In the elliptical verses, repeated themes and snatches of songs, he wove an almost biblical spell of a religious man going into the desert and confronting the true measure of his faith – can he live outside the confines of conventional human law but still stay on the side of right in the eyes of God? Can a man who gets away with murder and eventually finds peace with another lover still live with himself?

It is an examination of morality which would have been instantly recognisable to the likes of Paul English and the boys on Jacksonboro Highway twenty years earlier, and which contained Nelson's core character traits. He sits inside the shifting moral landscape of the *Red Headed Stranger* comfortably – a man with a spiritual thirst, a loner, passionate lover, dispenser of justice, outlaw. Even the title of the album was an autobiographical conceit, while the man who hunts down his wife, shoots her dead, then sing a haunted 'Blue Eyes Crying In The Rain' as he basks in her memory is not all that different in essence from the man who rolls from one town to another, cheats on his wife, and then sings heartbreaking songs about being abandoned and alone. As a cultural footnote, it's also worth remembering that Texas folklore decreed that a man was entitled in law to kill his spouse if she committed adultery. It wasn't actually true, but then the letter of the law wasn't always strictly applied in these matters.

It is a ballad record, raw as an exit wound, bitty, scratchy, cutting in and out of songs and weaving through saloon bar instrumentals. It is the sound of Nelson putting his money where his mouth is: if people wanted him to be the figurehead of country roots music, then here it was in all its harsh beauty. It was the first studio record he had ever recorded in Texas. It possessed none of the raucous fervour of the Family Band on stage, and after the beautifully produced suite of superior songs that was *Phases And Stages* it sounded unbelievably spare. It could have been recorded on a front porch or around a campfire. That was the point. In truth, as both a record and a narrative it ran out of steam a little towards its conclusion, but Nelson knew exactly what he was doing: the single line of vocal harmony near the end of 'Blue Eyes Crying In The Rain' is testament to how instinctively he pieced the record together.

He was determined to make the album he wanted, despite the inevitable expectations a new record company harboured. 'He just did that album because that was what he wanted to do,' says Paul English. 'Not because it would sell or anything, that wasn't what he was looking for.' Once again, he was testing the loyalty of those around him. He had done it with Martha way back in the fighting years, he had done it with his band, he had done it with Atlantic, and now he was testing those who worked for him, and his new employers at CBS. Nick Hunter had started working with Neil Reshen when Nashville's Atlantic operation fell apart, and he remembers a resolve within Nelson, a belief that this was the time to fully assert his desires.

Nick Hunter: He realised that this was the time. If he was ever going to make it, it was now. I was with him in the hotel room in Dallas when he signed the Columbia deal, and we talked about it. This was the next step. He was focused on his career then. Willie had figured out what he was going to have to do, and he kind of pulled it all together and got very, very determined about it.

Red Headed Stranger was presented to the executives at Columbia in the same way that a teenage girl presents a delinquent boyfriend to her parents, with a 'you're-not-going-to-like-this-but . . .' mixture of pride and defiance. The Nelson camp were prepared for battle and planned a pincer movement. In New York Neil Reshen took the acetate of the album into

Lundvall's office, while in Nashville Nick Hunter presented the record to Billy Sherill and executive Ron Bledsoe, who was running the CBS operation there. Reshen was accompanied by Waylon Jennings, despite the fact that Jennings was signed to RCA.

Bruce Lundvall: I said, 'Why is Waylon here?' 'Well, he's just Willie's friend.' So we played *Red Headed Stranger* on an acetate and I said, 'Wow, this is really kinda . . . special! Sounds like it was recorded in his living room!' And with that, Waylon practically jumped on my desk and said, 'That's what Willie Nelson is all about! He doesn't want to have a producer, he should never have a producer! This is what he is. This is what he's all about.' I said, 'Wait a minute. I'm not trying to be confrontational with you. Let me take it home and listen to it a little bit.'

According to Reshen, Lundvall hated the album on the first listen and Jennings screamed at him: 'You don't know what the fuck you're doing, this is why you lose all these acts.' Reshen himself was a little more persuasive: 'You don't give up on Willie Nelson just because he did what sounds like a thin, cheesy album,' he told Lundvall. 'You have to trust your art. He comes up with this album and it's his concept album, and you can't tell him: "You're really good but I don't trust you." You've got to at least let it play out. If nobody buys it then we go back and try again.' Lundvall was at heart a music man and he had signed Nelson on instinct rather than commercial judgment, so he was prepared to give it a chance. In Nashville, however, the reaction was even less positive. The executives were shocked and taken aback by the rawness of the album, the stark clip-clopping beat (where there was a beat at all) and raw acoustic guitar. They began talking about it as though it were a demo – with a bit of spit and polish, maybe some strings and a few overdubs it *might* make a decent album.

Nick Hunter: The record just stunned them. If you had gone to a Willie Nelson show back then – pretty much the same show it is now – you see this hell-raising, beer-drinking show with a lot of energy. Then you hear this record. It wasn't what they were expecting. I said to Billy, 'Look, if this record doesn't work and there's something you want to do, then we'll work out a way where you can produce Willie's next record.' When I told Willie that he didn't talk to me for about three weeks. He wasn't too thrilled about that comment. That was what he had spent his life trying to get rid of!

Lundvall and Sherill communicated over the weekend. Lundvall had listened hard to the acetate a few more times at home and had fallen for the record. He loved it. Sherill called him and told him he thought the album was a 'piece of shit. We'll never sell this record. It's not even *produced*.' To Lundvall this was all part of the charm. Once again, he pulled rank. 'It's a Willie thing,' he said. You either understood or you didn't. He had signed Nelson and he wanted to be seen to have the courage of his convictions: the record would come out as it was. He called a meeting with his staff at Columbia and explained the concept of the album and how important it was for Nelson, adding almost apologetically that it probably wouldn't sell many copies but it would be a solid catalogue album, ticking over, and would further bolster Nelson's reputation.

Originally, only 30,000 copies were printed. It would eventually sell over one hundred times that figure. Its phenomenal success surprised everyone, not least Nelson, but it was no accident. Neil Reshen was determined that the record wouldn't disappear down a long, dark cul-de-sac marked 'country'. Nelson was invited to the Columbia Records convention in Toronto. He played virtually all night long and everyone there simply fell in love with him: the salesmen, the promoters, the executives, the entire company. It was the same show he always played but most people outside of Texas had yet to see it. 'They wouldn't let him off the stage,' recalls Lundvall. 'It was one of the great moments at a record company convention – *everyone* talked about it.'

CBS were the gold standard of record company sales, and with the New York office onside and Nashville's nose out of joint, the record was given a national marketing push. Crucially, it was marketed to a pop audience rather than a country one. That the radio stations in Austin and Houston would love the record was a given – if they didn't receive a promo copy from the record company then they would go out and *buy* one if necessary because their listeners wanted to hear it, so they were bypassed in favour of important national stations. Nick Hunter had worked for Columbia between 1968 and 1972 and had a lot of good contacts. He personally sent a white label of *Red Headed Stranger* with an accompanying note to all 64 *Billboard* reporter radio panels in the United States – the stations that supplied the airplay data which made up the mainstream charts. That was how radio really got hold of the album.

Neil Reshen: This was his first release with CBS and he was meeting the top CBS sales to the station. That's what we wanted. That was the big argument I had with Willie and the band and everybody else: they didn't want to be a 'pop' act – well, 'pop' is short for popular. It just means people like you! So if I'm going to have the ability to ask for X amount of dollars in a budget, I want to use it to get the biggest stations. We insisted that the album be promoted as a pop album. Willie to this day doesn't understand that that album was promoted differently to all the other ones.

Reshen had other contacts which helped. The album received a glowing review in *Rolling Stone*, perhaps the most influential mainstream music magazine of its day, which concluded: 'Willie Nelson has recently recorded an album so remarkable that it calls for a redefinition of the term country music.' The writer was Chet Flippo, who happened to be looked after by Reshen's management company, Media Consulting Corps. Flippo was unquestionably a fine writer, knowledgeable about country music and a genuine fan of Nelson, but his position was perhaps a little compromised.

Neil Reshen: My deal with Flippo was: If you're going to pan it, then don't [write] it. But if you like it, write what you think. We represented Chet and [*Creem* magazine's] Dave Marsh and all these people, so we were able to pick up the phone [to the media] and talk to our own clients. But don't get me wrong, they didn't write anything they didn't feel.

It was, after all, not a difficult record to love. John Rockwell gave it a highly complimentary review in the *New York Times* of 8 August 1975, which reinforced in a prominent publication the notion of Nelson being the leader of a movement which advocated country music coming back to something fundamental. But what really made the album fly was 'Blue Eyes Crying In The Rain'. Written in 1945 by Fred Rose, it was an old-time sentimental standard, a death ballad with spiritual overtones: 'Someday when we're both up yonder/ We'll stroll hand in hand again/ In a land that knows no parting.' Nelson's reading was agonising, slow and empty, devoid of drums and unerringly beautiful, but it was a song that nobody in their right mind would have chosen as a single. CBS wanted to go with 'Remember Me', the only song on the album that had any real tempo at all, but the hypnotic magnificence of the song won out. Radio stations, especially ones like KIKK in Houston, started playing 'Blue Eyes Crying In The Rain' on air and getting a tremendous audience response. CBS relented, and the single exploded. It became Nelson's first country No. 1 in July 1975, but its real significance was in its crossover appeal: the single reached No. 21 in the *Billboard* Hot 100 in August. Suddenly, aged 42, Willie Nelson was on the pop charts, with perhaps his most uncompromisingly austere song yet. He admitted to being 'a little surprised',[3] but he had always believed this could happen.

Bee Spears: It really wasn't [surprising] because in Willie's mind, from the time that I first started and we were travelling in a station wagon, it wasn't a matter of if he was going to make it but when. He really believed in positive thinking and there was never any doubt in his mind. So he instilled that pretty much in us as well, just hanging with him. I mean, it was nice when it happened, but I can't say that I was really surprised by it.

Album sales rocketed on the back of the single, and the *Red Headed Stranger* hit No. 28 on the pop charts and stayed on the list for almost a year. It went gold in 1976, denoting over 500,000 sales, and eventually hit multi-platinum ten years later, with sales of over 3 million. Ultimately, for all the marketing push, great reviews and major label support, his breakthrough into the big league was one of those odd curveballs which ensures that the art of making music will always retain a little bit of magic and mystery amidst the harsh realities of big business. It really proved once and for all what Nelson had always argued: let me do my own thing, with my own band, and then sell the hell out of it. In essence, it was him they loved. It still is. He was simply being honest and people – given the chance – responded to his uniqueness and his ingrained spirit, and identified with him in some way as a survivor. Asked on the eve of the release of *Red Headed Stranger* what he had done differently with his new album, Nelson stared at the interviewer as though he had horns growing out of his head: 'Nothing,' he replied. And he was right.

Nick Hunter: One time we were talking about the record and how different it was and how kinda surprising it was that it was so successful, and he looked at me and he said: 'You know, it was my time.' Which in the long run may tell the whole story.

Legend states that the term 'outlaw music' was first coined by a journalist called Hazel Smith, who worked as a PR for Tompall Glaser and was probably riffing on Waylon Jennings' 1972 song 'Ladies Love Outlaws'. Jerry Bradley at RCA had also noticed a wild photo of Jennings where he had been given an electric shock by the microphone and remarked, 'He looks like an outlaw!' It was a tag which would later come to stick in the throat of some of those whom it sought to define, but it was a crudely essential label which became vital in selling this new musical movement to the masses. Jennings, the more serious of the pair, always thought it a little silly; Nelson rather enjoyed it.

Willie Nelson: It means you are not completely agreeing with the establishment. With that type of description I'd like to be known as fitting it. I don't run away from that word at all.[4]

It is one of the ironies of the so-called 'outlaw' movement that it was both a crassly commercial concept and also came to define a type of music which stemmed from an essentially conservative standpoint. Just like the phrase 'progressive country', which had been used to define the music coming out of the Austin scene, it was a misnomer. If you looked beyond the long hair, earrings and slightly comical piratical attitudes, the music was a throwback to old times and enduring values. It was the simplicity and harshness of the 40s, filtered through the expanded consciousness of the 60s, punched out with a thoroughly modern aesthetic; it was plaid shirts, jeans and denim dungarees versus gaudy Nudie suits and rhinestone; Nelson, Jennings, Johnny Cash, Kris Kristofferson and Tompall Glaser versus Kenny Rogers, Glen Campbell, and country carpetbaggers like Tom Jones, Olivia Newton-John and Engelbert Humperdinck. Soil versus silk.

The smash success of the *Red Headed Stranger* record did not go unnoticed in industry circles, and it wasn't long before the cash-in commenced. RCA were now sitting on a goldmine of old Nelson material which nobody had ever really heard. However, instead of merely repackaging old songs – which they would also begin to do with a vengeance – a grander concept was imagined. An album featuring four artists – Jennings, his wife Jessi Colter, Tompall Glaser and Nelson – which marketed them towards a non-country audience; in other words, the audience Nelson had just identified with his new record.

The record was called *Wanted! The Outlaws* and in reality it was a cheerful swindle. There was no new material on offer. Nelson's four tracks consisted of two songs from his 1971 RCA album *Yesterday's Wine* and two concocted duets with Jennings. One of them, 'Good Hearted Woman', was sold to the public as a live recording of the two in concert, but in actual fact it was a grand piece of fakery: a recording taken from Jenning's 1974 album *Waylon Live*, with Nelson overdubbing his vocals in a Nashville studio; they even added crowd noises and a cry of 'Willie' when Nelson came in, as though he were striding on stage. Chet Flippo wrote the sleeve notes. Despite the unmistakable scent of Nashville – the overdubs, the blatant commercialism – those concerned tried to put an 'outlaw' gloss on the project, from the mock Wild West portraits on the cover to pointing out that it was the first time that two Nashville artists from different labels had made a record together, which admittedly did free a lot of artists in the future. But it was a pretty shabby spectacle and not a particularly good record, although instructive in showing how far Nelson, and to a certain extent Jennings, were ahead of the competition.

For all the cheapness of the record, few could really blame the artists involved for capitalising on the moment. Jennings was the prime motivating force from the artists' side of the fence, believing this was a good, inexpensive opportunity to let people catch up with some of the decent material they had previously recorded. An inclusive man by nature, he wanted to share the good luck around, and if this was what it took to finally make people sit up and take notice, then so be it. The two men had become incredibly close, though they were very different. Jennings was borderline paranoid and wanted to keep a tight control on what he was doing and where the money he made was going. He was somehow more solid than Nelson, who was content to be allowed to make his own records after all this time and generally went with the flow. They fell out all the time but it never lasted long.

Jessi Colter: There was always brotherly rivalry, but their friendship outweighed that. Waylon described Willie as a free spirit, kind of like a gypsy. He went however the wind blew. I don't know how interested

Willie was in business and really taking control, whereas Waylon took control of all his own business, so there was a very big difference. But they really understood each other. They were a duo, but Willie is very private. He and Waylon were good friends and he was always sweet and engaging, but he's his own person and there is a part of him that is very much a loner.

Jennings' and Nelson's 'Good Hearted Woman' reached No. 25 in the pop charts in March 1976, while the album went into the Top 10. Both the single and the album won their categories at the CMA awards the following year, while the album went multi-platinum. There followed a tour by all four acts of the west of the United States which was hugely successful. Again, there was a very close eye being kept on the money, although Nelson was probably least conscious of all the financial aspects. Huge amounts of cash were changing hands – little wonder he eventually ended up with tax problems – and as soon as the final chord of the opening song died down Reshen or one of his minions would be on hand to collect. It was still a pretty rudimentary operation.

Mickey Raphael: One day we're stopping for gas. I open up the glove box and I find this pistol. I pull it out, thinking, What the hell is this? I'm in the front window of the van, and Paul is going [sotto voce]: 'Put that *down* . . .' Obviously it was loaded. Paul always carried one. He had to collect the money, and a lot of times the promoter would skip or say they didn't have the money or they got robbed or whatever. So Paul knew how to collect the money.

The tour was the final seal on the emergence of new, roots country into the cultural overground. Cue patronising articles in the national press about country music creeping 'out of the shacks and into the suburbs'. By 1977, almost one in every five records sold was a country record. In 1965, 250 stations played country music; a decade later, it was 1,150 and you could switch on your television and see Loretta Lynn dueting with Frank Sinatra.

Tompall Glaser: Everybody rushed out to buy the Outlaws' album: rock and rollers, kids, lockjaw types from the East, people who had never bought a country album in their whole lives bought that album.[5]

Inevitably, the image very soon passed into pale parody, but if it was a contrived fad at least it was a significant one and Nelson was surfing right at the top of the wave as the pre-eminent artist of national importance. He won an award for Best Country Vocal Performance for 'Blue Eyes Crying In The Rain' for 1975 at the Grammys in early 1976. He wasn't merely a singer with a big song – there were plenty of those. He was at the head of a movement, something completely new and odd and intriguing to the pop market, and he was grabbed and objectified almost instantly. His image helped: by now his hair was so long he was sporting pigtails, topped off with a bandana. He began to resemble the Nelson who is instantly recognisable today. It was a tidal wave of success which brought many changes. His natural lack of pretence and physical accessibility was a potent combination. He became an almost deified figure, and people would come to see him at all hours, expecting either a 24-hour party or some kind of spiritual or emotional guidance. The ranch at Fitzhugh Road was suddenly protected by six-foot high walls, electrified wire, closed-circuit TV, all designed to keep out unwanted visitors who 'thought I could lay hands on them and heal their crippled limbs'.[6]

Willie Nelson: It's hard to go anywhere and really just sit down and enjoy the evening. I only get two or three days off at a time and when I do I like to have complete isolation and privacy in order to rest.[7]

Success on such a scale marked the end of Nelson's free and easy home life, but it also abruptly ended his high watermark period of beautifully concise writing and record making. It is one of the anomalies of his career that he has very often created his greatest music when the fewest people have been listening. 'All of a sudden we had the ability to do what we wanted,' recalls Neil Reshen, and Nelson – so long denied – was indiscriminate about sating his appetites: every fondly harboured pet project came gushing to the fore, demanding to be heard, no matter how uncommercial or out of time it may have been. He had given himself – no, he had *earned* – the licence to do what he wanted.

After *Red Headed Stranger* he recorded a tribute album to Lefty Frizzel called *To Lefty From Willie*, which was literally cut in an afternoon on a stopover between Toronto and Austin. CBS weren't happy with it because the bass drum pedal squeaked and it sounded a little flat. They asked him to record something else and he came up with the plodding *The Sound In Your Mind*, one of his weakest records, which was released in March 1976 and was a little overshadowed by the success of the Outlaws' compilation, although it did contain a country No. 1 in the shape of 'If You've Got The Money I've Got The Time'. In March 1977, *To Lefty From Willie* was finally released, the bass drum pedal having been electronically oiled. It came six months after CBS had eventually issued Nelson's gospel album *The Troublemaker* in October, three years after it had been recorded in New York. It contained a significant dedication.

Paul English: Ever seen the back of that album? It says this album is dedicated to Carlene. He didn't say Carlene English or Paul's wife, he just said Carlene. He got the artwork done, locked off, and gave it to my son.

Nelson and Waylon Jennings reconvened in 1978 for another Outlaws style project, *Waylon & Willie*. Again, it was Jennings and RCA's Jerry Bradley who orchestrated the whole thing and again it smacked a little of expedience rather than genuine inspiration: the tracks were manufactured to give the illusion of genuine duets, the cover was a watercolour depiction of the two heroes with a silhouetted horseman thrown in for good measure, but it did the trick, going platinum within two weeks of release and hitting both the pop and country charts. Later, in 1979 and 1980 there would be duet albums with Ray Price and Leon Russell and an album of Kris Kristofferson songs. His sales plateaued over this period, averaging a healthy 350–500,000 copies per album, but his popularity as a performer showed no sign of waning: by 1978 he was playing to audiences of between 10–30,000 in huge auditoriums or stadiums and commanding $50,000 a show.

But one of the things that did stop, and it stopped very quickly, was his songwriting. Tellingly, the number of new Nelson songs on all of his combined album releases between 1976 and 1979 could be counted on one hand, marking a return to a familiar pattern. Necessity being the mother of invention, when the immediate financial need vanished and the time available to write shrank, the songs simply dried up.

Ray Price: The writing suffers, because you can't do two things at the same time. It affects you. The same thing happened to Kris Kristofferson when he got real popular – his writing slipped and fell by the wayside.

Nelson didn't head off over the hill with Price and the Cherokee Cowboys this time, but he did head over yonder and away down the long road. Some might say he never came back.

YOU NEED FRIENDS

Willie Nelson is talking about friends, but he is really talking about protection.

There have been times when he has needed protecting – from fame, from life, from being alone. When hard, true fame finally hit he created a mobile buffer zone between himself and the world, an ever-changing travelling party of cowboy courtiers who kept the world at arm's length when the need arose. And it arose frequently.

'I didn't want a lot of people around,' he says simply, and sighs. 'I just didn't know what was going to happen.'

The hotel room has never really warmed up and he huddles into his tracksuit top. It is not a subject he wants to talk about but he will. The words leave his mouth and form vague shapes, hinting at sharper images he will be picturing in his mind but will not reveal. He has seen almost every form of base criminality and the most extreme acts of loyalty and kindness pass before his eyes, many acted out in the name of friendship. Protection.

'At the time, I didn't want a lot of things to get out of my control,' he continues. 'I knew these guys were not the most politically correct in town, but they were good characters, good guys. I knew that if they had their eye on things everything would be cool. There would be no problem.' He laughs softly. 'I knew they wouldn't encourage a lot of people to come around.'

His entourage is unique in modern music – not even Frank Sinatra could claim such loyalty and longevity from his clan. He has been the centre of this show for over thirty years. He is the very reason it exists. He could make it all stop tomorrow and perhaps a hundred people would be left on the side of the road.

The line between employee, hanger-on and friend became blurred a long time ago, if indeed it ever existed. The relationship between the man and his human bubble is complex and comprises a multitude of mutual needs and wants. He doesn't want to hear it. Let's keep it simple.

'Oh, they're friends,' he says sharply. His eyes focus and darken the way they do when he feels a little anger rising. 'As far as needing, well, I don't know who needs what, but they're friends.'

He looks up from the floor and smiles, his brief passion spent. 'And you need friends.'

9. 1976–1978

The Fourth of July picnic at Gonzales in 1976 witnessed fifteen stabbings, seven rapes, one drowning, eighteen overdoses, one man on fire, 147 arrests, hundreds of openly copulating couples and more drugs, guns and bad vibes than Vietnam. The perimeter fence was knocked down and thousands of gatecrashers poured in. At Nelson's behest Hell's Angels were the powerbrokers, while cocaine, whisky and swaggering egos dictated the foul mood. It was country music's Altamont, the moment when all the good will which had been built up over the past few years folded in upon itself and soured, and Nelson was right in the eye of the hurricane. He bailed out, played a short set and flew to Hawaii before the picnic had even ended. He was sued by the site owner, the ambulance services and the electrical contractors. He lost $200,000 and cancelled plans for 1977.

If the term outlaw was contrived and essentially meaningless in a musical context, it had a wider social significance which was very tangible and not at all edifying. It is a fact that as the music became more and more sanitised post-1975, the lifestyle around it conversely became much wilder and flagrantly irresponsible. The outlaw tag had been taken at face value by many country artists. Not only were they granted exclusive access to the metaphors and imagery of the old West in song, which soon became hackneyed, but they also took it as an invitation to literally live beyond the law. It followed that the music attracted not just middle-class dilettantes who simply wanted to play a little with a new image, but also those who genuinely lived their lives on the wrong side of the tracks, who believed the hype and couldn't – or chose not to – recognise the line dividing artistic licence and real thuggery and bigotry.

Hence Gonzales, which became a virtual playground for all stripes of thugs, thieves, modern-day pirates of the prairies, bullies and predators – and hence the increasing mayhem and intimidating weirdness of Nelson's entourage. He had always been fascinated by these characters and now he began sailing even closer to the wind. He was on the road almost constantly following the success of the *Red Headed Stranger*, touring with the Outlaws' package, with Emmylou Harris, with Waylon. Things were getting faster, bigger, bumpier, wilder.

Rodney Crowell: It *was* wild. I remember being in a two-stall bathroom in Fort Collins, Colorado, standing in line for a long time in conversation and then finally looking down and seeing that the second stall was empty. 'Shit. What's going on?' So I went down there and took a piss, and that's when I realised that there was a pair of cowgirl boots turned backwards in the other stall and there was this line of road crew and hangers-on who were getting blow jobs from some unidentified woman in there. Guys waiting in line, drinking a beer, smoking a cigarette, and having a laugh. A little debauched? It was just the by-product of the culture revolving around the eye of the storm.

After years of station wagons, Winnebagos and even an old armoured bank vehicle which Paul English had decked out to look like a whorehouse, Nelson finally had a proper, full-sized tour bus, able to accommodate the more esoteric members of his extended family. A new coterie of hangers-on arrived and the atmosphere became seriously heavy. The band as well were let loose on the back of major league success, and soon the whole charabanc began to resemble an X-rated circus. In the middle of the madness was the bereft English who, half-joked Nelson, had become like the Red Headed Stranger himself: 'Don't cross him, don't boss him/ He's wild in his sorrow.' English provided the Mephistophelian swagger to the proceedings, hell-bent on self-destruction. In the bus, he would practise firing rat shot into paperback novels with his Derringer pistol – an apt piece of symbolism if ever there was one – and still ruled with an iron fist. It was funny. He would walk to the eating area and say, 'Don't use salt, it's bad for ya!' as almost every type of drug was being consumed around him. He even scared his own band a little.

His dark charisma and sense of danger undoubtedly created an atmosphere which allowed others to test the boundaries, as well as attracting a real social underbelly to Nelson and his crowd. The FBI trailed the bus sporadically, hoping that one of English's former associates, a man called Jimmy Renton, might show up. He never did, but plenty of others weren't so shy. There were numerous personalities: groupies, musicians and, according to Jerry Jeff Walker who toured with Nelson, 'a lot of weird hangers-on, biker guys with no teeth and shit. It was somebody's Saturday night everywhere we went.'

Nelson's personal involvements became more questionable. He invested $5,000 with a local character called Travis Schnautz, who used the cash to open a massage parlour in Austin. Schnautz was later assassinated by contract killers. In May 1976, just a few months after picking up his Grammy, Nelson was subpoenaed to appear before a grand jury in a multi-million dollar drug-running trial in Dallas, due to his close friendship with the defendant Joe Hicks, a former car salesman. He appeared in court in June to give evidence, and although there was never any suggestion of direct illegality on his part, there was a degree of guilt by association and a lot of bad press. Later, Neil Reshen's assistant Mark Rothbaum was jailed for distributing cocaine to the Nashville studio where Waylon Jennings was working. The package was intercepted by police in August 1977 and many suspected a set-up, but Rothbaum took the fall and would later be rewarded with Reshen's job for proving his mettle. Previously Nelson's criminal associations were run-of-the-mill – he was convicted of drink-driving in Texas in June 1974, fined and restrictions placed on his licence – but these events, combined with the ugliness of Gonzales, charted altogether murkier waters.

The way he was perceived changed somewhat. The papers began calling him 'Cocaine' Willie, which was ironic, given that he was practically the only one around who wasn't shovelling hundreds of dollars of the stuff up his nose. Cocaine was everywhere and became the primary engine of the touring escapades, but Nelson had never been a big fan of the drug. He had tried it enough times to have formed a negative opinion about it; Eddie Wilson recalls people spelling out W-I-L-L-I-E in lines of coke on glass-topped coffee tables backstage at the Armadillo in the early-70s but, as with speed and LSD, he dabbled before re-affirming that his drugs of choice were marijuana and tequila. However, once Nelson's career went through the roof and the band started earning good money every night, most of them were wired almost constantly. You could even hear it in their playing, which sometimes sounded like everybody was talking at the same time. Nelson would play a lick on his guitar and everybody would answer him on their own instrument, oblivious to the whole. In time word reached him that there was too much powder flying around and he attempted to put a stop to the cocaine use within the group: 'If you're wired, you're fired.' It became known as the No Blow Blues Band.

Mickey Raphael: It was pretty much non-stop drug abuse. I mean, *everybody* got high: even the executives at the record company were getting high. We'd be on an aeroplane and chopping out lines on the trays, because we were all pretty much hooked. Of course, Willie would go in the bathroom of the plane and smoke a joint too, but cocaine was a really bad drug – just the people who would bring it to us. The best thing about quitting that stuff is that you'd get rid of your playmates.

These 'playmates' brought their own brand of outlaw mentality into the camp. On the road, there were numerous tales of intimidation, guns being waved around, petty crime. The general tone of the times was encapsulated in the form of Peter Sheridan, one of the many Hell's Angels who latched onto Nelson's group – limpet-like – and refused to budge. Nobody quite knew how he arrived, they only knew that they weren't going to ask him to leave. Neil Reshen, who rarely came on tour for more than a few days at a time, had arranged for Sheridan to jump on the bus to watch Nelson's back, which was a worrying enough indication of the mood of the times. If the *manager* wanted someone like Sheridan on board, what on earth was going on?

Mickey Raphael: He was so obnoxious and so crazed that it really kept a lot of the riff-raff away. I think that was his main job. But it was also like having a pit bull as a pet: if it got bored it could turn on you.

Like some biker version of Conrad's Mister Kurtz, Sheridan soon turned native and became a genuine loose cannon, answerable to no one. He was intelligent, violent, articulate, drugged, loyal and unpredictable. He would walk around cutting people's T-shirts with scissors, grabbing pills and swallowing fistfuls at a time, hunting down and punishing miscreants for the tiniest misdemeanour. Connie Nelson admits to being 'really scared' when Reshen first introduced Sheridan into the Nelson camp, but she also saw another side to him.

Connie Nelson: My girls loved him and I grew to love him too. He took our daughter Paula outside in the dark at our ranch in Texas one time to see the fireflies. It scared my mother to death that I would let her go out in the dark with him, but Paula remembers that, to this day, as one of her fondest memories. Another time, he was tossing her up and catching her and bumped her head just a little on the static ceiling fan, but she cried. I thought he was going to start crying as well – it took him a long time to get over doing that. So, there were a lot of scary-looking guys out there that had a heart of gold. But not to mistake kindness for weakness – Peter would have *literally* killed for any of us.

It was the classic cliché of the roughneck with the soft centre, and Nelson was a sucker for it. The problem for those not in the know was judging which way these guys would turn. Mickey Raphael once lost his patience with Sheridan and pushed an ice cream into his face, and he just laughed. Then again, he could just as easily assert his power in unpleasant ways. He would stalk a security guy for not letting one of Nelson's family into the dressing room – an honest mistake – or steal a car and drive it over a field for no apparent reason. To anyone outside of the circle, visiting the bus was like stepping into a trial by fire. It was an instinctively hostile atmosphere. *Newsweek* magazine journalist Pete Axthelm had been commissioned to write a long cover piece on Nelson, and spent some time on the bus in 1978 when he was touring with Emmylou Harris and her Hot Band, which included Rodney Crowell, whose song 'Til I Gain Control Again' Nelson had started playing in concert. The writer was treated like a punch bag.

Rodney Crowell: Pete Axthelm was on the back of the bus and there was drugs flying around and what have you, and he was trying to find his comfort zone and be part of it so he could absorb the vibe. First of all, you need to understand that Willie is the centre of it. If you try to find your centre in the middle of all that, you're lost. Peter Sheridan would pick up on anybody's discomfort and really pick up on an impostor trying to insinuate themselves into the group. So I sat there and watched Sheridan just dismantle Pete Axthelm. I mean, he just took him apart. He was nearly in tears, when all he had to do was laugh and say 'fuck off'. Axthelm got up and left and Peter just looked at me and said, 'Pussy.' There was a lot of that.

The band's motto was 'Don't Try To Contribute'. In other words, 'You are a stranger here. You don't understand our life or our rules so keep quiet and back off.' People could step in and take their place in the outer edges of the swirl, but if they were caught trying to assert themselves or ingratiate their way into the banter they would be mercilessly exposed. It was a crude, macho system, consisting of constant tests and bluffs, and you either instinctively understood how to deal with it or you didn't. It was really a way of needling the new middle-class audience Nelson had stumbled upon, and underpinning it all was a very natural desire for honesty and truth – each visitor was scrutinised and any fakery or adopted attitudes were picked apart. After all, if Nelson and his band and his music and his life stood for one thing it was this: be who you are and be proud of it. Underneath the swagger there was a lot of humour and sweetness and camaraderie on the road, a drunken, stoned 24-hour party where you had to keep your wits about you but if you stood up for yourself and didn't take it all too seriously you would probably be OK. There was a fierce loyalty and a certain old-time courtesy which stemmed from Nelson, but it was often all but obscured by those around him.

The really interesting question, of course, is why he chose to surround himself with these people in the first place. This is a man capable of acts of astounding generosity and articulating profound sensitivity, who plays several low-key benefits each year and routinely gives money away, who is spiritually preoccupied, paternal and considerate to his band, who would listen to his harmonica player's girl troubles and always leave the door open. Indeed, to some observers he was not nearly firm enough with his band, either artistically or personally.

Neil Reshen: He'd be talking business with me and one of the band would come and sit down. I would just wait there and say nothing, and eventually they would get up and wander off. But Willie would never say, 'Oh excuse me, can we have a minute?'

His good nature and manners were really part of the problem. People gravitated towards him. They revered him and expected him to have answers in a way which was bizarre and slightly unnerving. 'There's a certain peacefulness in his eyes,' said actor and friend Jean Michael Vincent at the time. 'He's the guru.'[1] Undoubtedly, one of the reasons he – and Reshen – surrounded himself with some genuinely lowlife characters who seemed to take advantage of his financial largesse and his laid-back lifestyle and in return offered only a crude and perfunctory form of fealty and frontier justice was to keep these kinds of gushing disciples at bay. To literally scare them off. It was protection.

His loyalty and non-judgmental attitude to others was also a factor. He could see beyond the exterior and was always capable of recognising the good in people. Everyone deserved a second chance. He would insist on measuring someone's worth solely on how they treated him and behaved around him, and of course there was something about him that seemed to bring out the best in others. Most of these men had never really had someone or something to believe in, and Nelson gave them a cause. He liked the fact they were dependent on him, not because it gave him power but because it made him feel he was doing something good. They repaid him with almost embarrassing amounts of gratitude and unthinking loyalty, and he gave them due loyalty back in return. He was admirably dismissive of outsiders grousing about his gang.

Willie Nelson: I have friend's everywhere. I'm not ashamed of the people that I'm around. Even though some of them are probably what some people would call, uh, disreputable characters.[2]

But he was not unaware of how it all looked from the outside. At Gonzales some of his crew were kept off the payroll so nobody could trace their behaviour directly back to Nelson, but he was implicitly involved in – and therefore tacitly condoned – their activities nonetheless. On the tours with Waylon Jennings the crews would be at each other's throats over who would get top billing in each town. Nelson didn't care, he'd rather go on first and be halfway down the highway by the time Jennings came off stage, but he left them to it. He maintained a policy of see-no-evil which gave him huge amounts of protection while allowing him to continue being perceived as sweet-natured and laid-back. And he was. His good nature, his dislike of confrontation or saying 'no' to people was genuine, but it also became a canny tactic that could be used in all areas of his career. There is nothing in the script to say you can't be both a nice man and a wily operator.

Neil Reshen: We'd go to shows and somebody would come over to me and say, 'Hey, Willie just said that he's gonna play a benefit for this place.' I'd go over to the trailer and say to Willie, 'What are you doing?' And he'd say, 'Oh, I just figured you'd blow him off. You'd get me out of it.' So everybody loves Willie, and he lets somebody else deal with saying 'no'. He'd say: 'I wouldn't play for him. I don't even *know* him.' There are two sides to him, and the good side is *exceptionally* good, but we spent many years of our lives saying 'no' for Willie. He doesn't want to say 'no' to your face. He wants everybody to love him.

He enjoyed the element of surprise that his life on the road afforded him. 'I have no idea who may walk down the hall next,' Nelson said in 1978. 'It could be a politician, it could be a Hell's Angel.'[3] He wasn't exaggerating. They were fast, high times. He would hang out with Burt Reynolds, Jane Fonda and Candice Bergen. When he and Waylon Jennings played the Lone Star Cafe in Manhattan in April 1978, he was surrounded by the likes of Bill Murray, John Belushi, James Caan, James Taylor and, most improbably, Andy Warhol. A couple of days later he was in the White House. He had really become politically aware through his connections in Austin in the early-70s and leaned to the left, although his political views were pretty rudimentary.

Willie Nelson: We all know Democrats are better than the Republicans. The Republicans are for the rich guy. Everybody knows that.[4]

He had become friendly with the US president Jimmy Carter through fundraising for the Democratic party. In September 1977 he and Emmylou Harris popped in to see Carter at the Oval Office to pay their regards. A spokesman described it as the first time anyone had 'gone into the Oval Office in a tank top and on crutches', Nelson having recently broken his foot in a celebratory leap after he was released following a night in jail in the Bahamas for possessing marijuana. It was during the 1977 visit that he famously smoked a joint on the roof of the White House with a still-anonymous employee; Rodney Crowell recalls Nelson and the band coming back from that trip 'all huddled up laughing their asses off about smoking a joint – getting away with it'.

Carter and Nelson shared southern roots. The president was a spiritual Georgian who loved his music and in some ways he was the Willie Nelson of politics – easy-going, unpretentious, friendly – but his endorsement was also an indication of just how big Nelson had become. Presidents didn't hang out with B-listers, much less invite them to attend official functions and even book them to play in the grounds of the White House. For his part, Carter would occasionally turn up to shows, mouthing the words: his favourite album was *The Troublemaker*. As well as the president, Nelson had long ago befriended the Governor of Texas Anne Richards, a vivacious Democrat, socialite and recovering alcoholic who had been part of Darrell Royal's party set. And yet in the bus he was rubbing shoulders with drug dealers, crooks, borderline psychopaths and worse, and no one seemed to care much about the contradictions. Least of all him. It was this bizarre merging of social strata, the clash of conventions and the unease that it could create that he loved.

Rodney Crowell: I remember Lyle Lovett and me and Willie doing a TV show together. Before the show we're sitting out on Willie's bus and the governor of Texas, Anne Richards, walks in. We're sitting having this conversation and Willie just pulls out his baggie and rolls a joint and smokes it. After a while I couldn't take any more, and I said, 'Does this strike anybody as funny, smoking a joint across the table from the Governor of Texas?' Willie just kinda laughed it off. I don't think he even noticed. Willie exists outside of the normal conventions of society, in this rarefied and privileged place, just on the merit of who he is. I couldn't have done that. I don't have that much permission! He's unflinching in his determination to live his life.

It was his turf and his rules. No matter who he was with, he did what he wanted with the same quiet, non-confrontational ease he had always possessed, and he seemed to walk away unscathed and unjudged. The same impulse which was unimpressed when the Rolling Stones came knocking ensured he was not going to kowtow to a politician – he would simply accept everyone as they came and hope they reciprocated. It was a remarkable juggling act and a testament to the sheer force of his charisma and determination. It has been noted that Nelson can spend an hour talking to his fans and each one will come away convinced that they have shared a meaningful conversation in which he has agreed with everything they've said, yet he has probably uttered less than five words to each one. It was an illusion. He maintained that there was no reason ever to be rude to a fan unless they were rude to him, and he made time for all his followers after the show, looking each one of them in the eye and listening to what they said, but he protected himself. By being still, being himself and being quiet, he could let everyone project their own illusions upon him. He is fond of quoting the Bible: 'Be still and know who I am.'

On the bus, he was continually present but remained detached, available to all but committed to no one. It was a trick learned in childhood. He liked being the calm eye of the hurricane as all this lunacy boiled around him – and *for* him – and like a benevolent old king surrounded by a court of madcap jesters, minstrels and mercenaries, he sought amusement. He would watch the madness, smoke some dope, retreat when he wanted, go for a five-mile run in the morning, eat fruit salad and drink water. He had a balance, all things in moderation. He had recently decided to become healthy, having looked in the mirror one day and decided that he was 'disintegrating before my eyes'.[5] He didn't want to burn out, he didn't want to live fast and die young. After years of talking positively and trying to think positively, he now wanted to live positively. Coach Royal devised a fitness programme which involved cutting down on alcohol, eating healthily and exercising – push-ups, running – and generally taking care of himself. In many ways, the fact that Nelson has always attracted wildness and excess around him means that he doesn't have to go to the real extremes himself. He could live it vicariously, by proxy. The road, after all, could get pretty monotonous. Perhaps more than anything else he liked observing how people reacted in these extreme situations, how far they would go out on a limb for him, how much loyalty was on offer. He would play people off against each other and sit back and watch the results. It was all a bit of a game.

Mickey Raphael: Willie definitely [encouraged it]. He loved it. Willie's a shit-stirrer, he's always liked that undercurrent. It was entertainment for him. Peter Sheridan was so obnoxious that anytime somebody came around they had to *really* want to get to Willie to go through him. If it was somebody Willie would want to talk to or an old friend who Peter didn't know, Willie would call Peter off. It was like having this rabid dog around. That much obnoxious stuff has stopped. There are still people around us who are total fuck-ups, but you don't go to Willie and say, 'Oh so-and-so is drunk on their ass and making a fool of themselves.' We police it ourselves. If there's inner problems, we definitely don't take them to Willie. He finds out about it and he laughs: 'Well, that keeps things interesting!' It sort of becomes a circus.

He was a superstar, in the privileged part of the slipstream which existed beyond the currents of punk, or new wave, or whatever other cultural and musical shifts were taking place down below. He was courted by all layers of society, zipping from stadiums to A-list parties to TV shows, but his domestic life – if it could be called that – was inevitably suffering. His three eldest children had moved on. He was practically estranged from Susie, who was on her second bad marriage. Billy was difficult, drinking and running wild. Connie and her two young kids were spending more time in the mountains in Colorado, where she was skiing and making her own friends. When Nelson really needed some time away from everything that was where he would go. Texas was for business, socialising, playing, fun; Colorado was for rare sanctuary. But the incessant touring meant he was away from his family most of the time.

Connie would come out on the road with him occasionally. Either her parents would look after Paula and Amy and she would go alone in her Mercedes, staying on the peripheries of the vortex, or in the summer holidays she would come with the kids and they would all spend the vacation with him. In true country fashion, he would pull the children up on stage to join him in singing 'Amazing Grace', but it was not really a suitable environment for a child. Mostly he left his wife to bring up the children on her own.

Connie Nelson: It was like he belonged to the world and I was just a part of it. It's that gypsy lifestyle. You just have to accept that. I loved him and I always looked at it like I was moving into his life, he wasn't moving into mine, so it just would never have entered my mind [to ask him to stop]. I never wanted him to quit the road, that was his life, that was what he enjoyed doing. And he was great with the kids. When he came home he made up for when he was gone. He always did. He's always been a good dad and a great friend, but that's not to say that it didn't get hard, or things didn't come up when I wished that he was there instead of out somewhere, but that's just the way it was. He just wasn't a great husband.

There were perks, of course. They were financially privileged and Connie and the kids loved the sense of adventure of going on tour, of waking up in a new town every morning, a different view from the window. Nelson had first started touring overseas when he had joined Atlantic, and his wife would usually come with him on those jaunts abroad. At first, it was just the United Kingdom; later when *Red Headed Stranger* hit they went to continental Europe, but even then it was not always a happy affair. 'He was,' Connie says, 'always real glad to get back.' He didn't really like being away from his routine for too long, and with his lifestyle he had a fear of crossing borders. Back in those days people in Europe would come to the shows wearing 'little Western string hats', according to Bee Spears. The band felt the audience didn't really get the music, that they were regarded as something of a novelty.

Neil Reshen: He hated the idea of going overseas. I sort [of twisted his arm]. We spent a lot of time working on it and he cancelled the first couple, and then by the time he was at CBS he was amenable to go, but when he got there he was just horrible. He couldn't get any grass, and he just hated being away from where people knew him and loved him. He stopped smoking dope and he sort of relied on that at that time to keep mellow and everything. We were in France and we made arrangements to take him to some really good French restaurants, and he said 'yes', then he decided 'no'. He just didn't want to go out. So finally Connie and my wife went to dinner and I took him out, we went to have a drink and we wound up at the Crazy Horse [Saloon, a cabaret show in Paris]. He had these long talks with me. He was very morose because he was straight. He had a lot of interesting things to say. But he got over that. When we got back to playing in England, he was fine.

Later his overseas trips became easier. His popularity ensured a smoother passage and also meant he didn't have to work so hard to corral an audience. In time he travelled like a rock star, and singing to people who primarily didn't speak English only reinforced his beliefs that music was a universal force of unity, but despite his almost continual touring he was not always happy on the road. He would get tired, disorientated and dejected and would often resolve to throw in the towel, but he just couldn't stay still for long. Even when they were together at home, the fundamental differences in his and Connie's lives made things difficult. Connie was a mother, looking after her two children, trying to get them through school. She knew in her heart that her husband wasn't faithful on the road, but she would blame it on the advances of predatory women and only say something if it got too blatant. When Nelson was off the road he found it difficult to settle. They had few compatible interests.

Connie Nelson: One of the arguments Willie and I had, and it was probably because he was guilty over something else, was when he said, 'We don't do things together any more. You don't like doing the same things I do any more.' It was all about smoking pot. I said, 'Willie, I can't do it! It's not that I hate it or try to get you to quit, but it's just what it does to me. I'm a mom and I can't function.' His metabolism and mine are so different. I could smoke a couple of hits and I could sleep for fifteen, sixteen hours, but Willie seems to get energy from it. That's why he never liked speed or cocaine or any of that stuff, it made him jittery, made him feel bad and paranoid. But the pot just kind of levelled him out. It's so amazing. He can smoke something that would knock an elephant out! But I had to watch out for my kids. The only time I ever said anything about pot to Willie was when my girls were in junior High school. They had friends over and he had this stuff laid out all over the table, and I told him, 'Please don't do that. Please take it somewhere where kids coming in can't see it. That's not good for kids to see you smoking.'

Nelson spent a lot of time in Malibu in the mid to late 70s. Through touring he and the band had become good friends with Emmylou Harris, who lived in southern California. He sang and played and provided songs on some of her records, and Mickey Raphael – who had moved to Los Angeles and would soon be dating the actress Ali MacGraw – would also play harmonica with Harris and hang out with Rodney Crowell and other members of her Hot Band. It was a whole different scene from Texas but the routine didn't change too much. He was still a mysterious presence, slightly otherworldly.

Rodney Crowell: I remember being in Willie's apartment out in Malibu, with Mickey and all of us, sitting around smoking dope. Willie was lying on the floor watching television and I was just craving a conversation – just wanting to ask questions – and Willie, without being defensive or offensive, just sort of brushing it away. Chilling out and watching television. I remember thinking as a young man, Man, there's so much I could learn from him if I could just get him to open up. Then he'd turn around and say something just drop dead funny that kept it moving. For all of Willie's open accessibility, he is extremely adept at guarding himself.

His upstairs neighbour in the Malibu apartment complex was Booker T. Jones. It was a pleasing twist of fate. Jones was a songwriter, arranger, producer and multi-instrumentalist who had come up through the Stax label in Memphis as a house musician in the 60s; with his instrumental band the MGs he had been responsible for modern soul classics like 'Time Is Tight' and 'Green Onions'. He seemed a long way from country music, except nobody was that far away from country music any more. There was also a tenuous link: at the time Jones was married to Priscilla, the sister of Rita Coolidge, who had been married to Kris Kristofferson and was, of course, great friends with Nelson.

This was merely incidental. Jones had first spotted Nelson running along the beach in Malibu one morning. Later, the two met, talked a little and got to know each other. A plot developed. Nelson and Jones found common ground in their love of the great pop standards of the 20s, 30s and 40s, the songs of Hoagy Carmichael, Cole Porter, George Gershwin and Irving Berlin, the songs Nelson had fallen in love with as a boy in Abbott and which he still regarded as 'some of the most beautiful I'd ever heard'.[6] Later, they sat together and began to play.

Booker T. Jones: It was just an informal discussion of songs we both had admired over the years. Just a general acknowledgment of our similar admiration for music of the earlier era. That naturally led to informal jams and run-throughs of various songs, and Willie just said, 'Why don't we go to a studio and do this?'

It was an irresistibly nostalgic notion. It was still just about open season as far as Nelson's records were concerned. He was big enough and popular enough to be able to do pretty much what he wanted, although it would have struck CBS as ironic that aside from his debut smash with *Red Headed Stranger* his biggest records – those patched together collaborations with Waylon Jennings – were being released by RCA, the company who had let him go for $1,000, and not them. His other records were selling well but not amazingly so, probably because there were so many of them and the styles were so disparate. The record company were keen for him to keep on the straight and narrow, and his new project didn't sound too promising. It is easy to forget in these days, when everyone from Rod Stewart to Robbie Williams has recorded the great American songbook with great commercial success, that the notion of tunnelling back to the music of the 20s and 30s was not regarded as particularly appealing in general, and was simply unheard of within country music circles. All in all, CBS were less than keen on the idea. Rick Blackburn, who had taken over as president of CBS Nashville in 1976, suggested Nelson should stick to the outlaw country market and perhaps write some new songs as well. 'Stay with the mood that's hot,' he advised sagely.[7] Nelson predictably demurred. It wasn't just that he wanted to do this record, it was also that he felt in his bones that it had innate commercial appeal. He was always good at spotting the angles.

Willie Nelson: My audience right now is young, college age and mid-20s. They'll think these are new songs, and at the same time we'll get the sentiment of the older audience who grew up with these songs but don't necessarily know me as an artist. We'll bridge that gap.[8]

In late 1977 Nelson, Jones and the band set up shop in Emmylou Harris's house in southern California, which she shared with her husband, the producer Brian Ahern, whose Enactron mobile recording truck with its 24-track recorder was put in the driveway. The sessions ran along very informally. They set up a Christmas tree with decorations in the living room, hung out by the pool, ate lunch in the kitchen, and almost as a by-product recorded the biggest record of Nelson's career.

   Jones was vital in the pre-production process: he scoped out about eighty songs before the sessions, getting all the lyrics together and transposing the trickier chord progressions. Not all of the songs he dug up were aired, and the ones that were played really selected themselves naturally: 'Stardust', 'Moonlight In Vermont', 'Georgia On My Mind', each held a synonymous memory and meaning for Nelson from his childhood, taking him back to when he would hear Sinatra or Crosby on the radio, or sit with Bobbie as she picked out the melody on the piano. Jones had similarly close and warm associations to the music. There could probably be a profound sociological thesis built around the fact that a 33-year-old black man steeped in soul and a 45-year-old country shit-kicker from Texas found themselves sitting in California playing Hoagy Carmichael songs, but that would be missing the point. They were brought together by music they loved, and were just playing *for* that love. There was no real game plan. The band were used to things taking odd detours and were happy to go along with the flow. There were some new faces on board: Bee Spears had recently taken a brief leave of absence and when he returned he was sharing bass duties with Chris Ethridge, while Paul English shared the drums with Rex Ludwig. Indeed, for a short period Nelson was touring with two drummers on stage. But the balance hadn't really changed. They had all long ago learned to defer to Nelson's instincts and better judgment when it came to musical choices.

Paul English: Sometimes we have difference of opinions – I'm just talking about business-wise – but on the part of picking a song, I never do any of that. With music he's the main man. He just does what he wants to do, and [with *Stardust*] people thought just like he did: these are good songs!

Set up in the front room, they played live while Jones played organ. As usual, Nelson preferred a fast, no-nonsense approach, and one song led to another until it was more a matter of what to leave off the record rather than what to include. As was customary when he was working with a producer, once they were done Nelson left the leg work to someone else: Jones did most of the mixing, mastering, string overdubs, and also delivered the record to apprehensive and sceptical CBS executives.

Bruce Lundvall: The next thing I know he came in with *Stardust*, and everyone said, 'Oh my God, we're selling all these records with Willie and country radio loves him. Nobody is going to play this. It's all pop songs. It sounds like a Frank Sinatra record.'

It only sounded like a Frank Sinatra record to someone with malfunctioning ears. *Stardust* is a beautiful and timeless and brave record, but every note is perfectly in step with the man who made it. Anyone who had seen him in concert, or heard much of his 60s output, could not have been surprised that he had made the album, nor that he had done so naturally and without sounding forced or fake. He has called 'Moonlight In Vermont' his favourite song of all time and it was ideal for his voice and phrasing. There are no rhymes in the song's lyrics, they are a perfect, glacial prose portrait and hellishly hard to sing, but Nelson skips across the song impeccably. Throughout, Jones's organ playing is superb, giving the music a church-like ambience. People asked: was *Stardust* jazz, blues, country, pop, soul? Well, yes, it was all of those things. CBS were essentially worried that it was too old-fashioned, too middle-of-the-road, that it would dilute his appeal and alienate his core audience. Initially, they planned to make it a low-key release and hopefully move swiftly on to something more amenable.

Booker T. Jones: *Stardust* was the LP that wasn't supposed to be released! If you could find the invoices for the first pressings you would see that very few copies were printed in the beginning. I for one held on tight to my studio tapes because they were all I had to listen to for a while. It wasn't expected to sell big.

Bruce Lundvall made a trip to speak to the programme director for WHN radio (now WEPN), an influential country music station in New Jersey. They reassured him that it was going to be fine. 'This guy can sing the telephone directory, he's that special,' they told him. Wise words. *Stardust* was released in March 1978 and became the biggest selling record of Nelson's career, staying on *Billboard*'s charts for over ten years and going multi-platinum. Its three singles reaped two No. 1s and a No. 3 in the country charts, and he won Grammies in 1979 for his close to definitive reading of 'Georgia On My Mind' (he and Ray Charles share the honours), as well as his duet of 'Mamas, Don't Let Your Babies Grow Up To Be Cowboys' with Waylon Jennings, from *Waylon & Willie*. The cover of *Newsweek* said it all: he was 'The King of Country Music'.

The record did stick in the craw of some of the Nashville establishment. Nelson wasn't nominated for any CMA awards that year, but in truth he was far beyond having to worry about that. He hadn't attended the ceremony since 1976 and had asked for his name to be removed from the ballot in 1977; he didn't like being in competition with his friends and peers, and he probably detected a whiff of hypocrisy about the whole proceedings. He finally showed up in 1979 when they awarded him Entertainer Of The Year, but by then it was abundantly clear that labelling him as a country artist was merely a badge of convenience. The success of *Stardust* was further proof that his instincts were aligned to the mood of the times, while his communicative skills as a singer and song selector were finely attuned to his audience. He wasn't interested in elitism or musical boundaries.

Willie Nelson: I [did] 'Stardust' and 'Georgia On My Mind', because I [knew] that these songs are not only great and I love to sing them, but probably more important is the fact that everybody in that audience will like them, whether they've ever heard them or not. If you're a singer you can get up in front of an audience and sing songs that you know communicate. It doesn't matter what they are or whether you wrote them or not.

He had once sat down with Johnny Bush in the mid-60s when he was banging his head against a brick wall of indifference and told him: 'Of all the people who don't like what I'm doing now, look at the millions who have never even heard me yet!' He had always believed they were there. Now he had reached them.

I NEVER LISTEN TO THE BAND

W illie Nelson is talking about his band.

He has played with the same people for over thirty years. Two hundred nights a year for thirty years. Maybe 6,000 shows. And he still loves them.

'I'm guilty of taking them for granted, a lot of times,' he says. 'Most of the time.' He inhales deeply and considers the view outside. There isn't one. 'I know they're there and I know I don't have to worry about it. Being able to take them for granted is a compliment to them. Very same thing in the studio. I just do it and they're there behind me doing it with me. We do it two or three times and we've probably done it as well as we're ever going to do it.'

The band are all here. Somewhere. Filling the space on either side of Nelson, just like they do on stage, waiting for show time, waiting to slip into a routine as familiar to them as their own reflections, the long, unbreakable chain of music that begins with 'Whiskey river take my mind . . .'

It is left unexpressed most of the time, but the idea of Nelson alone on stage with just his guitar and a bundle of songs he hasn't played for a while is an alluring one. He knows it, but he won't do it. What would the band do while he was out there all by himself? And what would he do out on the road all alone?

'I've always thought that maybe, one day, when there is no band and there's just me, then I can always do that,' he says, rolling the idea around. 'It's not something I want to take off and do a year of right now, because I've got a great band and it's so easy to work with those guys.'

He talks like a thirty-year-old rather than a seventy-three-year-old. The restrictions of time are meaningless to him. It's so simple with the band. They don't even rehearse.

'It would be much harder, in a lot of ways, to go out there just by myself. It would be a challenge in a way and I'm sure I could do it and one day maybe I'll *have* to do it that way, but right now I've got the luxury of having the greatest musicians in the world right behind me.'

He operates a benign autocracy. He does what he wants and he has a band which enables him to do what he wants. They are the greatest musicians in the world, and they know their place.

'No, I don't ever listen to the band!' He explodes with laughter, and tilts his head almost imperceptibly upwards. He reaches for his lighter. 'I'd never be that weak.'

10. 1978–1984

Willie Nelson: As for being wealthy – well, what is wealth? There is just so much money you can spend.[1]

In his breakthrough year of 1975 Nelson had earned $581,000. By 1978 the figure was $2.1 million. By the mid-80s it was somewhere between five and ten times that amount. It was, for the first time, more money than he could easily spend, but he did his best. It was not the usual tale of rock star indulgences, although of course there was a touch of that. He had a shiny new Silver Eagle tour bus decked out with the latest home comforts (video golf, computers, faxes, state-of-the-art stereos, television, VCR), and over and above the ranch in Texas – which, almost apologetically, had all the tell-tale trappings of Jacuzzis, bars, grand pianos and superfluous things shaped liked flamingos, as well as real, live horses – he had two homes in Colorado, an apartment in Malibu, and he still owned Ridgetop and dozens of other investment properties scattered around, in Hawaii, Utah, Alabama. He has always loved making money and the freedom it brings, but in terms of his creature comforts or his most pressing needs it makes only a negligible difference to his life. He demands very little and has no interest in material things. He likes the fact that money enables him to cut deals, to hustle a little and see what might happen, to set sparks flying, but the accumulation of wealth and the tokens it buys is anathema to him. He will give away the Rolexes, the expensive Armani suits and $5,000 cowboys boots that people give him without a backward glance.

Mickey Raphael: Willie goes on the road with a tiny shaving kit, a pair of jeans, a T-shirt and a pair of tennis shoes. He picks up stuff, people bring him stuff. For his birthday – you wanna get him a Rolex, or a new guitar? No, I buy him socks and underwear. There's no material object that I would ever think about getting Willie. He just isn't attached to it. It means nothing to him.

Above all, money was for spreading about. Nelson's philosophy was simple: in the words of Eddie Wilson, 'You get your hands on the cash, cover your ass, and then pass the rest around.' He had always been generous in spirit and in deed, but the arrival of really big money illuminated the true breadth of Nelson's philanthropy. His almost manic desire to give it away could be psychoanalysed as guilt, or even as buying people's loyalty, but it was far too widespread and instinctive for that. It really began with wanting the people around him – his family, his Family Band and crew, his friends – to be well looked after and comfortable. It was good for his karma.

He bought a pool hall for his father in Austin and called it – honestly if unimaginatively – Willie's Pool Hall, where Ira could play a little music with his band and be settled. He cut Paul English a share of his song publishing company, Willie Nelson Music, first at ten per cent, then at twenty per cent. When the company was sold in 1990, English pocketed $360,000. Simply from hitting his drums with a stick, English earned $150,000 in 1978, an enormous amount for a hired hand. The rest of the band were all well paid, well fed and well looked after. They weren't on retainers, but because they toured so frequently and would get a cut of any album money if they played on it, they really could have no complaints financially. And if they were not quite treated as equals – after all, the entire operation was designed to ensure Nelson didn't have to even *think* about what he was doing next, it would just happen, and they were all part of that hierarchy – they were certainly treated like human beings.

Mickey Raphael: The other musicians I've met on the road, they meet Willie and they say, 'Man, we've worked with these really big stars but they don't *talk* to us. They don't even acknowledge we're there. We're like punch-the-clock employees. So you've got a great deal with Willie – as squirrelly as it may get at times, he's a human being. He acknowledges your existence.'

It was a laudable attitude and it came as naturally to him as breathing. It stemmed from his belief in loyalty, reincarnation and karma. The more good he did this time around the better off he would be in the next life.

He wasn't always able to put aside the basic temptations of the here-and-now in return for the promise of his heavenly reward – especially when it came to women – but he felt that spreading his good fortune might go some way towards redressing the balance. He had a long memory when it came to those close to him or those he felt he still owed something. He gave Faron Young a $38,000 prize bull in belated repayment for the $500 loan he had collected in Tootsie's back in 1961. He made Larry Butler, his mentor and helper at the Esquire club in Houston in the late-50s, a partner in a nightclub venture. In April 1981 he caught two planes and put down $6,000 of his own cash to play a fundraiser in Pleasanton at the behest of Dr Ben Parker, his old boss at KBOP. There were numerous other benefits: several for Native American Indians; for the mass unemployed in Lima, Ohio; for 1,500 prisoners in Missouri State penitentiary who had sent him a birthday card; for a local theatre in Hawaii; for abused children, where he displayed his singular sense of humour by suggesting that they play the old swing standard 'Beat Me Daddy (Eight To The Bar)' as an opener.

A few weeks after Bruce Lundvall had left CBS in 1982, Nelson ensured his entire family got front row seats at his New Jersey show. When he learned that Lundvall's son was in hospital for an operation, he and Connie sent a pinball machine and balloons. He would hear about sick children and arrange personal gifts and photographs. When Waylon Jennings' drummer Richie Albright got badly burned in 1981 working on his car, Nelson immediately handed him $10,000 to ease the medical costs. When his friend, roadie and business partner Tim O'Connor asked him to sign on as the guarantor for a $50,000 bank loan, Nelson simply gave him the money himself. Even relatively recent friends would find themselves swept away by his kindness.

Booker T. Jones: My memory is of him being hugely generous with his resources and energy. He must have had hundreds of homes, one of which he freely lent to me to stay in. Others were occupied by his children. I heard stories of Willie making operations available for sick people and the like. He was hugely popular in the Austin area.

There are literally hundreds of similar tales, and the majority of them are true. Sometimes he went too far. When CBS agreed in 1978 to let him set up Lone Star Records, his own record company, it was in many ways the crowning glory of his long fight against the system; his huge success and clout enabled him to release the occasional off-shoot record on his own label and put out other people's records as well, all with the backing and support of CBS. It was a golden opportunity and a recognition of the dues that he had paid and that he was now collecting on, but instead of nurturing the label he handed its day-to-day running over to Larry Trader, who had no idea what he was doing. The whole thing fell apart almost before it began.

The most noticeable downside of his generosity was that news of it reached out to a wider circle and attracted some vulturous characters. One of the other reasons Nelson had such a bewildering array of human wildlife hanging on to his coat-tails was that they scented money like sharks scent blood. Hangers-on, usually on the outer edges of the slipstream of his success rather than in the centre, would abuse his trust, siphon off cash, run up huge room service bills in his name and assume he had too much money and had smoked too much pot to ever notice. Even when those closest to him pointed out what was going on he was invariably infuriatingly obtuse and buried his head in the sand.

Lana Nelson: His immediate reaction would be to turn around and give that person everything he asks for, just to prove he's not making a mistake. He doesn't want to admit that someone has taken advantage of him, because it hurts his feelings and he doesn't want to deal with that hurt.[2]

Aside from those around him, there was also a whole sub-culture of supposed fans who would come to him looking for financial help: school fees, medical bills, handicapped family members, funerals, bank loans, business schemes, *life* – there was always a good reason for needing a little extra and Nelson was incredibly patient and forthcoming with his time and very often his money. Instead of signing autographs after gigs he would very often be signing cheques. He still does.

Paul English: He still helps a whole lot of people, and he still has people take advantage of him. He'll know it, but he don't care. It used to really make me mad but now it don't. I used to really get hostile over it but that's what friends are for. I always thought that I had to look out after Willie.

He never lost his faith in human nature. This was how it was supposed to be. In the dark days of the late-60s he had vowed privately that if he ever got the chance to play his music to people he would 'stand up there on stage as long as anyone will listen', and he also vowed that he would look after his friends. 'Where were *you* when we were sleeping in cars?' he would ask those who criticised his generosity. Rather than retreating into isolation and paranoia, Nelson clasped his people even closer to him. Rather than skulking behind closed doors to count his money, he did the opposite: he began building an entire infrastructure for himself and his entourage, and it is one which has – against all the odds – held together to the present day. Its creation was an extraordinary act of faith and friendship. For those members of his extended 'family' who had stuck close to him through penury and depression since the late 60s and early 70s, payback time was coming.

In May 1979, Larry Trader spotted a 'For Sale' sign outside Pedernales Country Club, a 76-acre expanse in the gentle hills of Briarcliff,

Spicewood, near Lake Travis and about half an hour from central Austin. The lot contained a nine-hole golf course, a clubhouse and a group of condominiums, but it was run down. Nelson bought it and began pouring money into the site: he restored the clubhouse and repaired the ailing golf course; he installed a hi-tech recording studio; he renovated the condos. Everyone got in on the act. Trader was installed as pro and general manager at the golf club; Tim O'Connor, another face from the early Austin days, was brought in to oversee the general developments; Jody Fischer, one of Neil Reshen's associates who had turned from gamekeeper into poacher, came in to run the recording studio. Core road crew members like stage manager 'Poodie' Locke, lighting manager Buddy Prewitt, bus driver Gator Moore, bodyguard Billy Cooper and others who had less tangible connections with the business came to live in the condos, often rent free. It was not luxurious accommodation – they were small, scuffed buildings sitting on the hill lining the road that led to the golf club, surrounded by grass and scrub – but the gesture and the spirit behind it was unmistakable. It was almost like a new Bandera on a larger, more ambitious and permanent scale. Bobbie moved into the house over by the sixth fairway. Even David Zettner, Nelson's old friend and bass player from the Record Men days, came back into the fold.

David Zettner: He basically retired me onto that ranch. He told me, 'I just want you here.' I've become his master graphics designer. I do all the graphics for T-shirts, CDs, posters, and I'm just free as a bird. I do all my watercolours and paintings.

Pedernales became something like a cross between a base camp, a den and a social club for Nelson and his friends. It is also where he has made the majority of his records since the late 70s. Everyone from the golfer Lee Trevino to Dennis Hopper – who dried out there – was welcome to come by, play some golf, kick back and relax. A few minutes and about a mile away from the country club, Nelson bought 700 acres of prime hill country land. He made plans for a cabin to be built there, which eventually turned into a magnificent country lodge with views over the rolling countryside, with deer and horses roaming around. Elsewhere he built a Western town in the grounds at a cost of $800,000, an authentic mock-up of something that might have come straight out of *High Noon*, with a saloon bar, a jailhouse, a single-room church and an Opry House. It was the outlaw dream taken to its most surreal ends: when he was on the road he had his gang all around him, and when he was home in Texas he could play king cowboy in the big house at the top of the hill, with his posse at hand and a permanent playground for them all to frolic in.

Poodie Locke: We'd get drunk and we'd ride horses through there – like kids! It was a fantasy: wind's blowing, a quart of tequila in you, the Texas sky. How many people can play cowboys like that?[3]

The end of the decade brought major changes in Nelson's personal and professional life. Ira died from cancer in Austin on 5 December 1978 at the age of 65. He had been in hospital for three weeks and it wasn't an altogether sudden passing. Nelson had managed to put the hurt of his childhood to one side and had established warm relations with both his parents since the mid-60s. He would see them often. Ira was just down the road from Pedernales at Willie's Pool Hall, and according to Connie Nelson father and son were fairly close when he died, for which Nelson must take the majority of the credit. And if the band were touring the Pacific West Coast they would stop in to see Myrle in Yakima, where she had lived since 1974 in the three-bedroomed house that Nelson had bought for her, and where she would – finally – mother him. She died on 11 December 1983, aged seventy, after a long fight with breast cancer, living life to the full almost until the end. He never could do anything other than love and admire her spirit, which was so close to his own.

Willie Nelson: Bring everybody, was my mother's outlook. Take all the buses and line them up out there, and everybody get off. It didn't matter whether it was me or Kris Kristofferson or whoever it was, Mother would stay up all night and cook and drink and carry on. God love her, that's the person she was.[4]

Outwardly he wasn't particularly affected by his parents' deaths: he had learned to live his life without relying on them. However, their passing reaffirmed his commitment to healthy living. They had both died from cancer and he blamed cigarettes, one of the few vices he is almost moralistic about in his opposition. He had smoked tobacco since he was in single figures, but he quit in the face of what they had done to his parents and other members of his family. He views marijuana as a far lesser evil.

Neil Reshen had also gone, although not quite so dramatically. He was fired in 1978 after a dispute which centred on the fact that Nelson felt his manager couldn't be trusted – he believed he wasn't looking after the money properly and was taking more than his share, all the while neglecting basics like taxes and invoices and accounts. He also didn't feel he was doing his reputation much good. Reshen's company, Media Consulting Corp, sued Nelson's companies for $1.1m in November 1979, and at the 1980 hearing it emerged that Nelson had initially believed that Reshen was both a lawyer and a certified public accountant, although he was in reality neither. He also claimed to be unaware that his erstwhile manager had previously pleaded guilty to embezzling stock from a Los Angeles bank. Even today, neither Nelson nor Reshen have anything to say on the matter. Reshen's assistant Mark Rothbaum came in as a booking agent and Nelson 'kept giving me responsibility' until he found he was fulfilling the role of manager, in fact if not actually in name. 'It was very understated and low-key.'[5] Rothbaum still prefers to be called Nelson's advisor. Like his predecessor, he was from Jewish, East Coast stock, and although tough and straight-speaking he was a little more urbane than his ex-boss.

Creatively, albums were taking a back seat to other things. Nelson was making them – lots of them, almost compulsively – but they were knocked off quickly and contained no new writing: duet albums with Leon Russell (*One For The Road*) and Ray Price (*San Antonio Rose*), a Christmas album (*Pretty Paper*) and a tribute to Kris Kristofferson. The album with Price marked a rapprochement between Nelson and his old mentor, who was still pretty mad about his old Cherokee cowboy shooting his prize fighting cock at Ridgetop back in the mid-60s.

Ray Price: He kinda did it as a surprise for me. He called and told me to come on in. Of course I live in Texas, and when I got up there he said, 'We're gonna do it tonight.' We cut it all in one night. It kinda had a rough edge to it, but that's what you want. I didn't realise it until after the thing was over that it was my birthday. That's the kind of person he is.

Such prolific, unstudied offhandedness would eventually run his commercial appeal into the ground, but for now he was still riding high on the success of *Stardust*. Movies had become perhaps his most pressing interest. It was really the *Red Headed Stranger* that led to Nelson's involvements in films. Even as he was writing the album he was envisaging it as a film – with him in the lead role, naturally. As much as he did want to be a cowboy – he wanted to say the things cowboys said and do the things they did – the Western town on his ranch was a serious undertaking, designed to be a movie set for the film. He was hot property and was courted by the film-makers. He sold the script to Universal for around $400,000 and set up a production company in a suite of offices in Burbank, Los Angeles, but he was entirely unprepared for the tedious process of getting a film off the ground and onto the screen. *Red Headed Stranger* didn't happen until as late as 1986, and in the course of waiting for the film to be made Nelson undertook a number of other roles. He talked with his friend, the Texan writer Bud Shrake, about various projects: at one point *Phases And Stages* was going to be made into a film, Leon Russell's 'A Song For You' was going to be adapted, something called *The Willie Nelson Story* was also mooted, and *Songwriter*, the humourous story of a writer based in Nashville who returns to Texas was also planned. It was clear he wouldn't be steering too far from autobiography.

But it was producer, director and actor Sydney Pollack who really got things moving on the screen and who, for a while, became 'sorta the Willie guy' in the movies. Pollack was – and remains – a highly respected figure in the industry, the director of *They Shoot Horses Don't They?* among several other films. In 1977, with the outlaw wave at its peak, he had been approached by an agent suggesting that Waylon Jennings could be a movie star. He barely knew who Jennings was but began listening to his music, and while doing so was struck by the sight of Nelson on the back cover of *Waylon & Willie*. Later he had dinner with Jennings in Nashville and Nelson tagged along.

Sydney Pollack: I got kind of mesmerised by Willie. In the middle of the conversation he said to me, 'Listen, I sold this album *Red Headed Stranger* to Universal, so I'm going to be in the picture business and I need to get some experience. I'd love to be in a movie with you sometime.' So I said, 'Um, *OK* . . .' Well, months went by. I started working on *The Electric Horseman*, and I got a phone call from Willie, saying: 'I know you're going to do this picture with Robert – he called him Robert – and I'd sure like to be in it.' And I said, 'Well, Willie it doesn't work that way. Yeah, it would be kinda fun, but . . .'

But Nelson was determined. *The Electric Horseman* was a movie about a rodeo star and would star Robert Redford and Jane Fonda. It would be the perfect place to go to school. He was quite deliberate about what he was doing. He didn't want to take just anything, and he reasoned that Redford and Pollack were the kind of people who would protect him and give him a little kudos. Ever since High school he had liked acting and he had always loved movies; his songs were often cinematic narratives and with his writing on hold, acting gave him another means of self-expression. In many ways it was a natural step.

Willie Nelson: I figured I'd just wait for something that was right for me. Truth is, I never know when I'm acting and I wasn't sure I could do it, but I thought it was time for me to find out.[6]

He called Pollack and said he was coming to California and could he drop in to see him? When he did the director was bowled over. 'He looked *so* amazing,' he recalls. Wearing a dark-brown suede Western jacket with fringes – exactly the same outfit he wore in the film – Pollack fell in love with the look and straight away said, 'Look, I've got a tiny little part I can give you, but you have to have an attention span. You have to repeat and just stand there, it's not like a concert where you sing and it's over with.' 'Oh no, that's OK, that's OK, I'll do it,' said Nelson. Pollack called his wardrobe people over and said: 'I just love the way he looks. Exactly like this, if you can just duplicate that.' And Nelson, ever the beacon of common sense, said: 'Hell, I'll just wear this!'

The conversation over his clothes was an interesting insight into his acting style: simply be yourself. He knew no other way. His role in *The Electric Horseman*, filmed towards the end of 1978, was as Redford's roguish manager. The part was small – although it kept expanding once Nelson came on board – and no real stretch. Pollack talked to him in simple terms: do the same thing you do when you sing a song. Just be yourself, be real, and don't try to act or listen to your voice. He did it well, at the same time pulling off the best line in the film, taken from the boys on the tour bus and ad-libbed straight onto the screen. Talking to Robert Redford's character, Nelson drawled that he was going to find a woman who 'could suck the chrome off a trailer hitch'.

Sydney Pollack: I thought the crew was going to fall in the swimming pool when he said it, because we didn't know that was going to happen. I'd never heard the line before, and the truth of the matter is it went past the censors. They didn't even know what the hell it meant!

His small but eye-catching performance in a mediocre movie was credible enough to lead to a starring performance in *Honeysuckle Rose* the following year. This time it was a hand-crafted role: a country singer called Buck Bonham torn between his wife and his lover, containing plenty of performance sequences featuring Nelson's songs and friends like Emmylou Harris, Hank Cochran, the Family Band and Johnny Gimble. How typical of him to ensure that everyone in the gang got a slice of the pie. Nelson had wanted Pollack to direct again but he was reluctant, and eventually he agreed to come in as executive producer. His co-stars were Dyan Cannon as his wife Viv and Amy Irving as the nubile young musician Lily, who leads him into inevitable temptation.

It was a pretty basic scenario with some truly bad lines, but most of the really compelling action was taking place offstage and when the cameras stopped turning. Life began to imitate art. Nelson and Irving embarked upon a less-than-discreet on-set affair. Irving was a pretty, 26-year-old Californian who was dating – and would later marry – Steven Spielberg, but it was an on–off thing which was very firmly off during the filming of *Honeysuckle Rose*. The affair wasn't particularly conducive to a relaxed working atmosphere, especially as the liaison was quickly mirrored by another one between Dyan Cannon and the director Jerry Schatzberg.

Sydney Pollack: Well, it was a mess on the picture! I go back all the way to Connie, and this thing started up. Willie's relationship was pretty rocky with Connie. It was an uncomfortable situation. There were these two affairs going on: Dyan Cannon with the director and Amy Irving with the star. I think there was this internecine tussle over protecting the size of the parts. Who the hell knows? But it was fun! He's a very attractive man. There's just something very unusual about him.

Nelson remained unapologetic. 'She was something else,' he later said of Irving. 'And I'd do it again.'[7] But he was famous now, and the kind of privacy he had been used to for over forty years was no longer on offer. The affair with Irving – conducted relatively openly within the confines of the set, although at the time he publicly denied the rumours that were flying around – could not just be ignored by his wife as so many of his previous flings had been, lost out in the vast emptiness and endless hours on the road, where temptations and loneliness meant that almost everything was instantly forgotten and – almost – forgiven. The affair ensured his marriage to Connie was becoming more strained than ever.

Connie Nelson: I guarantee you I knew about [the other women] from day one. I just tried to look at it like, Well, it's the women, it's not him. It's them coming on to him. It's not his fault. Denial. Total denial. There were a couple of times when I let him know that he'd better watch it because I *really* noticed, and then all of a sudden things kind of stopped. When it just got too blatant and I felt like it was real obvious, if I mentioned it then it stopped. So I would think, Well, it wasn't Willie, he just stopped it. It was just so ridiculous. The band were absolutely [protective of me]. It was funny, they tried to keep things from me for so long, and then they did the reverse. They'd want to tell me everything! I said, 'Wait a minute, I don't want to hear this!'

In the end, Connie and Nelson came back together for Christmas in 1979 and managed to patch things up, but it was an increasingly uneasy match. It could be that *Honeysuckle Rose* gives the audience a greater insight into Nelson's personality and his romantic appeal than is immediately apparent. As Buck Bonham he did a very good impression of someone who remains static as life happens around him. Attractive women compete for his affections with no apparent encouragement from him; his music and the mysterious force of his personality are enough. He is an oddly detached yet compelling personality. It was this kind of attitude which really held the key to Nelson's charisma in the eyes of the opposite sex. The calm, unshowy, take-it-or-leave-it presentation of his character and the to-hell-with-the-consequences shrug was very appealing, although not so much if you were on the receiving end of it, as inevitably one day you would be. But it's not true to say that he needed no one. He always needed *someone*, it just didn't have to be the same someone all the time.

Honeysuckle Rose premiered at Mann's Chinese Theater in Los Angeles in July 1980 and received mixed notices. Although it wasn't a commercial success, Nelson came out of it rather well. 'Its only clear focus is the redoubtable Willie Nelson,' wrote Janet Maslin in the *New York Times*. 'He commands attention absolutely whenever he appears on screen. In Mr Nelson's performance, and in his singing turns, the film achieves a precision in sharp contrast to the vagueness that afflicts it otherwise.'[8]

Then again, the *Washington Post* called him 'faintly preposterous'. There is certainly a thin line between an economical actor and one that resembles a tree, and Nelson sometimes crossed it. He certainly had presence and charisma, but he was not always convincing working with dialogue and exuded little in the way of warmth. But he was competent enough for it to lead to other films, which took up much of his time in the early- to mid-80s, some better than others: *Thief, Coming Out Of The Ice, Barbarosa* and *Songwriter*, perhaps his most successful film. He would generally either play a musician or a cowboy. He understood both. He was playing himself.

Sydney Pollack: The great thing about Willie is he's so fucking comfortable in his own skin. He had a kind of simple straightforward way of behaving, and an authenticity that I always found awesome. I wouldn't say he'll be playing *Hamlet*, but as long as he stays close to himself he's terrific. He's not trained as an actor, but what he has is a sense of truth that's essential to any kind of good acting. That comes from his life. There's not a phoney bone in his body. He's absolutely what he is and who he is. He's not trying to make an impression or impress or anything like that. He's the genuine article.

The process of making films, and in particular *Honeysuckle Rose*, pushed him towards the long process of writing again. *The Electric Horseman* soundtrack featured 'My Heroes Have Always Been Cowboys', a self-explanatory and rather downbeat reflection on the trials and attractions of men who live the transient life, which was written by Sharon Vaughn and became a sizeable hit for Nelson in 1979. Most of the soundtrack to *Honeysuckle Rose* featured live performances of old classics, recorded on location – including the Broken Spoke in Austin – on the Encarton mobile studio, and though the sound quality was dire the performances were often superb, excepting the contributions of the two lead actresses. But Pollack was adamant that there should be some new material for the film as well.

Sydney Pollack: I said, 'Willie, you gotta write something for this thing.' I used to get the Warner Brothers jet, and he'd get on the bloody thing and I'd have to stop him and his guys from smoking because the pilots were getting stoned! It was dangerous. The pilots kept coming back saying, 'Hey, you can't do this.' Anyway, I went down there to pick him up and he got on the plane and he starts scribbling shit on the back of this airline ticket envelope with a pencil. And then he said, 'How about this?' He read me the lyrics to 'On The Road Again' and I thought it was the worst song I had ever heard. [Intones without emotion]: 'On the road again I just can't wait to, er, be on the road again, um, the life I love is making music with my friends, um, I can't wait to get on the road again. On the road again I can't wait to, em, get on the road again . . .' And I said, 'Holy Shit! We're in trouble!' But then he turned it into this ball-breaking song that was a huge hit.

That 'On The Road Again' was a country No. 1 and a Top 20 pop hit in waiting was blindingly obvious upon its release in the summer of 1980. It is more than an anthem, it is a manifesto, simple enough to be learned by a toddler in a plastic cowboy hat. In many ways it shared territory with 'Night Life' and other early, great Nelson songs in its utter simplicity, economy and clarity of purpose. As Pollack suggests, without music it amounts to little more than a very primitive, almost banal statement of pure, obvious fact – 'The life I love is making music with my friends' – shot through with an enticing whiff of romanticism – 'Like a band of gypsies we go down the highway' – but the rumbling joy of the melody and the playing lifts it sky-high. And in any case, why say more? The one really interesting choice of lyric in the song is found in the line: 'Insisting that the world keeps turning our way.' Not 'hoping' or 'asking' or 'praying'. *Insisting*. A powerful and significant choice of word from a man who had fashioned the world into a shape he could recognise.

The other new song on the album soundtrack, 'Angel Flying Too Close To The Ground', was more complex and profoundly beautiful. It had been written in 1976 and kept aside for one reason or another, and was as elusive as it was heartfelt: Nelson says it is an ode to Connie in one of their many times of difficulties, although she doesn't appear to agree; Pollack claims it is a farewell to one of his underworld pals. 'It was about a guy that got hurt that he liked particularly a lot in the Hell's Angels, and that's what the angel was,' he says. There's also a compelling suggestion that it is about his mother: 'I knew one day/ You'd fly away/ For love's the greatest healer to be found/ So leave me if you need to/ I will still remember.' It is about all these things and more; like many of his great songs, it sings of love without possession and has a universal resonance.

The other intervention of fate which resulted in a resurgence in his songwriting was a major health scare in August 1981, when he suffered a collapsed lung while swimming in Hawaii, where he was spending the summer at his holiday home. Nelson still owns the property on Laulea Place in Spreckelsville, between the towns of Kahului and Pa'ia on the small Hawaiian island of Maui. Over the years the house became first his primary base outside of Austin, and then his main home away from the road.

Following the accident he was taken into emergency care and spent over a week in hospital, and although no surgery was required a chest tube was inserted to drain the lung. He cancelled dates and took the whole of September and October off to recuperate in Hawaii and Colorado. He rested, cut his hair and shaved his beard, and generally took a good look at himself. He used the rare time away from the helter-skelter to finally write a full album, the first since *Phases And Stages* to be almost entirely self-written and a conscious return to the narrative, cycle-of-song that characterised that album and particularly *Red Headed Stranger*. His brush with illness resulted in a sombre reflection of mortality, mythology, faith, karma and reincarnation.

The idea for *Tougher Than Leather* took seed with the title song, a lovely rolling country ballad which told the story of an old gunslinger in the even older West who kills a young rival and is then haunted by the memory of the dead man's girlfriend, symbolised by the talismanic image of the 'rose' which appears throughout the record. Over the rest of the album, the gunslinger dies and is reborn as an urban cowboy in modern-day San Antonio, where he is imprisoned and then executed for a robbery and murder he didn't commit. 'Was it something I did, Lord, a lifetime ago/ Am I just repaying a debt that I owe?' He had written the songs in late 1981 but the album didn't come out until over a year later, in March 1983. It was regarded by many as a mere pale retread of *Red Headed Stranger*, with its stripped down instrumentation, its downbeat feel, its recurring musical themes and morally inquisitive narrative. Even the painted cover and the cartoon-strip depictions inside – lovingly drawn by David Zettner – were echoes. And it's true it did invite comparisons, but in many ways it is a deeper and darker record than Nelson's acclaimed breakthrough, the only real chink of light coming on 'A Little Old-Fashioned Karma', where he explains his spiritual beliefs in typically low-key fashion by singing, 'If you wanna dance you gotta pay the band.'

The narrative was a little confusing without repeated listens or explanatory notes, and it failed to really grab the public imagination. Partly this was because it was a record whose mood sat oddly with the brashness of the early-80s: in 1983 other superstars like the Police, Prince, David Bowie and Michael Jackson were releasing slick, modish, landmark records such as *Synchronicity, 1999, Let's Dance* and *Thriller*, and Nelson later felt that such a delicate, subdued record fell through the cracks and got trampled on. It was partly his own fault. There was simply too much music out there, and much of it was his own. He was releasing a cascade of albums: three in 1982, five the following year, to the extent that Columbia were refusing to release some of his recordings on the basis that they were overworked and couldn't fit them into their release schedule.

He was both over-exposed and in direct competition with himself, and his suite of new songs suffered by comparison. At the same time as *Tougher Than Leather* was making small waves – the album reached No. 39 and its single, 'A Little Old-Fashioned Karma', went to No. 10 in the country charts – his duet with Merle Haggard on Townes Van Zandt's 'Pancho And Lefty' was hitting No. 1 in the country charts.

'Pancho And Lefty' had been recorded by Emmylou Harris on her 1977 album *Luxury Liner*, which is where Nelson had first heard it. Like almost anyone with a functioning pair of ears, he fell in love with the song on first listen and transcribed the maze of words by hand. A few hours later the song had been cut, becoming the title track on the duet album he was recording with Merle Haggard. The record was produced by renowned Nashville songwriter, musician and producer Chips Moman, who had worked with everyone from Wilson Pickett and Dusty Springfield to Neil Diamond and Elvis Presley.

Merle Haggard: My bus was there parked at the studio, and I'd been up for more than a day. I wasn't doing any kind of speed or anything, I was just up on adrenalin. I'd been asleep not more than forty minutes [when] I got that terrible feeling when someone wakes you up and you feel like your head's in a barrel or something. Well, Willie woke me up! And only for Willie would I have got up. He said, 'Hey, I think I've found the kinda song we need for the title song for this album.' Willie spent about three hours taking that thing down off Emmylou's record. It was hard to make out the words. There was not any manufactured piece of paper big enough to hold all these words, and he'd written it out in pencil on this old, ripped open paper bag. I said, 'My God, that's good. I'll have to learn it'. He said, 'Well, the band's nearly got their part, they're in there right now. By the time they get theirs you'll have your part!' I said, 'Go ahead and record it and I'll put my part on in the morning. I'm out of it.' He said, 'No, you need to be on the ground for this one, it's going to be great.' He literally dragged me out of there and we went in the studio, and I didn't know the song at all, I'd never heard it before in my life, and we made that record you guys hear right there. I got one pass at it. One pass. The next morning I said, 'Hey, I'd sure like to do my part over,' and Willie said, 'Oh hell, they've mixed it. It's all closed up. It's great.' I didn't even get to hear my part back until the record came out! Willie has a rule. If you get him [in the studio] on something that's all you're going to get. He ain't going to go back and do it because he's too busy.

'Pancho And Lefty' was a beautiful, mysterious song in any guise, and although Haggard has expressed a few misgivings about Moman's rather clinical production, it was a memorable single and has since become a highlight of Nelson's live set. But it was something of an exception to the rule. Nelson's career had so swiftly ascended into the stratosphere that things like 'Pancho And Lefty' and *Tougher Than Leather* sat oddly with the bulk of much of his own current output, drowned out by the rather less subtle sounds of the rest of his music. Much of the music he was making had travelled so far from *Red Headed Stranger* that many people could not make the connection back: they identified him instead with the lushness of *Stardust*. They may not even have known – or cared – whether he was a songwriter or not. As the more involved, considered songs and albums found favour amongst his long-term fans who appreciated that they contained the core essence of Nelson's art, he was busy playing to the galleries with a series of albums and songs which consolidated and indeed boosted his status as a pop performer and a showbiz icon, but did little for his long-term reputation. With hindsight, he was sowing the seeds for his own downfall.

He had recently released the *Always On My Mind* album, which reached No. 2 on the charts in the summer of 1982. It was his most blatantly commercial record ever, containing versions of such classic songs as 'A Whiter Shade Of Pale', 'Bridge Over Troubled Water' and 'Do Right Woman, Do Right Man'. It was recorded without the Family Band and given a glossy, contemporary production sheen by Chips Moman and his band of studio musicians, which included songwriter and guitar player Johnny Christopher. He managed to find some flicker of a heartbeat in the rather saccharine but seductive title cut, but it was both a song and performance which dealt with emotions in big, bright primary colours, with none of the finely etched light and shade of his best work. Despite – or more likely because of that – the song had given him a No. 5 single on the pop charts, his biggest ever single success. Apparently he wasn't even aware that Elvis Presley had recorded it ten years earlier.

Merle Haggard: No one else could have done 'Always On My Mind' following Elvis. I turned that song down. We were in the studio and [the song's co-writer] Johnny Christopher jumped up because he didn't like the song we were recording at that moment. He was very rude, actually. He jumped up in the middle of the session and said, 'Man, I got a better fucking song than this in my pocket!' I don't know if he'd taken anything but he had a lot of nerve. All the musicians' faces went red, they didn't know what was going to happen – we might kill Johnny! He'd interrupted our take, jumped up and killed our record. He suggested 'Always On My Mind' and the room went quiet, and I said, 'God, didn't Elvis have a big hit with that?' I didn't even consider it because Elvis had got it, but Willie was standing behind me, and he said, 'I'll cut it.' I turned around and looked at Will and I said, 'My God, *you* could. You could have a fucking hit on this.' And lo and behold, of course he did.

Nelson's mainstream, pop-balladeer's reading of 'Always On My Mind' won a Grammy in 1983, while the album went platinum. Later the same year he went back into the studio with Booker T. Jones to record *Without A Song*. If *Tougher Than Leather* had flirted with being an imitation of former glories, then *Without A Song* dived in with both feet. It was unapologetically *Stardust Part II*. One of the problems with Nelson having his own recording studio on hand constantly at Pedernales was the danger that some of the intensity and urgency could drift away from a project. *Without A Song* was recorded mostly at night, after many long golf and tennis days for him and producer Booker T. Jones, who along with the band was set up in the condos. There was a much more relaxed attitude than on *Stardust* and it took longer to cut. It was a pleasant record, comprising ten standards, but it somehow lacked the freshness and unity of *Stardust*. The strings were recorded in London, the horns in Hollywood, and the soul of the record was misplaced somewhere along the way.

Perhaps more significantly, Nelson's duet with Spanish superstar Julio Iglesias on 'To All The Girls I've Loved Before' was also recorded during the *Without A Song* sessions in mid-1983. It has often been said that Nelson will sing with anyone on almost anything, but he should have drawn the line at treacly, chauvinistic Euro-pop power ballads. The song marked the nadir of his career creatively and musically, and yet pushed him to even greater heights of celebrity, a sure signal that he was letting his standards drop to new depths. It was the type of record that would have Hank Williams twitching in his grave and Waylon Jennings – one would hope – reaching for his holster, the kind of over-produced slop that put anything Nelson had ever done in his RCA days in the shade. The difference here was that he was under no pressure to record the song, and indeed seemed genuinely pleased to do so. There were three options: either his critical faculties were failing him; he really couldn't say 'no' to anyone; or he just wanted to hang out with his new friend Julio. It was probably a bit of each.

It had been Connie who had alerted him to Iglesias after she'd heard him singing on the radio while Nelson was playing in London in June 1982. He had liked his voice, thinking he was some unknown singer rather than a European superstar, and called Mark Rothbaum, who arranged a meeting. They quickly agreed to work together, although unusually, the song wasn't really discussed. 'With Julio it was his singing that attracted me,' Nelson later said. 'But as a rule it is my feeling for the song itself that urges me to cut it.'[9] Iglesias – the self proclaimed 'love-aire' – came down to Pedernales with his entourage and limousines, rubbing shoulders with the rough and ready Nelson crew, who arrived in golf carts.

Booker T. Jones: I remember being interrupted [during *Without A Song*] by a visit from Julio Iglesias to record 'To All The Girls I've Loved Before' one night. That was a big deal. Willie pulled out all the stops for Julio: a big dinner and reception. I watched the recording from the control room. It was a pleasure to watch him work with another artist and producer, me being only a spectator.

Nelson cut his vocal in Austin with producer Albert Hammond, who had written the song for Sinatra; it is, in many ways, a 'My Way' for wannabe gigolos and ageing lounge lizards. The rest of the track was completed without him in Los Angeles, so he can't really be held responsible for the sickliness of the finished product. The song was predictably and depressingly enormous, a No. 5 single in March 1984, and the sum total of perhaps two hours work in the studio on a summer's night put the seal on his populist, showbiz status. It attracted a transient audience who would not stick around. It is still the song that many people who have little interest in Nelson's music remember him by.

He continued making some distinctly odd career moves, diluting the true essence of what he did. The line in the sand denoting the crucial difference between elegant, heartfelt truth and syrupy sentimentality had been washed away. He could write and record the sublime 'Forgiving You Was Easy' in a day, proving that when he was being pushed he could come up with the goods. On the other hand, he also cut his version of the wretched 'The Wind Beneath My Wings' during the same period, and this time there was no Julio to blame. What was he thinking? One obvious clue lay in his age. He was fifty-years-old, not an age where most artists are expected to be peaking. His commercial summit had arrived unusually late, between the ages of 42 and 52, while his creative prime, it could reasonably be argued, came at various stages between the ages of 26 and 42, a much more familiar time frame for an artist to blossom. The intensity and regularity of his talent had diminished and the soundness of his judgment was by no means infallible, but any notion that he was being seduced by the notion of being a pop star seems unlikely.

Connie Nelson: I never remember Willie trying to make it big: 'I'm going to be the next pop star.' Never. I never ever saw that side of him. I don't think there was ever that side of him. He honestly just wanted to make his music, he never vocalised that he wanted to make it big. It was about selling more records and making a good living.

Nelson had really become a national institution first and an innovative musician second; the embodiment of the spirits of Bob Wills, Nat King Cole, Zebulon Walton, Jesse James and Burt Reynolds fused together. He was tracing wild curves on the map: he would show up on everything from Bob Hope's *Pink Panther Thanksgiving Gala* to *Miami Vice* and *Saturday Night Live*. He toured Japan for the first time and struggled with the language barrier and cultural differences; he was scheduled to play a series of shows with Frank Sinatra at Caesar's Palace in Las Vegas in June 1984, a true thrill for the boy from Abbott, but the edge was taken off the entire event when Sinatra could only fulfil one night before pulling out with a throat problem, while Nelson attracted criticism for – uncharacteristically – crossing a picket line to perform; in early 1985 he appeared alongside the rest of America's A-list singers on the USA For Africa single, 'We Are The World', the rather tepid response to Band Aid's 'Do They Know It's Christmas?' A few weeks later he turned up to play at the Oscars. He had become an industry, a one-man mass market. A single name would suffice: 'Willie'.

And still the money was rolling in, and still the money was pouring out. By the mid-80s his average gross annual income was estimated conservatively at around $10 million, including royalties from his own songs, income from his albums and tour revenue. His expenses were monumental, however. The daily payroll for the thirty-strong crew on the road was $12,000, plus at least the same again in expenses and hotel rooms. The lowest paid 'member of staff' was on a minimum of $40,000, literally for bringing the beers to the table and making the coffee. An average of 150 shows a year – it was often more – amounted to annual tour overheads of at least $5million, and that wasn't including the hundreds of people – from Mark Rothbaum and his office to recording engineers and golf club staff, from script writers and interior designers to business partners and marijuana suppliers and those who did 'chores' for him of an unspecified nature – who sent their bills for Nelson to pay. It was mostly dealt with in cash, which would explain why there was an Uzi sub-machine gun on the bus. Mix in the hand-outs, charity requests, Connie and the kids – *all* the kids – and other family members, and the cost started adding up.

In 1983 he began leasing a private seven-seater Lear Jet – 'AirWillie' – at an annual cost of $400,000, to take him from film set to concert hall to home to awards show and back again. He once landed the plane because Ray Price wanted to piss on *terra firma*, not in the cramped toilet. That cost over $2,000. He later bought the Lear outright for $1.7 million, but it surely could have been only a minor surprise to him when the day arrived when it had to be sold. AirWillie was leaking fuel. From his vantage point high up in the clouds it was hard to tell, but financially, commercially, creatively, he was already starting to lose altitude.

IT WILL HAVE TO BE SOLVED SPIRITUALLY

Willie Nelson is talking about politics.

He has been holding the cold, unlit joint in his right hand for about ten minutes. He may have forgotten it is even there.

Politics is almost indistinguishable from personality for him. If he gets a good feeling about someone he will be inclined to back them, especially if they have empathy for the common man. 'I was supportive of President Carter,' he recalls. 'I was supportive of Dennis Kucinich when he was running in the Democratic election. So yeah, I've had my guys that I've supported.'

He is an American. It defines everything he does. He is most in touch with the soil beneath his feet and the people who live on it and with it. Like his music, his beliefs are unsuited to the grand gesture or the concerns of the few.

He favours small changes that make a difference to real people. His new pet project is Biodiesel, an alternative fuel source derived from vegetable oils. He loves it: farmers can grow the plants year after year which can then be turned into fuel.

Now even his own tour bus runs on soy extract. He calls it BioWillie.

'I've been involved in a lot of things that will keep us from being dependent on foreign energy,' he says. 'Biodiesel is a great one, because farmers can grow it and truckers can get immediate use from it. But there's also solar and hydrogen, all different things you can do in addition to petro-chemicals, which are quickly diminishing. There has to be thought about what's going to replace it. Biodiesel is a natural replacement because it's something the farmers can grow.'

He is, he says, still aware of the bigger picture. He is still a politically engaged man. 'Yeah, I think so. I still like and dislike a lot of things that are going on.'

He pauses. He is thinking of an example. 'I think the war in Iraq is wrong. That's wrong. Unfortunately, it's not going to be solved politically. It will have to be solved spiritually.'

The room is silent for a few seconds. A little rain is falling outside. The television is turned off but its black, lifeless screen is concealing any number of atrocities throughout the world. A spiritual solution seems a long way away.

'Maybe not so far,' he says softly. 'Maybe not so far.'

11. 1985–1990

D uring his nervy, somewhat shambolic turn with Ronnie Wood and Keith Richards at the Live Aid concert in Philadelphia on 13 July 1985, Bob Dylan had mumbled, 'I'd just like to say I hope some of the money that's raised for the people in Africa, maybe they could take just a little bit of it – maybe one or two million maybe – and use it, say, to pay the mortgages on some of the farms . . . the farmers here owe to the banks.' Given that he was the closing act at a concert designed to help raise funds for the millions who were currently starving to death in Africa, it struck many as a peculiarly insensitive, ill-judged and poorly expressed sentiment. Certainly, Live Aid organiser Bob Geldof was watching Dylan on television from Britain with his head in his hands, and not just because 'Blowin' In The Wind' was out of tune.

Bob Geldof: I wasn't really pissed off, but I just thought it was very American – not getting the plot. They were foreclosing on the farms in the mid-West, but Dylan should have understood the greater context in which Live Aid happened. I was in despair.

Also looking in from somewhere out on the road was Willie Nelson, who found himself nodding in agreement with Dylan. Nelson had already commented to Ray Charles at the recording of 'We Are The World' earlier in the year that famine relief was of course all well and good, but what about their own people? It was a question he was not alone in asking at the time. For all his universal mind, Nelson often displays a very local frame of reference, well attuned to the mood of the American people. He hadn't played at Live Aid but its ability to generate both awareness and funds had inspired him and confirmed, once again, that nothing could quite beat music for bringing people together. Farming was a cause he could easily get passionate about and there was no question that the grievances hesitantly outlined by Dylan were legitimate in a national context, if rather secondary weighed up against the totality of the world's evils.

It was the Reagan era and farms were being foreclosed all over America, 'the first symptom of a widespread and systemic failure of farm policy to keep family farmers on the land,' according to Farm Aid's mission statement. At heart, Nelson's fledgling Farm Aid organisation was a grass roots movement for the working man, squarely aimed at the small family farmer whose livelihood was being threatened by increased industrialisation and the onset of globalisation. In essence, he was paying homage to the roots of country music itself, to the very soil that he came from. Farm Aid harkened back to an idyllic rural America, the one of his youth, where small community banks would be sympathetic to the troubles its own people were experiencing. Now, if a farmer who wanted to run with the times couldn't keep up his loan payments he was being evicted from the land which gave him the means to survive. Family farms were disappearing and a whole way of life and livelihood was going with it. It was the erosion of old-time values: first the farmer, then the local store, then the service station across the street. Nelson wanted to do something to try and alleviate the immediate discomfort and pain of at least some of the individuals and families who were suffering the most. They were, after all, his audience.

Willie Nelson: The family farmer is a small farmer who loves the land. We can't take that away from him. Farmers are still not getting enough money for their product and are still going out of business at the rate of several thousand per month. Something has got to be done.[1]

Within a month of Live Aid, Nelson had rung around his farmer friends to take the temperature on the ground and picked up the baton, creating the seed of the idea for a Farm Aid benefit concert. Recognising the need for some political muscle, he joined forces with the Governor of Illinois, James Thompson. Thompson was an old friend: he booked Nelson each year to play the Illinois State Fair and even had it written into the contract that he would get to eat chilli on the bus with him. He was happy to help. Nelson hit the phones: Neil Young, Waylon Jennings, John Cougar Mellancamp. Bob Dylan could hardly say no. The whole event was conceived, announced and organised within a six-week time span; the show was hastily arranged for 22 September in Champaign, Illinois, right in the heartlands of the farming community. Everything seemed to happen simultaneously: acts were added to the bill daily, while Nelson set up a board with Governor Thompson and like-minded musicians such as Mellancamp and Young, both of whom hailed from farming communities. There was heavy presence from the Nelson camp: Paul English sat on the panel as, in time, did Nelson's daughter Lana, manager Mark Rothbaum, and road manager David Anderson.

They admitted to being unsure exactly how the money was going to be used. That detail would be pondered later. Nelson was in at the sharp end; hands on. He met farmer groups to discuss how to distribute the funds, talked to politicians from several states, corralled the acts. It was ultimately decided that he would not only be the public face and central voice of Farm Aid, but that he would be responsible for the distribution of the money, signing every cheque that went out. It was an immense vote of trust, confirmation that he was the perfect figure to be at the head of the movement. It also meant that Farm Aid became, as had Band Aid for Geldof, a much bigger commitment and a heavier load than he had ever envisaged. But he stayed the course.

The September concert was a genuine event. By the time the day arrived the bill had undergone a dozen revisions and swelled to include such rock luminaries as Lou Reed, Randy Newman, Bon Jovi, the Beach Boys, Roy Orbison, Tom Petty, as well as the cream of the country establishment: George Jones, Johnny Cash, Merle Haggard, Charley Pride, Loretta Lynn and Glen Campbell. It was in many ways a more impressive and all-encompassing line-up than the US leg of Live Aid itself. Nelson introduced it on the day with the pointed words: 'Welcome to Farm Aid – the concert for America.'

The 78,000 tickets had sold out in three days, and despite the drizzle and gusting winds the event was a success, the crowd comprised of an unusual mix of college students, rock fans and farmers. Nelson, naturally, opened the show, accompanied by Neil Young on the downbeat 'Are There Any More Real Cowboys Anywhere?'. Fourteen hours later he closed alone with a set including 'On The Road Again', 'Always On My Mind', and the inevitable 'Whiskey River'. As the fans exited, fireworks lit up the sky and a tape played 'America The Beautiful'. During the concert pledges rolled in on the toll-free phone line: 1-800 FARM AID.

In total, Farm Aid 1985 raised around $7m. Ticket sales for the concert were responsible for $1.3m, and the rest came from $3m in pledges and corporate donations and roughly the same amount in broadcast rights. There was some surprise at the relative paucity of the figure – euphoric pre-concert estimates had ranged from $30m to $50m – but it was academic in many ways. The US farm debt in 1985 was $212 billion, accruing interest at a rate of $58m per day. It was an insurmountable sum.

Indeed, there was criticism from the American Agriculture Movement and others along the lines that the proceeds of the concert were 'not even a drop in the bucket' of what was required, but it's hard to imagine who or what could have dented a hole in a debt of that magnitude. The concert certainly raised consciousness – it was broadcast live and attracted huge amounts of press coverage – and succeeded in helping those most in need with immediate aid. Nelson was unapologetic.

Willie Nelson: Be idealistic. Never mind if people call you an idiot. Just because your idealism can't instantly cure all the ills in the world, don't be cynical about it. Be idealistic and take a step forward.[2]

And the money did reach some of the most needy. The first cheque, written the day after the concert, sent $100,000 to the National Council of Churches for distribution to emergency food pantries serving farmers. A $25,000 donation to the League of Rural Voters was cancelled when it was suggested that monies given to a lobbying group amounted to a political donation from an avowed apolitical group; Nelson replaced it with $11,700 from his own pocket and added that he was 'angry that our government isn't doing enough', just to make the point. The business side of the Farm Aid organisation found its feet very much through trial and error, but soon the money started pouring out of the office in leafy Connecticut to the agricultural heartlands: grants; the building of an emergency help network, including a telephone helpline; legal aid; food aid; scholarships; education programmes. And it has endured. At the press conference at the end of the first Farm Aid concert Nelson promised 'this is just the beginning'. He has kept his word, through the concert's insurance problems, general compassion fatigue, not to mention his own personal traumas.

Farm Aid II, held in Texas on 4 July 1986 in conjunction with Nelson's annual picnic, was both less successful financially and less gripping as a musical event. Falling foul of the curse of the sequel, the event raised a disappointing $1.3 million, although it did feature a once-in-a-lifetime opportunity to see Nelson singing Aerosmith's 'Smokin' In The Boy's Room' with Mötley Crüe's Vince Neil. There has been a concert almost every year since, and although it has inevitably slipped down the media agenda and has never again attracted the line-up or level of donations of the inaugural concert, the organisation has been a quiet success and remains an important strand of Nelson's legacy. Prior to Farm Aid III in 1987, the office issued its report, led by its director Carolyn Mugar, outlining its commitment to the long-term alleviation of farmer's troubles. Nelson also visited Congress – resplendent in black baseball cap, black T-shirt and white sneakers – to reprimand a Senate agricultural sub-committee over its lack of action, and has personally contacted countless farm families who turned to Farm Aid for assistance. He would step outside the box as well: in 1989 he headlined a benefit for Dixon Terry, a farmer from Iowa and president of the Family Farm Coalition who was killed by lightning, leaving his family $300,000 in debt, and has consistently rallied the cause in all manner of ways.

It has not always been a fashionable cause, but he has remained involved and in the loop throughout, despite the fact that Farm Aid has survived far longer than he ever imagined. Between 1985 and 2004 the concerts raised a total of $26,739,467, and $21,510,477 has been spent on a whole raft of programmes. It employs five full-time members of staff and its remit has widened, to include the promotion of local, healthy produce; emergency relief for farmers hit by hurricane Katrina; and measures to curb and control the long-term effects of everything from the depletion of soil deposits and genetic engineering to environmental damage. But in many ways, Farm Aid's greatest legacy has been the countless individuals it has helped at the frontline of severe hardship. The larger issues have not gone away: there are ever decreasing numbers of farms in America and if anything the underlying problems have only got worse.

Willie Nelson: The idea is to make people aware of the issue, maybe to buy the farmers a little time until long-term answers to their problems can be found. What we really want to do is change the attitude of the average American towards their ham and eggs in the morning.[3]

He said these words in 1985, but they still hold true today.

He was due some fun and games. He went off to film *Stagecoach* in New Mexico with his buddies Johnny Cash, Kris Kristofferson and Waylon Jennings at the beginning of 1986. He had already wrapped up filming the previous summer on his beloved pet project *Red Headed Stranger*, made for under $3 million, having chipped away at the script with his friend Bill Witliff over the years. The glory days of his Universal film contract – which had set aside a budget of $13.5m for *Red Headed Stranger* – were gone: Nelson shot the movie in 39 days at the Western town on his ranch in Austin, and also co-produced and co-financed the project. Paul English and Bee Spears had roles. Darrell Royal raised funds. It did not prove to be a wise investment. The film bombed and was described in the *Washington Post* as 'vintage Willie-ism. Nicely produced, stiffly acted and every twist of the interminable plot telegraphed well in advance. Not recommended.'

Stagecoach was a much more successful and light-hearted romp. It was a made-for-TV remake of the classic 1939 John Wayne Western and his co-stars were a significant bunch: his new band of collaborators. In September 1985 Nelson had released an album under the guise of the Highwaymen, a catch-all for himself, Cash, Jennings and Kristofferson working as a somewhat grizzled country super-group. The previous November, of 1984, they had all travelled to Switzerland to take part in the recording of Johnny Cash's annual Christmas TV special, which was being filmed in Montreux. While there, they batted some songs back and forth in the hotel room in a loose manner, at the end of which Jennings suggested that they might bring the quartet into the studio. He had, in fact, mooted the idea before, to Kristofferson at least, of Nelson, Jennings and Kristofferson working together on a kind of expanded Outlaw project. Kristofferson didn't think it would work. At the Montreux show between 12 and 17 November, Jennings tried again and the response was more positive.

Jessi Colter: It was like four big stallions trying to pull in one direction! I think Waylon had a lot to do with that. It was some time before Waylon re-introduced the idea, maybe Waylon and Willie talked, and then they brought John in. They found a way to do it.

The following month in Nashville, Chips Moman was producing a duet between Nelson and Cash called 'They're All The Same', ear-marked for Cash's *Rainbow* album; Jennings and Kristofferson came by the studio separately to visit. The quartet began singing the Jimmy Webb song 'The Highwayman', which they had toyed with in Switzerland, about a creative and impulsive spirit which lingers through the centuries, from the dirt roads of the age of the highwayman to the era of space technology. It was really about the many guises and incarnations of the deathless Spirit of America, and the song would have appealed to Nelson's sensibilities in particular. Once they had finished 'The Highwayman' they 'did another, then another', according to Jennings, with the result that an album was in the can before Christmas.

The backing band consisted of some of Nashville's finest, men like Bobby Emmons and Reggie Young, but the tracks were a bit sloppy, and featured a strange mix of voices and tones. Although a compellingly unusual project, in many ways they struggled to find a song big enough to accommodate them all. It was all a little gruff and nobody quite sounded at ease. Nonetheless, the atmospheric title track was a country No. 1, its success built on the back of a video film which took five weeks to shoot, each star playing the character they represented in the song: Nelson's highwayman, Kristofferson's sailor, Jennings' dam-builder, and Cash's singularly unlikely jet fighter. The idea to make *Stagecoach* really grew as an extension of the video experience, offering the opportunity for the four overgrown cowboys to build some more on-screen chemistry together. It was an ensemble piece, with Nelson playing Doc Holliday, and it wasn't a happy set in many ways: there were tensions between the producers and the Apaches who were extras on the film, and Nelson 'was appointed by Johnny Cash'[4] to step in to complain about their conditions. There was even a threatened walk-out at one point over the lack of direction.

In a more profound sense as well, Nelson's time might have been better off spent keeping his own house in order. All the wives had gone down to

New Mexico for the shoot – June Carter Cash had a small role in the picture – but Connie had made the difficult decision to stay behind to look after their daughter Paula Carlene, who at sixteen was now heavily involved in drugs.

Connie Nelson: I knew Paula was into drugs. There had been some major things that had gone on, there was no question, but I couldn't ever catch her at it. I just couldn't leave her with my mom and go off and have fun knowing this was going to happen. I felt like it was her *life*. So I told Willie: 'I can't go. It's not that I don't want to, I can't.' It was going to be a real big buzz, but I stayed home and I did find proof that she was doing drugs. I put her into rehab in San Diego and my mom came out to visit me from Colorado. I put my mom on her plane a week later, she called me that night – and the next day she was dead. I went to her funeral. I hadn't seen my oldest brother Mike in about five months and he looked *bad*, really sick. I asked him if he was OK and he said he had bronchitis and he was taking medication. A week later, he was in hospital with AIDS. He'd contracted it from a transfusion after a bad car wreck . . . it was just unbelievable. And while all this was going on, Willie is having an affair with the make-up girl on the movie. I hated him for that. There was a year when I hated him. Absolutely hated his guts.

Nelson met Ann-Marie D'Angelo on the set of *Stagecoach*. She was a dark, attractive 29-year-old from California with Hispanic roots. As a make-up artist she had worked on a handful of movies, including *Bachelor Party* in 1984, and also appeared as a bit-part actress in the abundantly silly TV movie *Starflight: The Plane That Couldn't Land*. D'Angelo became the mother of his two boys, Lukas and Micah, and finally his fourth and current wife when they married on 16 September 1991 in Dallas, in a service overseen by the Episcopal priest and Rosicrucian, the Reverend A. A. Taliaferro, whose taped sermons Nelson often listened to on the bus.

He later commented that 'they say you marry what you need. Kris Kristofferson married a lawyer and I married a make-up girl',[5] but it is unlikely he had such firm intentions when the couple first came together. The affair with D'Angelo was by no means a one-off during this period. In 1990 Nelson was sued by a journalist called Nancy Helen Watson, who claimed she had a six-month affair with him in 1985. 'I almost felt like a virgin because I had never before experienced sex with that depth and clarity,' she told the television programme *A Current Affair*. 'And I don't expect ever to find it again.' Hence a rather optimistic $50m lawsuit, claiming that he broke his promise to marry her and that she also broke her ankle at his ranch. $25m for each catastrophe, apparently.

The writing had been on the wall with Nelson and Connie for some time. The serious affair with Amy Irving aside, he had written the beautiful, self-explanatory 'Is The Better Part Over?' in 1984 (it finally ended up on the *A Horse Called Music* record in 1989), detailing the sad decline of a once-powerful, all-consuming relationship: 'Is the better part over/ Has a raging river turned into a stream?' Even so, judging by past history it looked odds-on that he would return to the homestead and the kids at some point, but this time it proved to be the end. It was much more than sexual betrayal. However painful, that had become somewhat routine and had been faced up to and dealt with before. This was a breach of loyalty, respect and support to his wife during the time she had needed him the most.

Connie Nelson: He was surprised when I filed for divorce. I don't think he expected me to leave him, but there was no way I could stay either. I just had to cut my losses. I just couldn't deal with everything. I had to let [the marriage] go and deal with the rest of it.

It would take her some years to forgive him, but the bond was too strong to be severed for ever. They divorced in 1988 and she toyed with writing a tell-all book, but eventually abandoned the idea. Paula Carlene came through rehab and went on the *Oprah Winfrey Show* to complete her journey through the standard American rites of passage. She now writes and sings and works as a masseuse in Colorado. Connie moved to San Diego to be near Paula Carlene and began to get her own life together again, away from Nelson. Slowly the wounds healed. Nowadays they are great friends, talking at least once a week and seeing each other regularly. She prefers, in the wise words of her ex-husband, to remember the good times.

Connie Nelson: My brother died in 1990, and while he was in the hospital Willie came in with all the band. Now Willie *hates* hospitals, but he came to the hospital and saw my brother. By this time I knew all the AIDS patients in every room, and while he was there Willie went with me and visited every single one. After he'd left I thought, What's really, really important? Willie did this for me and my brother and all these people. This is the real Willie. How can I hate him? I just kind of put things in perspective – that he's a good guy. The marriage just didn't work. He had a different view of marriage than I did.

The impact of her departure on Nelson is hard to gauge. Those closest to him unanimously vote Connie as their favourite of all the wives and maintain that he lacks something without her. There have been grumblings about Annie, or the 'new wife' as she is still called, nearly twenty years after they got together. Merle Haggard, like some playground rebel whose partner in crime starts dating the prom queen, mutters that 'she doesn't like me. She don't like me, I don't know why. Maybe because Willie likes me. I'm hoping that's what it is.'

Others at Pedernales have less kind things to say. Annie bases herself in Maui and has never really relished spending a lot of time in Texas. She is involved in political activism and environmental issues and chooses a quiet life for herself and her children. She will bring her boys, both musicians, out on the road in the summer, but other than that she leads her own life. She possibly didn't envisage having to spend her married life competing for her husband's affections with a coterie of frequently stoned, no-nonsense, good-time Southern gentlemen who could also lay claim to being 'family'. She has never gone out of her way to court Nelson's entourage.

David Zettner: Connie was the favourite. She was the darling. All the musicians loved her. Everybody loves Connie. Willie still loves Connie! She was the one who put the life in him. She was always thinking for him. This new wife, I don't know if she does that for Willie. Her first trip into meeting us, we were recording in the big studio, and we could tell she was either scared or something. She didn't want to say much anyhow. I never really did get to know her before she bought that place down in [Maui]. I don't think she wanted to be that friendly with all of us. Roger Miller told me right before he died: 'Yeah, the new wife comes in, the old friends go out.' Of course, Willie's deal is that there are a bunch of us!

The usual relentless round of touring was continuing apace, although basic human fallibility made the occasional attempt at slowing down the bus a little. Nelson fractured his left thumb – on his chord-forming hand – riding his bicycle at home in May 1986. It made guitar playing impossible and meant he had to take the best part of two months off the road leading up to Farm Aid II, although it had no long-term repercussions on his playing. In April 1987, Paul English suffered the effects of smoke inhalation during a fire at his home in Dallas caused by sawdust catching alight, which caused $150,000 worth of damage to the building and $50,000 worth to its contents, including gold discs, equipment and old memorabilia. It also had another impact.

Paul English: I can't smoke [pot], not since 1987 when my house burned down. I was in it. I got lung damage so I can't inhale anything. But that's all right. Pot is a thing that comes and goes with me, and it came and it went.

Marijuana was still firmly on the agenda for Nelson and many of his cohorts, but the insanity of the Family Band's cocaine years had largely passed. Things had settled down. Nelson smoked his weed, played video golf, watched movies, jogged and hit the stage night after night, while road manager David Anderson juggled the co-ordinates, handling communications between Nelson's HQs in Connecticut and Austin and his mobile office, situated in a cubbyhole under a bunk bed on the bus. It was furnished with an IBM XT computer, a fax machine and photocopier, a modular phone, a cheque writer and a machine gun, and in this cramped space the outside world and Willie Nelson somehow connected. Elsewhere on the bus, christened first *Honeysuckle Rose* then *Honeysuckle Rose II*, there was satellite TV, comfortable couches, a kitchen well stocked with vegetables and watermelon, thick velvet curtains to maintain a little privacy, mahogany panelling on the walls and heavy carpeting underfoot. Bee was the practical joker, horsing around, gaffer taping shut the doors on the bus where others were asleep. 'Just too much free time,' says Mickey Raphael.

There was still a smattering of the old, heavy vibe, provided by the likes of Larry Gorham, his bodyguard and an ex-Hell's Angel, but a seat on the bus was just as likely to be occupied by a man from Wrangler jeans, with whom Nelson had just signed a 3-year, $7 million sponsorship deal. The deal allowed Wrangler to promote one hundred of his concerts each year and distribute front row tickets to their dealers. The outlaw movement had always been a corporate-driven notion, this was just a more overtly commercial use of the brand name. Nelson now occupied a unique niche in American music and indeed culture: the benign face of the anti-establishment, wearing rebellion as a logo. He would endorse the 'Don't Mess With Texas' anti-litter campaign in 1989: the dope-smoking pirate urging the nation's youth to put their roaches and Rizlas neatly in the nearest bin.

Musically, he was spreading himself far too thin and suffering from burn-out. He was not alone: Dylan, Bowie, Neil Young, Johnny Cash and others were all struggling to understand where they fitted into the rather barren musical landscape of the mid-80s. Nelson occupied a safe haven in the sense that he was a celebrity who no longer needed to make hit records in order to keep doing what he loved, but his releases were increasingly disjointed, containing mere moments rather than whole sides of inspiration. His 1986 single 'Living In The Promiseland' was a country No. 1, but it was an unexceptional, all too socially aware slice of rock-tinged MOR, taken from the equally unexceptional, jumbled up and often somnambulant album *The Promiseland*. His time spent hanging out with Mellencamp and Neil Young seemed to have turned his head, but the bottom line was that the bulk of the material simply wasn't good enough and he in turn seemed suitably uninspired.

Commercially, his star was waning. There were no further crossover hits on the pop charts, and his albums of the era were a paradox: schizophrenic and jumpy, and yet containing too many pales echoes of ideas he had already investigated with greater success in the past to attract anything other than a niche market. *Island In The Sea* from 1987 was a laid-back slice of old-time textures, including Hawaiian music, yodelling, folk and country, with four over-produced tracks by Booker T. Jones tacked on at the end; 1988's *What A Wonderful World*, which again revisited standards from the early part of the century, was produced by Chips Moman and featured Julio Iglesias on, somewhat inevitably, 'Spanish Eyes'. It failed to reach even the lower reaches of the pop charts, a sure sign that the formula was failing through overuse. Nelson seemed unconcerned. He was simply doing what he wanted.

His collaboration with Fred Foster on *A Horse Called Music* in 1989 promised much, and delivered to a certain extent. Foster had produced Nelson's magnificent 'Forgiving You Was Easy' back in 1984, not to mention 'I Never Cared For You' in 1964, and often encouraged Nelson to keep things clear and uncluttered. *A Horse Called Music* contained the wonderfully fresh 'Nothing I Can Do About It Now', which had been written to order by songwriter Beth Nielsen Chapman. An upbeat country two-step in the mould of Lefty Frizzel's 'If You've Got The Money I've Got The Time', it was his last solo country No. 1 to date and featured such absolutely on-the-money lyrics that most people assumed that Nelson had written it himself: 'And I could cry for the time I've wasted/ But that's a waste of time and tears/And I know just what I'd change/ If I went back in time somehow/ But there's nothing I can do about it now.'

The song was embraced by his slightly disaffected constituency in the south-east as a kind of homecoming, and he sang it with an energy and abandon that had become rare. The track clearly highlighted his dilemma: such songs were hard to come by, and if he wasn't going to write them himself then there were few people that could. Elsewhere there were the usual re-recordings of his own classic songs – in this case 'Mr Record Man' and 'I Never Cared For You' – and other people's songs, like 'If I Were A Painting', which couldn't cope with the company they were keeping. *A Horse Called Music* also included the poignant waltz of 'Is The Better Part Over?', his long, slow farewell to Connie which tracked the universal cycle of a relationship's fast, bright beginning and slow, regretful ending. Foster counts it as his favourite Nelson song. Significantly, he used the demo version.

Fred Foster: It's such a great song. We tried to do it with the band two or three times and never could make it. I said, 'Willie, just you and the guitar is so great, can I just take it and let me play with it?' He said, 'Sure, I'll trust you.' I took him just him and the guitar, it's magic, but I wanted to do something because the song was so special. I took it to Nashville and created an overture on the strings. Just the strings and a bass that I added to Willie. I just think it was brilliant. I think it would have been a hit single if Columbia would have released it.

Even on stage, the first and last bastion of Nelson's art, the real beating pulse of his music down through the years, things had become tame, a bit predictable. Many reviewers had cottoned on to the seemingly lazy, perfunctory concerts. Nashville session supremo Grady Martin had joined on third guitar, but little changed: if you caught Nelson as he wound his way around the country (and there was a good chance you would, he was still on tour for nine months out of every twelve), you either accepted and embraced the very narrow parameters in which he and the band would work or you were going to come away disappointed and a little confused.

The sets were virtually identical night after night and unsurprisingly low on energy. He opened with 'Whiskey River', played a medley of 'Funny How Time Slips Away', 'Crazy', and 'Night Life' which gave each of those classic tunes pretty short shrift, performed mini-suites of songs by Kris Kristofferson, Hank Williams and tracks from *Stardust*, Jody Payne would get a chance to sing, Bobbie would lead an instrumental 'Over Yonder', there would be a handful of gospel songs and then a reprise of 'Whiskey River'. Unvarying highlights from the rest of his classic songbook were crowbarred into the cracks. His vocals travelled between economical and simply offhand and disinterested. There was much to be admired in the instinctive, almost telepathic interplay between the band, but at what point does telepathy simply breed boredom?

He had, in all truth, ceased moving forwards. 'Formulaic and uninspired,' ran a review in the *LA Times*; while *Newsday*'s John Anderson was scathing but perceptive in his review of an 80s New York show at Pier 84. '[He is] a walking contradiction. The self-described redneck hippie was once acclaimed as a songwriter but ignored as a performer; now his biggest hits are pop standards and his own songs go unrecorded. He plays for free for farmers and Native Americans but also does the casino circuit. He's written and performed some passionate songs, but Nelson has lost any passion for singing them. He wears braids and plays golf. He's Frank Sinatra in a Stetson. "How'm I doing?" Nelson asked in a lyric. Don't ask.'

Another reviewer called his band the Past Their Prime Players. In that same way that listeners were becoming grateful if a new record simply contained one or two good – or even original – songs on it, so his concerts were now defined by those rare moments when he diverted his eyes from the script. Things really only came alive when he added a new song like the lithe and energetic 'Still Is Still Moving To Me' – written in 1988 – to the set, or dug up a rarely performed gem like 'I Never Cared For You', but the distance Nelson travelled between such moments during his set stretched out and over the horizon. He seemed, in part, to be playing the songs that he thought people wanted to hear, rather than pushing himself creatively. It was a fatal course of action for any artist.

Bee Spears: We're pretty much locked into what we do, because we've changed it around before and people would always come up and say,

'Well, I'm very disappointed you didn't play "Good Hearted Woman" or "To All The Girls I've Loved Before",' so we just kind of have to cover all the highlights. There was a while when we were playing everything, but that's pretty gruelling. Well, I mean the audience loved it.

Perhaps it's true to say that only when an artist has slowed down creatively is it possible to see them clearly enough to describe them as an icon: Nelson was definitely an icon. He was at that stage in his career where people start handing out awards for simply lasting the distance, rather than for making a current impact: the Grammy Living Legend Award in 1989; the Special Merit Award at the American Music Awards the same year; Lifetime Achievement Awards from the Songwriters Hall of Fame and the National Academy of Popular Music in 1983; the Pioneer Award from the Academy of Country Music in 1991.

But he could still attract controversy. In October 1987, alongside Kris Kristofferson, Joni Mitchell, Jackson Browne and comedian Robin Williams, he scheduled a concert at the Pacific Amphitheatre in Costa Mesa, California, under the banner 'Cowboys For Indians and Justice for Leonard Peltier'. Peltier was a founder of the American Indian Movement and had been convicted in 1977 of murdering two FBI agents at the Pine Ridge Indian Reservation in South Dakota in 1975, although his supporters claimed the initial trial was highly irregular. An appeal to the Supreme Court for a new trial had been refused.

Special Agent Richard T. Bretzing, head of the Los Angeles FBI office, announced in a letter that he was 'utterly revolted' by the concert in support of a man who had killed two of his colleagues. The concert went ahead nonetheless, and most of the people who came were initially unaware of the political connotations and simply came for the music. One of the audience said she particularly liked Nelson's duets with Julio Iglesias. A picket line on the outside of the venue holding placards and a leaflet outlining Peltier's plight handed to the audience on the inside made them aware of both sides of the argument. Nelson, whose politics stemmed from his humanism rather than his polemic, played Hank Williams's 'Hey, Good Lookin' ', which not even the most fervent activist could interpret as a subversive act. Even so, two country music stations dropped his records from their playlists, and the following year police called for a boycott of his concerts in Rhode Island, Boston and West Virginia. 'We don't take kindly to anyone who supports cop killers,' said FBI agent Wayne Sacco, who organised a 400-strong picket line at the shows.

Nelson was forced into action. The concert had placed one of nature's unifiers and emollients in an awkward situation, caught between two of his natural constituencies: the Native Americans and the police. Or, in broader terms, the liberal activist lobby and the conservative caucus that contained many of his old-time country fans. His solution was to propose a joint benefit concert for the American Indian Relief Fund and the

National Police Memorial Fund. He met with the American Federation of Police Officers and issued an apology, something of a rarity: 'I deeply regret that so many police officers and organisations were offended by the Indian concert,' he said. 'In the future I will certainly consider all aspects of any benefit concerts so as not to offend anyone. I have nothing but respect for all lawmen and under no circumstances do I support cop killers.' The old guard won this time.

He also became embroiled in a rather odd, macho row over playing a concert in Belfast, Northern Ireland. For the first three weeks of April 1988 Nelson and the band were on a ten-city tour of Europe, during which he was scheduled to play Belfast until the date was cancelled, he claimed, without his knowledge. There were whispers that he was worried about the latest violence in the long-term sectarian struggle between Catholic and Protestant terrorist groups in the province. Nelson's response was pure cowboy indignation, no doubt fuelled by a recollection of the nights of guns and chicken wire back in the skull orchards of Fort Worth. Bombs? Bring 'em on.

Willie Nelson: I'm not afraid to play anywhere. We're ready for Belfast. It's just another beer joint. It'll be a piece of cake. You can call me a lot of things but a wimp isn't one of them.[6]

He pinned his colours to the mast in 1998, offering his support to Sinn Fein, the then-political wing of the IRA, and as recently as 2005 he entertained Sinn Fein's president Gerry Adams on his bus in Dublin. The extent of the Nelson entourage's knowledge of the complexities of Irish politics can be judged by the fact that one of the band was heard to ask: 'So, is Gerry Adams a terrorist?' He returned from Belfast unscathed and clicked back into the old routine, rolling around his homeland for the rest of 1988. He took a little time off towards the end of the year to prepare for the arrival of his and Annie D'Angelo's first baby. Lukas Autry Nelson was born on Christmas Day in Austin, Nelson's sixth child and his second son. His first, Billy, was now 31.

The new father took it easy over the festive period: hanging out in Austin, watching the basketball at the University of Texas, playing golf. He went to Hawaii for a spell and played a benefit show on Maui, and in March 1989 he began recording the new Highwaymen record, again with Chips Moman producing. It was more of the same, perhaps even a little less successful than the first record. The album was rushed and although their pleasant version of Lee Clayton's excellent 'Silver Stallion' was a minor hit single, there was nothing quite as powerful as 'The Highwayman' this time to really pull it all together. The tired, old-timer cowboy theme was established from the outset: 'I'm going to chase the sky forever with a woman and a stallion and the wind/ And the sun is going to burn into a cinder before we ride this way again', to which the listener might have added slightly irritably, 'Yes, yes, we know.' That four of America's all-time great songwriters were struggling to find decent material was virtually beyond belief. There was a little too much emphasis on message songs and grizzled, heavy-handed philosophising, while Moman was much too liberal with the synthesizer.

Waylon Jennings: It could have used a little more time spent on it. We ran in and out too quick, and we didn't have that one great song. It's hard to find material that goes over with four people, each with strong, let-it-all-hang out opinions.[7]

Highwaymen 2 was released in March 1990 and reached No. 79 on the *Billboard* chart. In many ways its most significant reason for existing was simply providing a compelling excuse for the four titans to play some concerts together. They had played at Nelson's picnic in 1985, but that was a one-off. They had all been busy around the time of the first album and there had been logistical problems in the sense that each musician was devoted to their own touring band – Kristofferson was especially reluctant to abandon his Borderlords – but they finally came to an agreement, with Nelson managing to negotiate the inclusion of Mickey Raphael in the excellent nine-piece group. They kicked off with eleven one-nighters across the country in March and then added more dates in the autumn. It was a mixture of their own greatest hits, played ensemble, during the first half and then some – but not too much – Highwaymen material at the end. Nelson couldn't resist a crack at the expense of Kristofferson's rather limited vocal capabilities.

Fred Foster: Kris said to Willie, when they were about to go on stage on the Highwayman tour: 'I don't think I'm in very good voice tonight,' and Willie said, 'How could you tell?'

It was illuminating to hear Nelson's songs played by a new band, although he was still persisting with what one reviewer described as 'dumping his lyrics at the beginning of each melodic line as if they were giving him a bad taste in his mouth'. There was a heavy feeling of nostalgia in the air, a sense of hard-won survival and tough romanticism. Both Jennings and Cash had undergone bypass surgery in 1988: Jennings had finally quit cocaine, while Cash eulogised the virtues of a fruit protein drink he imbibed religiously each morning. Kristofferson ran and worked out with weights, while Nelson was still sticking to his own healthy regime, now with fifteen-month-old Lukas and Annie D'Angelo in tow on the bus. But they still hung on tight to their mythology.

'Willie's the outlaw coyote,' said Kristofferson. 'Waylon's the riverboat gambler, I'm the revolutionary communist radical and John's the father of our country.'[8] Each had their own bus, and they would travel in convoy down the dark highways after each show, in a silent and separate show of solidarity. All in all, the tour was more successful than the record, although it was a measure of how times had changed that they struggled to sell out the arenas they were playing. There were new country stars: Randy Travis, Clint Black, Dwight Yoakam, Lyle Lovett, k.d. lang, who had moved the genre on, and outlaw had passed into history, embodying a poignant, gruff, defiant nostalgia.

He continued touring with the Family Band after the Highwaymen went their separate ways, meeting tragedy head-on in late March when a car ran into the bus in Nova Scotia, killing the car's driver. Off the road, he was still thinking up new methods of entertainment for his people at Pedernales, planning other business ventures. He had recently paid $1m to Act III Entertainment for the rights to more than 4,000 vintage country music TV shows, featuring Dolly Parton, Portner Wagoner, Marty Robbins *et al*, old Western films and shows like *Bonanza* and *Wagon Train*. He planned to broadcast the material on a new cable channel he was setting up called Cowboy Television Network. As usual he managed to give it a personal spin.

Willie Nelson: Travelling around the country or around the world, it's very difficult to find what I want to see, which is a good Western movie or some good music. That's exactly the reason I got into this.[9]

In fact, he had been approached with the idea by promoter and fellow Texan Mack Long, one of the numerous local characters who had been in business with Nelson over the years, and he had instantly handed over the cash. Long was installed to run the operation from Spicewood. Technological guru, archaeologist, inventor, computer expert and pirate entrepreneur Bob Wishoff was brought in from his home in Jacksonville, Florida to design a twenty-first century television studio for the CTN, but the reality was considerably less slick. News of Nelson's Cowboy Television Network was reported in the press with due fanfare, but the view from the ground was very different. This was another attempt at building a home-cooked cottage industry, planting its roots in the eccentric soil beneath the sprawling network of condos at Pedernales. The practical results of CTN were heroically farcical and came as close to defining the madcap spirit of Nelson and his set-up at Pedernales as anything really could. The venture was beset by legal problems and business wrangles with persons of various shades of unpleasantness, and when it did hit the screens briefly – as the Outlaw Music Channel – it shared its satellite space with a horse-racing channel.

Bob Wishoff: Whenever there wasn't a horse race, we would slip in our midnight to 6 a.m. broadcast. It was guerilla broadcasting at its finest. We had one truck and two VCRs and in between shows we would switch tapes and it would basically go to static! In condo number three one night we decided to go on the air live. We had a satellite truck in the parking lot, one camera, three cheap mikes, no show planned. Willie just broke in and said, 'Hi, I'm Willie Nelson and we're going to do a live broadcast for you.' Suddenly Willie decides to take calls. We had one telephone and you couldn't hear the other end, you could just hear Willie talking. He sang 'Happy Birthday' to at least fifty people. At 2 a.m. in come a load of people like Kimmie Rhodes and David Zettner, just back from a gig at the Broken Spoke. We said, 'Come on in, we're on air!' The living room was packed with people and cameras. We had a hand-painted sign on the fireplace with the logo on it. People would walk past with doobies, bottles of whisky, shouting 'Roll another one!' Willie kept asking for people to call him from France, and you had me on air explaining to him how cable TV works, that they couldn't see it in France. We did that two nights in a row. It was gonzo as all hell. About a week later we got a bill from ASCAP for $5,000 for singing 'Happy Birthday'. It was mad. We had a $1m satellite truck, all this stuff, and we were putting out crap!

Unsurprisingly, CTN didn't last long, and it wasn't until 1998 that Nelson attempted to relaunch the Outlaw Music Channel, this time walking into a dispute with the Kickapoo nation tribe in Kansas, who ran a large casino in the state and invested money in the venture. In its clumsy way it was all part of Nelson's desire to communicate directly with people over a long distance, to bring them directly into his ranch and his country club.

He has since become much more savvy in his use of new technology, but back in 1990 his understanding of it and the nature of the technology on offer was much more limited. It was the time of the Gulf War. He had heard a Kris Kristofferson song coming over shortwave radio from Saudi Arabia and had loved the idea of that universal reach in a time of conflict. He asked Wishoff to set up his own radio show, which he duly did on a Costa Rican shortwave channel. It was called Outlaw For Peace.

Nelson played a few concerts on air and offered free time to anybody in the world who wanted to make a radio show. For two years they made all kinds of programmes, giving air space to everyone from Aborigines to local characters in trailers who would scratch the records on air. They also broadcast Farm Aid 1992, where Wishoff originally ran into problems with licensing until Nelson asked him: 'Uh, well who *is* Farm Aid, Bob?' 'Well, I guess it's you Willie!' Even so, it transpired that Farm Aid had sold the radio rights to Clear Channel, and in the end Outlaw For Peace only managed to broadcast the concert by blagging passes from the band, hanging a broomstick out of the radio booth at the Texas Stadium and then attaching a microphone to it. Wishoff still thinks it was a typically mischievous test from Nelson.

Bob Wishoff: That started a three or four year adventure of Willie playing with my head! Saying, 'Go ahead and broadcast, this year we'll get it right.' Next year in Iowa, I still don't get the broadcast rights. They kept unplugging me and taking passes away from me. Willie will play tricks on you: 'You want to be an outlaw so I'm going to let you be an outlaw. We're not going to help you.' Willie is an underground kind of guy. That's the heart and soul of him.

It was just the normal fun and games, if a little tamer than the old days: provide the context and the opportunity for chaos and then sit back and watch. See how far your entourage will travel for you, see how they cope under their own steam. Wishoff became another generic member of the gang: performing tasks, messing with pirate radio and computers, and doing Nelson's sometimes eccentric bidding.

The conflict in the Gulf began in August 1990 and later that year Nelson sent a copy of his anti-war song 'Jimmy's Road' to Wishoff, asking him to 'do something' with it. Wishoff devised a plan where the public could send him a blank cassette and he would tape them the song, along with a reading of Mark Twain's 'The War Prayer', and send it back to them. He was deluged, to the extent that half the Pedernales community spent their days home-taping in the name of peace. In some ways it was simply business as usual. In other ways, 1990 was a strange and significant time to be part of Nelson's circle. It was manic. Hyper. Super-charged. There was trouble on the wind.

Bob Wishoff: It was weird. It was very insular, and everybody had these stress levels like something was about ready to happen. They were very nervous. And of course it did happen. The tax man came.

BAD

Willie Nelson isn't talking.
  'I won't admit there is anything evil,' he says. 'Or bad.'
And he relights his joint.

12. 1990–1992

For a man who believes passionately in karma and reincarnation, Nelson must have wondered many times what he had done in a previous life to have warranted the desperate chain of events which afflicted him in the early 90s; or perhaps he attributed it to the fact that it was simply payback for some of the sins committed during his current time around.

Probably he blamed the incontestable vagaries of fate and tried not to think too much about it. What he couldn't deny, however, is that the events which battered his life had been signalling their arrival for some time, building their force and energy from actions he had taken – or often had failed to take – many years ago. When the consequences finally cornered him they tested his belief in positive thinking to its very core and attacked the heart of everything he truly believed in: music, family, freedom, the ability to keep moving.

On Friday, 9 November 1990, the cloud that had been hanging over him and his family for over five years finally burst, unleashing a torrential storm. The Internal Revenue Service seized properties in five states to satisfy a $6.5m tax debt that he owed, which through a series of penalties had risen to $16.7m. It was a momentous day, still talked about darkly by those who witnessed it at Pedernales Country Club: the lines of black cars slipping ominously onto the property; helicopters hovering overhead;

agents with pistols and men and women in suits clutching clipboards, demanding to know where all the real riches were being hidden amongst the everyday detritus of lives lived without fuss.

Larry Trader: I'll never forget that day. They came storming in. There were rumours to that effect, but Willie's sort of headstrong and the worst thing you can try to do is intimidate him. We had a feeling but we never knew it would happen. Then that Friday they came in and put chains and locks everywhere.

As Trader suggests, nobody could say they hadn't been warned. Nelson's complicated financial mess had two central causes: the reign of negligence overseen by Neil Reshen in the mid-70s; and an even more calamitous tax shelter scheme Nelson entered into on the advice of the accountancy giant Price-Waterhouse in 1980. The reason he was unable to deal with the financial fallout from these events was more straightforward: his tremendous generosity over the years and continuing vast expenditure, combined with a *laissez-faire* attitude to responsible finance in the face of declining record sales and concert profits. In a nutshell, he was close to broke.

It was a conspiracy of inevitability he knew was on the horizon and yet refused to acknowledge. The Nelson empire – from Pedernales to the *Honeysuckle Rose* – ran on a system of benign neglect. Nothing was confronted, everything delayed. No one wanted to be the harbinger of negative news, even if the consequences of denial were dire. He was surrounded by people in whose best interests it was to avoid presenting him with a clear view of reality, and he certainly wasn't inclined to go looking for it himself. The mantra of positivity and 'living in the moment' was all very well, but it could not be applied successfully to everything in life, especially money, but he simply didn't see the world in that way. While he ploughed cash into doomed white elephants like the Outlaw Music Channel, there were no trust funds or protected investments for his children; no real intelligent thought put into the way his money could be used for his long-term security. That's not to say that people didn't try, but that kind of talk bored him and went against the grain. It had always been that way. As Eddie Wilson said: 'Cover your own ass and then pass the rest around.' Except he had spread it around so much and so often that he had left himself exposed.

Nelson had been presented with countless opportunities to face up to his tax issues over the years, yet nothing satisfactory had been done until it was much too late. That his problems stretched back as far as the late 60s was hardly surprising. He had been fingered for non-payment of taxes in 1967, 1968 and 1969, and into the 70s he was still being hit with penalties, but the sums involved were relatively small, reflecting the days when his salary was collected nightly in cash with a gun for back-up. The real problems arose when Nelson started earning decent money.

In November 1978 the IRS filed a $71,991.75 lien against him and Connie, effectively claiming first right to their property in Colorado in lieu of unpaid taxes in the last quarter of 1977 and the second quarter of 1978. Soon, it transpired the problem was far more extensive. The period particularly under dispute was 1975 to 1978. It was later discovered that all Nelson's financial records for those years had been destroyed, and the IRS were especially concerned about discrepancies between the huge attendances at the Fourth of July picnics in 1975 and 1976 and the relatively small profits declared to the taxman during this time. If they had known the madness that swirled around these events they would have had a better understanding of how Nelson's operation worked and of how difficult it was to get an accurate handle on his incomings and especially his outgoings, but that was not their problem. They just wanted more money.

When Neil Reshen left Nelson's pay in 1978 their dispute centred on the tax issue. Reshen has consistently denied that it was his job to pay Nelson's taxes. His employer disagreed and blamed him for the mess he was in. By 1985, the mistakes and negligence of the 70s had left Nelson with an IRS Notice of Deficiency totalling $2.2m: this related to the years between 1975 and 1978 and comprised a debt on undeclared income to the tune of $1.4m plus penalties of $730,597. The figure was contested in the US tax court in Washington but Nelson's legal team lost.

This was all worrying enough, but there was another, even more concerning tax issue gathering pace at the same time. In 1979 Nelson and Mark Rothbaum – in an attempt at taking greater care of business after Reshen's departure – met with representatives of the accountancy giant Price-Waterhouse. The firm urged Nelson to defer paying his taxes by investing in First Western Government Securities. Nelson invested $30,000 in 1980 and $165,000 the following year. Later, Price-Waterhouse recommended that Nelson move his money into cattle and cattle feed. These were perfectly legitimate tax deferment schemes: buy cattle and feed, deduct the cost of the feed as a business expense and then sell the cattle, making enough money to both pay your taxes and make a profit. That was the idea. In reality, it was poor advice and cost Nelson over $1m. It also meant that the money he had invested to pay his tax bills simply wasn't there.

Connie Nelson: We were in Lake Tahoe when the guy from Price-Waterhouse brought the tax deal to Willie. It was to put some money in cattle feeding down in Texas, and the money made from that would go not only to pay your taxes, but you would make money on it too. This guy said there was no way it could fail. Of course it did fail and all the money that was put into it that would normally have gone to taxes was all gone. It made it look like Willie just didn't pay his taxes. It was Price-Waterhouse, so how could you not agree! If this guy said it was a good idea, well, it's got to be a good idea.

The upshot was that in 1988 Nelson and his now-estranged wife were slapped with a Notice of Deficiency for the years 1980, 1981 and 1982, the period where the Price-Waterhouse scheme was running – and failing. This time it was really serious: he owed nearly $5m, not including interest and penalties, which were escalating daily. By the spring of 1990 the long, drawn-out process was nearing its endgame: for the combined follies of financial mismanagement and bad investments in the years between 1975 and 1982, he and Connie – it was always a shared tax bill – owed an astonishing $32 million to the taxman, for the official citations of negligence; failure to file a tax return; and failure to pay taxes. Nelson never argued over the fact that he owed money on back taxes, but he balked at the astronomical sum.

Willie Nelson: I'm not trying to skip out. The only argument I have with them is the penalties and interest, which at this point are growing at like $5,000 a day. I would like to negotiate that a little bit. But other than that I admit I owe them the money. I guess I could file for bankruptcy and eliminate the debt but that's way down on the list of things I want to do. Since 1983 I've paid them $8m in taxes, so it's not as though I'm a tax dodger.[1]

He worked hard to find a compromise: he employed prominent New York attorney Jay Goldberg to fight his corner. Goldberg negotiated with the IRS and on 6 June 1990 managed to reduce the sum owed to $6.5m, plus a further $9m in penalties and interest to be held over. A charge of civil fraud was not pursued. Effectively, Nelson had three months from that point to make a substantial contribution towards paying the $6m bill – a half or even a third of that sum would have sufficed initially – and he would have blocked any further immediate action and bought himself some time.

Finding $2m in ninety days shouldn't really have been a big ask. Looking in from the outside Nelson was a superstar, continually raking in the money from his tours, still pulling in royalties from his many records. However, the reality of his situation was somewhat different. His touring income had shrunk from $10m in 1986 to $3.3m in 1990. His record sales had plummeted, a victim of the changing times, lack of quality control and general over-exposure; by 1990, his annual royalties hovered around the $400,000 mark. It sounded like a lot of money but it was not, in all honesty, anywhere near enough to support his lifestyle and his prevailing circumstances.

Lana Nelson: He had more expenses going out than he had coming in. We've been living hand-to-mouth for the last couple of years. He didn't have 6 million. He didn't have 1 million. He probably didn't have 30,000.[2]

He was going through a divorce; he was still supporting all of his kids, not to mention his partner Annie D'Angelo, Lukas and his seventh and final child Jacob Micah, born on 25 April 1990. He owed Columbia around $3m in advances that hadn't been recouped, so he was making no money from his record sales. Then, of course, and most significantly, there was the huge, rolling, money-swallowing machinery of his extended family and the system that kept them all on the road and in jobs and homes. On top of that, the money he handed out to hangers-on, strangers and friends was frequently unaccounted for. Charity is normally tax deductible, but not when it is given freely at every turn. He did not, after all, ask for receipts. The bill for all those hand-outs was bound to arrive someday, and now he was paying the tab.

Throughout the second half of 1990 the Nelson organisation scrambled around in pursuit of funds. In July he put the ranch at Evergreen, Colorado up for sale for $3m, but it failed to sell. He could have sold his land and his houses in Austin and elsewhere to raise the cash but he was unwilling to do so, not least because it would mean uprooting all the people who lived there and who depended on him. He could also have declared himself bankrupt, but that didn't strike him as a particularly attractive option either.

He did agree to sell Willie Nelson Music, his publishing company, for $2.27m in August, finding himself back in the position of having to offload his songs to get by: the sums and stakes were much higher than they had been back in the late 50s, but the principle was the same. As a further indignity, none of the money from the sale went to the cause. Instead, it was earmarked to cover outstanding bank loans while Paul English, as 20 per cent shareholder, received $360,000. Some suggested English should have given up his share, but even if he had offered the cash to Nelson it would not have been accepted. He spurned charity, rejecting the idea of turning the Fourth of July picnic into a fundraiser.

Central to his reluctance to pay the bill right away or make any drastic, life-altering moves was the belief that – although he undoubtedly owed the IRS substantial amounts of money – none of this was really his fault. To that effect, in August he launched a $45m lawsuit against Price-Waterhouse, claiming that the firm did not investigate his investments despite him paying $1m to them in fees, and furthermore that the tax shelter had been recommended and suggested to him by Price-Waterhouse, which contravened acceptable practice. The argument would rumble through the courts for the next four years.

In the meantime, the IRS deadline of 6 September came and went without any significant payment being made, with the result that $16.7m in liens was placed on his personal property. From that point on it was only a matter of time before the IRS finally lost patience and came calling for their money. As well as the estate at Pedernales – the golf club, the recording studio, the condos where his friends lived, his Western town over the road and his fishing camp – his unsold property in Colorado was seized on 9 November, alongside his mother's old home in Yakima, Washington and property in Hawaii and Alabama. In San Diego Connie, who on paper was liable for half the unpaid tax, had been unable to buy a house for years because of the debt hanging over her: she rented until the early 90s. The band were also affected, as much of their equipment was stored in the country club. Now it was behind padlocked doors.

Nelson wasn't in Texas when the IRS came. He was in his manager's house in Hawaii. He had already ensured 'Trigger' was taken care of, which was his main concern. The guitar had come to define his entire career: battered, eccentric; neither one thing nor the other; traditional yet unconventional. It was a talisman, a tool and a symbol of where he had come from. Without it, he claimed he would give up. With it, he could do anything. Everything else was up for grabs: gold discs, photographs, personal effects, bandanas, shorts, golf clubs, all his master tapes, light fittings, even wallpaper. It was all unceremoniously hauled away and itemised, ready for auction. The IRS didn't spot the cannabis plants growing behind some of the condos, but that was about all they missed.

Johnny Bush: The IRS came down and took everything that wasn't nailed to the floor. I mean *everything* in that studio: the glass out of the control booths. Everything. If his guitar hadn't been on that bus and that bus hadn't have been on a lease, they'd have got that too. They took it all. He had his clothes and his guitar and that's about all he had.

There were desperate attempts made to rescue things. David Zettner recalls receiving a call from Lana Nelson in the afternoon telling him to drive up to the ranch in his car, come straight around the back and not to speak to anyone. She loaded his boot up with tapes and he drove away. The war tales have inevitably become mythologised over the years – everybody has a story from the front line of the Day The IRS Came – but unquestionably possessions were spirited away under cover of darkness. People would gather at the house in the middle of the night and pass furniture over the fence, to be driven away from under the eyes of the government agents. But these were small victories.

Suddenly everyone was out of work: the studio was closed, the golf club shut, the film set out of bounds. Even if they had been open there was no money to pay them. Bob Wishoff recalls later having to pool their money to buy petrol for the bus. The haven had finally been breached. The party was over. There were a lot of very worried people pacing around. In many ways, in the long run the IRS bust sorted out the wheat from the chaff and cleared out some of the human detritus that had helped Nelson get into this mess in the first place.

Tim O'Connor: I'm pretty frustrated by the outer layers of bark and moss that have grown around Willie's tree. And I think it's burdened the tree. As far as I'm concerned, this is a great shakedown. Everybody should give the man room to breathe for once.[3]

In Hawaii, Nelson was lying low, trying to keep his cool and planning what to do next, although it was a little late to now start turning his full attention to the matter. He cancelled a scheduled New Year's Eve appearance and cracked a few classic Willie-isms to the press along the lines of how funny it all was and that everyone should send 25 cents to the IRS and be sure to ask for a receipt. He had been aware that this was coming and so wasn't panicking or feeling sorry for himself, but he and his advisors were peddling furiously nonetheless.

He began rallying his friends: Darrell Royal, the farmers, lawyers, used-car salesmen and politicians such as Ann Richards who had formed the core of his powerful and protective circle in Texas for two decades. Neil Young advised him to head for the hills. There had been huge swathes of press coverage – some of it negative, most of it wry and broadly affectionate – but in his home state there was an immediate outpouring of goodwill.

Dave Crowe, a used-car salesman from Waco, launched WillieAid, while the Broken Spoke put an enormous pickle jar on the bar saying 'Where There's A Willie There's A Way' and asked their regulars to shove a few dollars in. On 2 December they organised a dance show and auction. Owner James White sent the proceeds straight to Hawaii, along with all the other correspondence he was receiving in support of the star. Nelson admitted to being overwhelmed by the response, if a little embarrassed by the money.

James White: I was getting donations from all over the country, from prisons, the troops in the Gulf. Real heartwarming letters. They wanted to help him. We had a fundraiser for him and sent him $10,000 and he said, 'I want to thank you from the bottom of my heart. I'll be home after Christmas and come up and eat a chicken fried steak, drink a cold beer and do a little pickin'.' He told me: 'They can't take the smile off my face and they didn't take 'Trigger' so we'll be OK. We'll be all right.' I never heard him complain much about it.

Nelson spent Christmas in California with Annie's parents and then returned to Austin – via Abbott and Hillsboro – in the early New Year. He stayed with friends. He was making a TV film, *Another Pair Of Aces*, with Kris Kristofferson, and as promised the two came in for a jam session at the Broken Spoke, acting as though they hadn't a care in the world.

Later in the month the auctions began. On 23 January his personal effects went under the hammer: everything from garbage cans, posters, personal photographs and golf carts to gold records and furniture were on the block. The sale raised around $68,000, and already there was evidence of the support network closing in. Jeanne Oakley, of the Willie Nelson and Friends Showcase Museum in Nashville, bought many items for several thousands of dollars. They would all find their way back to Nelson.

There was a huge amount of loyalty in the area: two days later, Pedernales Country Club – including the golf course and recording studio – and the Western town went up for sale and failed to attract a single bid. Aside from anything else, Nelson was good for business: his estate attracted musicians and film stars and people from all walks of life to the area, and the local economy benefited. There is no evidence that there was any intimidation, but word had got around that this was no ordinary sale, while Nelson's friends ensured that nothing would go smoothly.

Bob Wishoff: We would purposely disrupt the auctions, making bids we had no intention of fulfilling and things like that!

When the country club was re-auctioned in March, Darrell Royal bought it for $117,150 and promptly announced, 'I'm going to sell it back to Willie any time he wants it. And he wants it bad.' However, because it was bought at less than the reserve price, the property was reclaimed by the IRS and auctioned a third time in May. This time it was bought by a company outside of the inner circle but another Nelson ally, his nephew Freddy Fletcher, subsequently bought it back privately. It was Nelson's whenever he needed it, and as early as the summer of 1992, he was leasing Pedernales and using the studio again.

And so it went on. On 29 January, his old ranch at Fitzhugh Road, now Lana's home, was sold for $203,840. It was bought by an Arkansan lawyer, John Arens, who represented the American Agriculture Movement, who worked closely with Farm Aid. Arens went straight to Nelson with the news. 'I really don't know what to say,' Nelson said at the time. 'It's just another indication of how important friends are.'

Mickey Raphael: We just felt very defensive of him. It was interesting to see the people who were there buying the stuff back. The ones who bought for a nickel on the dollar and gave it to Willie, or the ones who took it like scavengers. It was kind of interesting to see.

Of course, it had been planned well in advance. 'I have friends who have offered to buy property for me and save it until I can afford to get it back from them,' Nelson said in 1991. 'I was assured of all that months ago.'[4] Local musicians would buy up his amps and guitars and put them in storage, ready for him to collect any time he wanted. It was an astonishing vindication of the values of loyalty and friendship which he held so dear, and a fitting response from the community he had treated so well over the years. He was not, however, entirely immune to all the pain that events were causing. He was angry at the people who had got him into this mess and dismayed at where it had all lead. He was angry at himself as well, for following such dubious advice when all his instincts – his most trusted radar – had told him not to. It wasn't easy to watch his life being laid out on a table and sold to the highest bidder.

Connie Nelson: Willie was furious to some extent, but I think it hurt him too. The fact that the IRS came in and auctioned off his stuff, you know, that physically hurt him. Stuff that he'd saved for years, things that people had given him, they just took it all. It hurt more than it made him mad. In a way it's just *stuff*, but it still hurts. Things that people have given you over the years that you care about, sentimental stuff, that's the part that hurts. Whereas a car is just a car.

By April the dust was starting to settle and he cut a deal with the IRS. They had by now realised that Nelson was not living a decadent lifestyle and that there was no way they were going to recoup $16.7m from his possessions. They thought he might as well start earning some money. The arrangement meant he could continue to tour and keep some of the income for his own living expenses, but the IRS would require a full, month-by-month account of how all earnings were being spent. It effectively meant that the free-for-all of the old days was over – there was no room for extravagant gestures or a coterie of hangers-on. However, there *was* still room for a little bending of the rules, a bit of the old outlaw spirit. Soon after the IRS had struck Nelson and the band played the Night Life club in Houston, which he part-owned.

David Zettner: [They] told everybody in the band: 'Make sure if anybody asks, tell them you're not being paid. This is just for fun.' So Poodie got all the money and put it in a paper bag for Willie and kept it on him, and three days later he saw Willie on the golf course and just threw it in the back of his [golf] cart: $100,000. He just 'found' it there. In other words, it had been filtered so nobody could say, 'Oh, Willie owes on this.' Everybody was helping him out. It was incredible.

His other master plan, which he had negotiated with the IRS, was to release an album to help pay off his debt. Rather like Marvin Gaye's *There, My Dear*, which had formed part of the divorce settlement to his wife, *Who'll Buy My Memories?: The IRS Tapes* was designed to help wipe the slate clean by allowing him to make money doing what he did best.

He had negotiated access to the more than 300 cardboard boxes of master tapes that the IRS had seized from his studio, and from them he pieced together a 25-song album consisting primarily of classic old songs played on just an acoustic guitar, recorded at intervals through the years. The plan was to sell the album for $19.95 using television adverts and an 1-800 number – it wouldn't initially be available in the shops. Nelson's cut of the action was $6 per album. 'Three million copies would give me $18m and I'd have a million to get drunk with,' he said, and he wasn't quite joking.

Willie Nelson: I think if we give it enough publicity there's no limit to what we could sell. Within four or five months, the whole debt could be wiped out. We'd take a negative thing and turn it into a positive thing for everybody.[5]

The IRS Tapes was released on 3 June and marked the apex of the dreamy philosophy that governed Nelson's life: namely that he could – as Johnny Bush puts it – 'turn horseshit into lemonade'. It was a hopelessly optimistic venture from the off, but he nonetheless seriously seemed to think it would bail him out, and nobody within his entourage appeared to contradict him with a straight dose of common sense. He explained how *Stardust* had gone multi-platinum and yet initially nobody had rated it at all, but these were very different times and he had as much chance of selling three million albums as he had of visiting the moon. In any case, only $3 from his $6 cut was going towards his IRS debt, which meant he would in reality have to sell six million records to break even. In the event *The IRS Tapes* sold around 200,000 copies, and was not blessed with good luck. Nelson appeared on ABC's *Prime Time* TV show with the wrong phone number emblazoned on his shirt; then the Television Group, the company selling the album through telephone orders, went bankrupt. Sales had effectively ground to a halt by January 1992.

The irony of it all was that it was his best album in a long time, a wonderfully raw and heartfelt reading of some of his most beautiful and downbeat songs from the early and middle parts of his career. Alongside solo versions of 'The Sound In Your Mind' and 'Permanently Lonely' that knocked spots off the originals, there was a lovely song called 'If You Could Only See' which had never been released. Many wondered why these recordings had languished in the vaults for so long when he had lately been churning out mediocre material year in and year out. It is one aspect of Nelson's work that is hard to understand, but in reality it was simply an extension of his live-in-the-moment philosophy. He created in the moment as well, and when the moment had passed he didn't linger. It was often down to mere circumstance and fate what actually got released into the public domain. Later, *The IRS Tapes* was released with a companion album, *The Hungry Years*, recorded in Bogalusa, Louisiana in 1976. It was an equally strong set, and there are hundreds of other recordings still lying around in the Nelson vaults. He has had instant access to his own studio for the past 25 years and is constantly cutting material, either alone or with his visitors, and then filing it away. He recently admitted that he was planning to spend some time finding out exactly what was in there.

Merle Haggard: He's got about forty songs down there at his place that we've done together that nobody's ever heard. We just came out of his golf course down there one day and we just kind of fell in to an unplanned situation. There's some really neat stuff. We did [Jim Reeves's] 'Am I Losing You?', we did a Bob Dylan tune, 'Don't Think Twice, It's All Right'.

In February 1992 Nelson negotiated a final compromise with the IRS. He owed them a total of $9.6m in unpaid taxes, interest and penalties, of which $3.6m had already been paid – raised through his touring, the album, the auctions and the sale of his properties in Colorado and Yakima. He now had to pay a further $2.4m within three years (with $1m being paid within ninety days) and a final $3m within five years. In the meantime the IRS would receive 40 per cent of *The IRS Tapes* sales and a significant slice of any monies received in the lawsuit against Price-Waterhouse, which was still rumbling through the courts. In the end, it was this lawsuit that bailed him out.

All along, Nelson had alleged that the firm's management and account-ants had urged him to defer paying his taxes and had recommended the investment into First Western Government Securities, despite the fact that the company were aware that the scheme was flawed and fraudulent and attracting interest from the IRS. Nelson also alleged that he was misadvised over the cattle feed investments. In January 1994 Price-Waterhouse filed a summary judgment claiming, 'The evidence in this case demonstrates without question that Price-Waterhouse acted in good faith throughout its relationship with plaintiffs. Price-Waterhouse cannot be liable for fraud or racketeering simply because plaintiffs did not obtain the tax benefits they desired.' Nelson's lawyers filed a detailed, 51-page opposition in April, and in August the dispute finally settled in their favour. The exact terms of the agreement remain confidential, but in essence Price-Waterhouse settled his outstanding tax bill with the IRS. He was even.

Connie Nelson: As it turned out, it was illegal for the guy at Price-Waterhouse to bring the deal to Willie. If somebody else had said something to Willie about it and then Willie had gone to Price-Waterhouse and they had said, 'Sure, go ahead,' it wouldn't have been illegal, but this guy worked for them and brought it to Willie and that was illegal. Someone that worked in Price-Waterhouse had proof that this guy had done this eight or ten other times. She snuck the paperwork out and got it to Willie's attorneys, so they had proof. That's when Price-Waterhouse settled and everything got paid. They paid everything. The only deal was we couldn't go to the press and say what happened.

Nelson could now buy back his country club and studio at Pedernales and his ranch at Fitzhugh Road from his friends. He had pulled it off. Of course, there were some things that had been lost forever in the fire sale, but in the main it was a remarkable feat of preservation. Larry Trader was still manning the golf club; Bob Wishoff was still hatching gonzo schemes in the condos; David Zettner was living up in a cabin on the ranch, producing bands and tending his artwork; many of the road crew were still living in the grounds of the country club; Bobbie was still on the sixth fairway; Lana was back at Fitzhugh Road; the bus was still on the ranch, awaiting use. If you looked around it was hard to tell that the IRS had ever been there at all, but nobody would ever forget it.

He had endured a bruising and potentially humiliating process with humour and grace, had surfed the media onslaught and the frequent limp jokes and cracks about him being a 'tax dodger' with little complaint. It had never really been a story of greed, but instead a meandering narrative featuring many characters, encompassing loyalty, naivety, abused trust, recklessness, black humour, hopeless optimism and canny tactical moves. Above all it was a tale of determination, the determination that nobody could ever force him to change the way he lived. And against all the odds, he had won.

Just as he was dusting himself down from the worst of his early skirmishes with the IRS, another long-running source of heartache finally played out to its conclusion, this time with truly tragic consequences. His son Billy committed suicide on Christmas Day 1991 at his home in the suburbs of Nashville, hanging himself with a cord. He was aged only 33.

Billy had always been a difficult man. He had problems, many of which unquestionably related to the haphazard manner in which he was raised. Martha had died in 1989, but she had only ever really been a mother in name. Shirley had disappeared from view at a vulnerable age and Connie was never embraced as a surrogate. Billy had never settled comfortably into either his skin or his life. His father had never been around enough, although Nelson involved him in his business, as he did all his children: Billy had a role in the 'Pancho And Lefty' video in 1983, doubling for Merle Haggard, and they also recorded an album of gospel songs together the same year, finally released posthumously in 1994 as *Peace In The Valley*.

But Billy was not a satisfied soul. His drinking had long been a problem. Observers at Pedernales recall the day he drove his car through the window of the local store in Briarcliff to get some alcohol – Nelson had to go down and smooth things over – and in May 1990 he was found guilty of drink driving in Nashville and sentenced to 20 days in jail, a

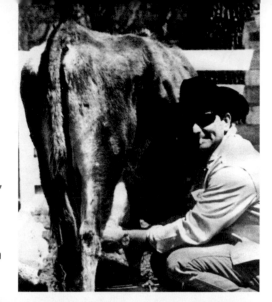

Right The gentleman farmer: milking a cow – and smoking a cigarette – at Ridgetop in the mid-60s

Below At the inaugural Farm Aid in 1985, with Neil Young and John Mellencamp (© Bettmann/Corbis)

Bottom Performing at Farm Aid: the organisation has raised over $25 million in twenty years (© Timothy D Easley/AP/Empics)

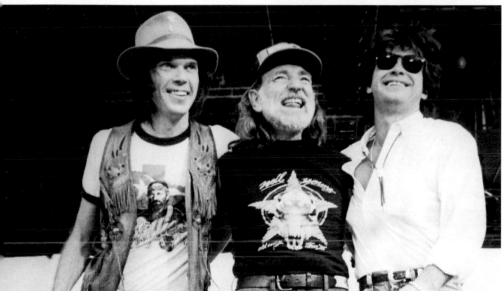

Above Drummer Paul English and Nelson's eldest daughter Lana, relaxing in 2005
(Courtesy of Mickey Raphael)

Below left Mickey Raphael, harmonica player in the Family Band
(Courtesy of Mickey Raphael)
Below right Johnny Bush: friend and collaborator for over fifty years

Above left Nelson surveys the scene at his Texas ranch following the IRS bust in November 1990 (© Time Life Pictures/Getty Images)
Above right Under lock and key: the IRS come calling at Pedernales
(© Time Life Pictures/Getty Images)

Below A promotional flyer for *The IRS Tapes* in 1991

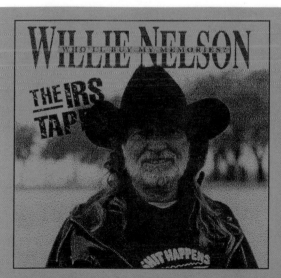

Above left On the golf course with Annie and Lukas in the late 80s
(© Time Life Pictures/Getty Images)
Above right Mr and Mrs Nelson step out at the Grammys in 2000
(© Mark J Terrill/AP/Empics)

Below On stage with Lukas (© Brian Kersey/AP/Empics)

Top Two of the great
voices of America: Nelson
toured with Bob Dylan in
2004 and 2005 (© Robert
Galbraith/Reuters/Corbis)

Above With his friend
and co-conspirator Keith
Richards (© Robert
Galbraith/Reuters/Corbis)

Right Relaxing with Julio
Iglesias and Ray Charles in
the 80s (© Bob Wishoff)

Above Willie Nelson Drive is the main thoroughfare through the Wild West town at Nelson's Texas ranch
(© Graeme Thomson)

Left The Opry House in the western town
(© Graeme Thomson)

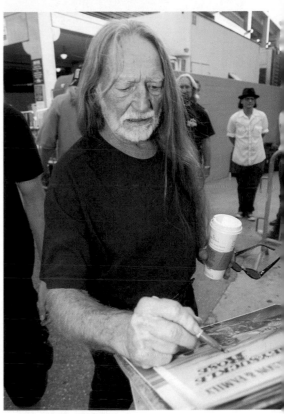

Above left With Emmylou Harris and Daniel Lanois during the making of *Teatro* in 1998 (© Chris Cuffaro)

Above right Nelson still signs numerous autographs after every show (© Getty Images)

Right Loading up with BioDiesel, his new environmentally friendly passion (© Paul Natkin/AP/Empics)

Left Trigger: the most famous guitar in the world
(© Lynn Goldsmith/Corbis)

Below Still on the road: Farm Aid 2005
(© Getty Images)

$1,000 fine, a 1-year ban and 160-hours community service. At that point Connie attempted an intervention.

Connie Nelson: I had Billy talk to this doctor up in Palm Beach who was a drug rehab doctor, and helped Thomas 'Hollywood' Henderson get sober. Billy came with me to meet with him, and he talked with him and just had suggestions. I told Billy he could come and stay with me – he wouldn't do it – but the main thing was Billy came to see this guy with me. I did that and it didn't work. I always feel like I wish I'd have just handcuffed myself to him. I mean, I tried a lot of things and Willie tried. Willie did as much as he could, but I feel like he still feels guilt. I still feel guilt, so I know he does.

Billy killed himself on Christmas Day, which also happened to be Lukas's third birthday. Some of Nelson's friends believe that his marriage to Annie three months earlier and the arrival of two more sons into the family had a detrimental effect on Billy, who was for so long the sole male heir. Others mutter about Nelson's neglectful parenting skills and lack of attentiveness to his children. But who in life can accurately identify the source or measure the quantity of every little hurt? What can be said is that the real problem with Nelson's stoned, egalitarian principles, his insistence on treating all people with equal respect and courtesy, was that it neglected the fact that the individuals within his family circle deserved to be regarded as special – to be allowed to feel more important than others.

It's a little ironic that his fans, the people who view Nelson from afar, feel that they know him while those with an up-close view have constantly battled to attract his attention and his interest. His wives suffered because of that, but his children were the worst affected. When he wrote 'It's Not Supposed To Be That Way' for his daughter Susie in 1973, he later confessed that 'it occurred to me that it was easier to sing it than say it'.[6] It's a telling remark. Sometimes they needed to hear him say it. He certainly shouldn't be held responsible for all their brushes with misfortune, all the abusive marriages, divorces, alcohol and drug abuse, unhappiness and suicide, but his absences and laid-back devotion to fate certainly couldn't have helped. He was simply not a dedicated father.

Johnny Bush: He doesn't like it, but he doesn't deny it. Willie's the same to everybody. When the crowds gathered around the bus when it pulls up, I've seen one of his children in particular hanging out in the crowd waiting for Willie to come out, when someone should have said, 'Come on in.' I don't think he means to be that way, but there's so many, many people. Some people blame him for Billy's suicide, but I don't. Billy just had some problems and I know that grieved Willie a lot, it hurt him terribly, but I don't believe it was because he was pushing Billy out.

All his family had grown up with the knowledge that they had to play second fiddle to his pursuit of a life that worked for him. Nelson was aware that it hurt but he wasn't able to change his lifestyle to make it better. He loved them all and he had always loved knowing that he had a home and a family waiting, just as long as he didn't have to actually be there too often. 'I refuse,' he later said, 'to stay where I'm not happy.'[7] He provided materially for his children, but even when he was off the road during their childhoods he was rarely around to provide solid emotional support.

Willie Nelson: I always feel I need a home base. There's something in me that makes me want to know that wherever I am, and whatever I'm doing, I can always go home to someone, someplace. Truthfully, it's not so much that I enjoy being there.[8]

Nelson had visited Billy in Nashville not long before he died. According to one newspaper report his son had asked for some money which Nelson, embroiled in his tax problems, was unable to give him. He was buried back in his home state of Texas and one of the pall bearers was Paul English, one of the few people around Nelson who understood what he was experiencing, having lost his own wife to suicide in 1973. English had since re-married but had never forgotten the impact of Carlene's death. He tried to speak honestly.

Paul English: I told him, 'I know what you're going through. I can't say anything, no one else can say anything that will help. I know how it feels.' It's a very big catastrophe. There's no closure. It's still going on. My wife has been dead since 3 January 1973 and I think about her a lot.

Nelson retreated, tried to make sense of it all. His belief in reincarnation helped, as did his espousal of something he called 'instant reincarnation', which forwarded the idea that body and soul were in constant regeneration; that effectively you were a different person now than you had been one minute or even one second earlier. He almost never talks about Billy, but on one rare occasion he commented: 'Well, you have all these guilts and regrets, but you can run yourself crazy. You're not the same person now you were then, so why take responsibility for something you didn't do?'[9] It sounded suspiciously like an excuse, and one he didn't even swallow himself.

Combined with the stress of the IRS inquiry, it is a wonder that the events didn't kill him or send him into a self-destructive tailspin. Even Bobbie, his closest and most constant support, feared for him. Not even his best friends know how he dealt with it; he guarded his emotions and his responses well. Perhaps what Kris Kristofferson once said is true:

'Willie wears the world as a loose garment.' When in doubt, he did what he always did: he kept working.

He toured the States with the Highwaymen in February, and joined them in Europe for the first time in April. In between he focused on the Farm Aid concert that had been organised at the Texas Stadium in Irving on 14 March. He brushed aside any comparisons between the fate of the farmers and his own financial situation.

Willie Nelson: I have the ability to make a living. I still have my talents and a band and a promoter and a beer joint somewhere to play my music in. These guys have lost their farms and are now part of the unemployed. They need help more than me.[10]

But he did have to make some difficult choices in recognition of his financial plight. He signed a deal with the fast food chain Taco Bell, singing a somewhat parodic song on a television commercial; the chain also sold discounted cassettes of his albums with certain purchases. Jose Cuervo Tequila signed up for a two-year sponsorship of his tours, while copies of his forthcoming album would come with a mail offer for a free pair of Willie Nelson signature shot glasses.

Later he would endorse almost anything: 'Willie jeans', the Gap, Old Whiskey River Bourbon, adverts with Waylon Jennings for Pizza Hut's stuffed crust pizza and, finally, the inevitable commercial for an account-ancy firm. It wasn't just the money that was important in these matters, though it was obviously welcome. The deals were initially designed to illustrate publicly that Nelson was still in business – that he wasn't destitute or hiding away, but was out there doing what he had always done and was, in Mark Rothbaum's phrase, 'corporately attractive'.

Nonetheless, it opened him up to a certain amount of criticism and ridicule. One of fellow Texan Bill Hicks's comic routines at the time centred on his detestation of musicians who advertise products. 'You do a commercial, you're off the artistic roll call for ever, and that goes for everyone . . . except Willie Nelson. Twenty-four million dollar tax bill, Willie was a little looser than the rest of us. I just avert my eyes when he sings about tacos, you know what I mean? Is he finished yet? No? Oh, poor Willie. Poor fucking Willie. Oh God, let's pass the hat. Get him off the Taco Bell commercial! We gotta save Willie!' Nelson was having none of it.

Willie Nelson: Hey, don't even start on me about selling out. I've heard it all before and my dues are paid – in full.[11]

There was a more serious impact on his routine. In late 1991, he signed a contract to perform throughout the spring and summer of the following year in Branson, Missouri, a pretty resort in the Ozark mountains. The deal had the merits of a steadier, guaranteed pay cheque which was easier for the IRS to keep tabs on, as well as fewer travel and booking costs. Branson had started with one venue in 1983 and had ballooned. Now, with two dozen theatres almost exclusively devoted to country music acts, it had become a gold mine.

It was a down-home theme park, a place where acts came when they were sick of the road: they would buy a theatre, plaster their own name on it, and come and play extended residencies for long periods throughout the year then go away and count their money. Big touring acts such as Kenny Rogers, Loretta Lynn and Glen Campbell would pop in, but some of the regular acts were of a lower calibre: Shoji Tabuchi, for example, the Japanese violinist who incorporated a little country fiddling into his schmaltzy, Vegas-style routine.

How the idea of dropping anchor in such a place was conceived and agreed upon by Nelson is hard to fathom; perhaps his hands were tied. Branson – more specifically the Ozark Theater – was to be his home and primary work place for the next six months, during which he was supposed to play 144 shows with Merle Haggard also on the bill. 'It will be nice to sit in one spot for a while,' he said beforehand, presumably through clenched teeth and with his fingers crossed behind his back.[12]

Predictably, it soon became a trial. Branson was only a small town, with a population of 4,000, and it was utterly consumed by its new industry. An estimated four million people passed through each year, and acts were expected to be accessible to the public. Although Nelson was always happy to sign as many autographs as he could directly after a show, he did not relish living in a goldfish bowl.

Paul English: Branson was very, very hard. It was like doing time. Willie and I stayed in a hotel that was on the same parking lot as the theatre. When you got off from work there was a big crowd there – you [couldn't] go to a restaurant or something like that. We had to buy food and keep it in the little mini-suite in the hotel. We had a microwave and a very small refrigerator, and we had to keep cereal and everything and just made the best of it. It was like doing time.

Nelson arrived in May, and every Sunday he and English would play golf together. One day they played 45 holes and then performed a concert in the evening. There was not much else to do. It felt like premature retirement, a slow, living death. The audiences wanted more than just a singer: they wanted someone to crack jokes and show off, an 'entertainer' in the most vacuous sense of the word. For all his penchant for Vegas, he was not programmed for cabaret. He cut and run less than halfway into the contracted engagement, and a second Branson season planned for 1993 was quickly and quietly abandoned with the explanation – directly contradicting his earlier statement – that 'he didn't like being in one place for a long time'.[13]

In later years when he performed 'Me And Paul' in concert Nelson would substitute Branson for Nashville when he sang the line 'I guess Nashville was the roughest.' He was relieved to get out of there. It had been no fun, but it was another one of those tests of fortitude and mutual loyalty that brought everyone closer together.

Paul English: We worked five or six nights a week. Most people would put their band on salary, right? And the crew. Well, Willie didn't do that. We all got paid just like we were on the road. For every show. We made more per show than the other musicians did per week. The driver got paid every day, and he drove about fifty yards forwards and then backed up fifty yards. That's how you keep people together for 35 years.

He came up for air and toured from July through to the end of October with the Family Band, relishing the feel of the tarmac beneath the wheels on the bus. Along the way he proclaimed his support for independent Presidential candidate Ross Perot (although Bill Clinton was a nice guy too, apparently, and he performed at his inaugural concert the following year) and ducked out for a few weeks in August for a series of shows with the Highwaymen.

On 1 November, the day after the tour ended with two shows in Austin, he played a free concert on the steps of the State Capitol to raise funds for a restoration programme for the building. The Nashville Network dropped some coins in the box and filmed the show, capturing a flawless piece of work and a rare opportunity to see him perform solo. As those dark eyes looked out from the steps onto the sea of people below him, then gazed over their heads to scan Congress Avenue and the Austin skyline stretching beyond, Nelson probably didn't linger on the thought that it was almost exactly two years to the day since the IRS had shown up on his doorstep, just thirty miles away from where he now stood. Everything in the past was dead and gone. He was shook up, cleansed by the fires of adversity and ready to take his talent seriously again.

I'VE BEEN OUT HERE SO LONG

Willie Nelson is talking about promotion.

It's an ugly word. He doesn't care about it at all. He does things backwards: most artists will only tour in order to promote a new album, but he releases a record simply to remind people he's still out there on the road. If a new song isn't up to scratch it won't make it into the set list of his show. Very few do.

'It's hard to put new stuff in there,' he says thoughtfully. 'If I start putting new stuff in there just to promote a new record, to me that's just not a good enough reason. Just because a record came out doesn't matter to me.'

He is playing a show tonight. It will closely resemble most of the shows he has played for the past twenty years. He will play precisely no songs from his latest record. Few people in the audience will really care.

He smiles. He is getting to the point.

'Really, I like the old stuff better,' he says. 'It's already proven itself to be good for me. Just because something is new doesn't mean it's great.'

Perhaps it's a long, slow revenge on the record companies that messed him around for years. 'Oh, the record company really doesn't realise where I'm at or where I am or what I'm doing,' he says all at once.

The voice is slow and completely devoid of any unpleasant emotions. He wears a look on his face which strongly suggests he hasn't even *thought* about doing anything other than exactly what he wanted for quite some time. He flicks ash onto the table, and it rolls towards the cardboard No Smoking sign.

'It's not their fault and it's not my fault,' he continues. 'I could guarantee you that I could go the rest of life and not play a song from my latest album and nobody there would know. They don't check on me that much. It's not like I'm a new artist where they're there every night to see what I'm playing. I'm not really dependent on what my last record did. I've been out here so long . . .'

He trails off and looks around, reminding himself of where he is. He comes to the conclusion that it doesn't really matter. It's a hotel. There is a show to play later. He is 'out here'.

'I've been out here longer than they have,' he says finally. 'That's just a fact.'

Nobody argues.

13. 1993–1998

S tanding backstage at Bob Dylan's thirtieth anniversary concert in Madison Square Garden on 16 October 1992, waiting to perform Dylan's 'What Was It You Wanted?', Nelson watched Sinead O'Connor wilt beneath a violent, ugly tide of hostility. Two weeks earlier the Irish singer had torn up a picture of the Pope on *Saturday Night Live* with the words 'Fight The Real Enemy', and now the torrent of boos and catcalls from the crowd swept her off stage in the embrace of Kris Kristofferson before she had even started to sing. Nelson gave her a couple of minutes to compose herself and then gently enquired, 'Now, you're still going to come and sing with me tomorrow, aren't you?'

The following day O'Connor duly ducked into Power Station studio in New York and recorded an apt version of Peter Gabriel and Kate Bush's quivering duet 'Don't Give Up' with Nelson for his new album, *Across The Borderline*. The context of the recording was significant, for it was partly Dylan's rejuvenation as an artist which charted a navigable course for Nelson to follow through the 90s.

Also in attendance at Madison Square Garden that night were two men who had steered Dylan out of the murky waters of the mid-80s and helped him dream up a meaningful future: Don Was and Daniel Lanois. Creatively, Dylan had made his return to the land of the living in 1989 with *Oh Mercy*, which had been dragged out of him by U2 and Peter

Gabriel producer Lanois; the follow-up, *Under The Red Sky*, was produced by Was, bass player with professional eccentrics Was (Not Was) and a man increasingly in demand as a producer.

With his manager Mark Rothbaum doing the groundwork, Nelson hooked up first with Was and then Lanois in the 90s, and their participation similarly revitalised his own slumbering muse, coaxing and cajoling some of his very best music out of him. In between, he returned to Texas and cut a self-produced album with his family and friends that was so personal, so honest and stark in the face of everything he had gone through in the past few years that it's a wonder he ever released it at all. At the end of the decade he could reflect upon three wildly diverse albums whose quality and consistency were unmatched by anything he had recorded since the early 70s. In doing so, he was able to trace a line back to 1992 and the making of *Across The Borderline* with Don Was.

'Don't Give Up' was an unusual choice of song for Nelson, but far from randomly selected. From the start, Was was firmly in control of the vision for the album and determined to impose a clear identity and focus upon it. Throughout the recording process he placed Nelson's talents in the hands of crack musicians and – in general – let them loose on tremendous songs. It was the same trick he had pulled off a few years earlier with Bonnie Raitt's *Nick Of Time* album. As Nelson admitted, the producer's long reach gave him the freedom to simply concentrate on the emotions of the songs and, more importantly, on his singing, while Was booked the sessions, drilled the musicians and hand-picked the songs.

Willie Nelson: Don brought the songs to the studio, and there were several of them that I said, 'Well, that's a great song but that's not me.' 'Don't Give Up' was one. But the more I listened to those songs, the more I said, 'Yeah. There is an infectious *something* there.'[1]

Was had chosen songs that subtly toyed with perceptions of Nelson as he neared his sixtieth birthday, conjuring up a mood that veered between elegiac and defiant: when he softly sings 'you paid the price to come so far' on the title cut, it is almost unbearably moving in light of his own troubles. On Dylan's 'What Was It You Wanted?' he conjures up the edgy, paranoid contempt of a man who spends his time constantly surrounded by people who are looking for something from him, whether it be a member of his family, his clique or the IRS. Small wonder he initially rejected the idea of singing it, but he digs deep and finally unearths a steely, slightly scary new voice to express the sentiment.

The personal resonance of 'Don't Give Up' is ultimately self-explanatory; Willie Dixon's classic jazz-blues 'I Love The Life I Live' is a wry reflection on the ups and down of an easy-come-easy-go attitude to money. On Lyle Lovett's 'Farther Down The Line' Nelson plays the amused old sage who has loved and lost a thousand times, passing on his sympathetic advice to a younger cowboy whose heart keeps being painfully unsaddled.

His own 'Still Is Still Moving To Me' is a Zen update of 'On The Road Again', a less equivocal, more philosophical exploration of the body's vibrations and his constant need for motion: 'I swim like a fish in the sea all the time/ But if that's what it takes to be free I don't mind.' Even Paul Simon's 'Graceland', which Simon had first offered to him back in 1986 and which Nelson wasn't keen on initially, held a deeper, more personal meaning than he realised.

Paul Simon: [Willie] thought it was about Elvis, whereas it's about losing a love, and healing. But I didn't want to say it to him: 'You've lost a son.' Willie finally did get the song as he sang it in the studio, exulting that 'this is a great fucking song. There's a lot more here than "let's go to Graceland".'[2]

This combined effect created by these song choices was both powerful and deliberate: to create a myth-like Nelson, at once outlaw, preacher, sage and above all survivor. But without being in any way burdened by a concept, *Across The Borderline* also read as a modern day parable of the American dream, opening with a reading of Paul Simon's hymn to the immigrant, 'American Tune', a song which on paper seems singularly unsuited for Nelson but is, in actuality, one on which he simply shines. 'Across The Borderline' was a beautiful, cautionary serenade to the plight of Mexican immigrants and indeed anyone trapped or stymied by their circumstances. 'Don't Give Up' is a hymn to all blue-collar workers, John Hiatt's 'Most Unoriginal Sin' relocates the story of Adam and Eve to an archetypal saloon bar, while 'Heartland' is an elegy to a way of life that was dying.

'Heartland' was credited as a co-write between Nelson and Dylan, but it was not quite as dramatic as that sounds. Dylan had given Was a cassette of a hummed melody with the word 'heartland' sung at intervals, and Nelson had taken it away and finished it. It is an explicit if clumsy war cry on behalf of the farmers: 'The bankers are taking my home and my land away/ My American dream/ Fell apart at the seams.' Dylan came in to the studio to sing his part.

Willie Nelson: It's one of those surreal things that happen in your life. One of those times when you say, 'Well, God, that just happened didn't it?' You still can't believe Bob Dylan was just sitting over there and he was just singing and now he's left. He wasn't there long. He came in and did his part and left.[3]

The album was studded with such cameos: Paul Simon, Bonnie Raitt, Lyle Lovett, Mose Allison, David Crosby, O'Connor, but they were used unobtrusively. Indeed, the much touted 'duet' concept – which had recently become a cliché, used by everyone from Sinatra to Ray Charles with great commercial success – instinctively put some people off, but it was a misreading of the record. Only three of the songs were truly duets, and it was far from being a bitty, gratuitous album. Despite the fact that it was created piecemeal – a song here; a song there – throughout 1992, the record flowed.

The majority of the work was done at the Power Station in the autumn, but as always there was a Texan angle: four of the songs were recorded at Pedernales with the Family Band and Johnny Gimble, while a further two were cut in Los Angeles. The achingly lovely title song, written by Ry Cooder, John Hiatt and Jim Dickinson, had been the first track recorded, cut in Dublin while the Highwaymen were on their European tour in April, the stage band and Kris Kristofferson lending support.

The principal studio band in New York consisted of several Highway-men – including Mickey Raphael – and assorted session players, and they achieved a tasteful and energetic mix of understated acoustic textures. Above all, Nelson's voice was used to brilliant effect, in many ways illustrating how little he exerted himself on stage, too often skating through his songs on autopilot. It was not, however, a record that heralded the return of Nelson the songwriter, although there were suggestions that he had tried.

Willie Nelson: Sometimes I get guilty because I haven't written in a while, and I'll make myself sit down and write something. But usually it's not that great because it's forced. The best stuff I write comes whenever I least expect it.[4]

Aside from 'Still Is Still Moving To Me' and the Dylan collaboration, the only other new song was the simple 'Valentine', written for his son Lukas and only just avoiding pure schmaltz. However, the album reaffirmed his peerless talents as an interpreter of both songs and emotions. More than that, *Across The Borderline* indicated that the man still cared about his craft, and remains one of his most enjoyable records. It received a whole host of great reviews and sold 400,000 copies within three weeks of its release in March 1993, climbing to No. 75 on the pop charts, his best showing for almost a decade. There is no question that the IRS publicity had put him back in the spotlight and the record benefited from that, but it was also a recognition of the quality of the work. He was back on the map.

It was shaping up to be a landmark year. He turned sixty at the end of April and threw a musical birthday bash in Austin. *The Big Six-O* was filmed over two days and featured a cast to die for: B.B. King and Bonnie Raitt doing 'Night Life', Ray Charles on 'A Song For You' and 'Seven Spanish Angels', Bob Dylan joining Nelson on 'Pancho And Lefty',

Waylon Jennings on 'Good Hearted Woman'. Paul Simon and Emmylou Harris were also there, as were a good representation of the Nelson clan, from Lana, the eldest at forty, to Micah, the youngest at three, who at one point grabbed the purse of a woman in the crowd. 'That's how we're paying off the IRS,' smiled his mother.

There were more celebrations. In September, Nelson was inducted into the Country Music Hall of Fame at the CMA awards in Nashville, introduced by Johnny Cash with a heartfelt tribute. As he stood on the stage, he gently mocked his old contrary stances towards awards. 'If you think I'm going to come up here and accept this award when all these guys are just as deserving as I am – you're damn right I am!'

At precisely the same time as he was being immortalised by his peers, however, he was being evicted from his musical home of eighteen years. His deal with Columbia expired in September and the somewhat half-hearted negotiations foundered primarily on the label's desire to remove Nelson's creative control. They were off-loading many of their older acts: country music had become an enormous industry again, in part thanks to the mass popularity of rap and grunge, which alienated many mainstream listeners and drove them towards the unthreatening sounds of new country, dominated by Garth Brooks and a succession of other fresh-faced young men with enormous hats and very small microphones.

The era of Shania Twain, Faith Hill and Lonestar was just around the corner, in which the line between bad pop-rock and bad pop-country would become almost non-existent. Nelson, thank the Lord, was no part of that. Instead, despite the obvious success of his latest album, he was regarded as a piece of living history, and even then he was doing better than most. Merle Haggard, Kris Kristofferson, Johnny Cash and Waylon Jennings were all struggling to find a comfortable place.

Columbia had been an unhappy hunting ground for a while. All the old faces had changed, and when the sales began to dry up in the mid-80s the label started exerting more control over Nelson's product. He had recorded several records which they had refused to release: *Sugar Moon*, a set of Western swing classics recorded with Merle Haggard's band, the Strangers; *Willie Sings Hank Williams*, a truly brilliant record which reunited him with Jimmy Day and reaffirmed the link between one country pioneer and another on classics like 'Move It On Over' and rather more obscure gems such as 'Why Should We Try Anymore'.

'I love that album, I really do,' Nelson later said,[5] and so he should – both records finally showed up on the mammoth *Classic And Unreleased* box-set in 1997. *Moonlight Becomes You*, a standards album recorded some years previously and only released after he'd left Columbia, was also turned down. His problems with the label gave the lie to the frequently quoted misapprehension that he had 'creative control'. It was an issue which could still fire up the old Nelson ire, over thirty years after he had first thrown in his lot with the money men at the record labels.

Willie Nelson: You want to fight that same battle again with the same prick that you popped before, but [only] if you really want to go through that again. Sometimes I do, because I know he's out there. And it's gratifying to pick those fights. In the first place, I know I'm right. If I don't think I'm right I shouldn't be there. It's gotten to the point where I just think it's funny. You either have to laugh or you kill somebody. Even when they tell you you have artistic control, you don't. Unless you see it in big letters in your contract: THIS MAN HAS COMPLETE ARTISTIC CONTROL, then you don't have it.[6]

In truth, Nelson missed a golden opportunity with the considered success of *Across The Borderline*. He slipped straight back into the same old bad habits. 'I read one place that the new album is like hearing about a friend waking up from a coma,' he said. 'To me it didn't seem that way. I'd still been working.'[7] It was a comment which dismayed, illustrating as it did his failure to distinguish between run-of-the-mill product and genuinely fine work. What he should have done – and it wouldn't even have crossed his mind – was give the Family Band a holiday, set up with a vibrant new five-piece group and tour *Across The Borderline* alongside a new, rejuvenated selection of his classic songs, then follow it up with a record of new original songs. It would have been a mouth-watering prospect and could have taken him onto new levels, both commercially and particularly creatively. He did throw a few of the songs into the achingly predictable live set with the Family Band, but that was the extent of his concession to change.

Instead, the follow-up to *Across The Borderline* was a standard Nelson release, *Moonlight Becomes You*, put out by the independent Justice Records, run by his long-time friend Randall Jamail. It had been recorded years earlier with his old Houston pal Paul Buskirk, and was another slant on the Nelson-sings-Tin-Pan-Alley angle. It was far from being a bad record, but it lacked pizzazz or any element of surprise and failed to capitalise on the attention *Across The Borderline* had generated. For the next two years he was back on the wheel, bouncing between record companies, touring with the same sextet and the same old songs, releasing too many albums which slipped between the tracks: *The Healing Hands Of Time*, for example, where he performed a mixture of standards and six of his own oft-recorded classics with a slushy 63-piece orchestra slowing and sweetening each and every song. Even if they hadn't, everyone got the feeling they had heard it all before.

On one level, it almost beggars belief that Nelson had never been busted for drugs, especially when one considers how openly he smoked it and endorsed its benefits. On the other hand, he was particularly well protected, in Texas particularly, and friendships and alliances built over the years generally ensured he was not targeted. Back in the 70s he would travel around the state with a stack of albums in his back seat, handing them out to traffic cops who might have expressed an interest in how fast he was travelling, how much he'd been drinking or what precisely he had been smoking. It usually worked.

Times had changed somewhat, but it still came as a shock and an indignity when he was arrested on the morning of 10 May 1994, on the I-35 at Hewitt, about ten miles south of Waco, right in the middle of his home turf. He had been playing poker with his old sparring partner Zeke Varnon in Hillsboro all night and had decided to pull over on his way back to Austin when the weather turned foggy. Police discovered him at 9 a.m. lying fast asleep in the back of his grey Mercedes, and upon closer inspection they also discovered the roach of a joint in the ashtray and rolling papers on the dashboard. Nelson was then arrested, at which point he indicated there was more marijuana under the floor mat in the front passenger seat. He was taken to McLennan County Jail and charged with possession of less than two ounces of pot, and released on a $500 bond.

David Zettner: Next day, I was over there at the golf course and here comes Willie, the cop, the judge and the lawyers, all playing golf. I asked him afterwards: 'How's everything going?' 'Oh, cool,' he says. 'Nothing to it.'

At a pre-trial hearing on 1 March 1995, Nelson's lawyers pushed to get the charge dropped on the basis that the two police officers had conducted an illegal search. They also highlighted inconsistencies in their testimonies and audio gaps in the police videotape recordings. Matters seemed somehow to be panning out in Nelson's favour: one of the policemen who had arrested him, Sergeant Michael Cooper, had already been dismissed from duty. The defence team even called the sheriff of McLennan County, Jack Harwell, as a character witness for Nelson. 'I've known Mr Nelson since the early 50s,' said the sheriff. 'Anything Mr Nelson told me I'd believe. I'd go to the bank with it.'

Soon after, the county judge ruled the policemen's evidence inadmissible on the grounds that there was insufficient cause for a search of the car, and threw the case out of court. Nelson – who was facing six months probation, revocation of his driver's licence and mandatory drug testing – announced that he had not accepted a plea bargain on principle because his rights had been violated. Nobody, of course, was denying that Nelson had been in possession of the marijuana, it was just that, well, someone somewhere hadn't been reading the script closely enough.

Willie Nelson: It was a small community cop. I don't know what he was trying to prove, I think he was just one of those zero-tolerance type guys. Most of the law enforcement people that I know, and know *real* well, think that it was kind of overreacting, especially since it was a misdemeanour. A ticket or a fine is normally satisfactory.[8]

Soon after the end of his legal adventure he was back on the road with the Highwaymen, promoting the last instalment of their decade-long adventure, *The Road Goes On Forever*, which proved to be an inauspicious title. This time Don Was took care of production duties and pulled the best performance out of them yet, wisely keeping their unison singing down to a bare minimum – those voices never did blend – and instead focusing on one solo performance apiece and elsewhere letting them trade lines. They toured the States through June 1994 and in November visited Australia, New Zealand, Bangkok, Hong Kong and Singapore, a far-flung jaunt which was to prove their swansong. 'I guess it's pretty well done for,' said Waylon Jennings. 'We're not going to do it any more. I don't intend to. Too many people got involved.'[9]

Nelson and Cash discussed the possibilities of a reunion in 1999 but it came to nothing. Jennings was in serious ill health by that point. The Highwaymen had only succeeded in staying together so long through sheer force of will and mutual affection. Musically, it had been a struggle. In truth, all of them were so bull-headed and set in their ways that the project had been beset by compromises and small disappointments all along the way, from song choices to musicians to business.

Jessi Colter: They found it challenging with just one band, [but] they found a way to do it. Even with opposing managers and this and that, the brotherhood was strong.

Nelson returned from the tour of the Eastern hemisphere, put in a quick stint filming the vacuous *Gone Fishin'* with Danny Glover and Joe Pesci, and then headed straight for California in mid-December, playing some unrehearsed and slightly shambolic acoustic shows with Leon Russell at the Coach House. While out West, he spent three days recording at Ocean Way studios with Don Was, who had broached the so-bad-it's-good idea of taping some of Nelson's songs in a reggae style. It was a conceit which Nelson was reluctant to embrace; he had very little knowledge of the form and what he had heard didn't convince or convert him. Nonetheless, he relented. The album had all the hallmarks of a novelty project.

Mickey Raphael: I think he likes Jimmy Cliff, he likes Toots [Hibbert]. For a while I'd bring him stuff and we'd go through different phases. Willie listens to everything. I'd bring him everything under the sun, anything but country music, unless I found a great writer. Somebody said, 'Well, we can do your tunes with a reggae vibe,' so that's kind of how the project evolved.

Was chose twenty Nelson originals for consideration which were then boiled down to around ten. They had already cut a reggae version of 'Undo The Right' in Los Angeles earlier in the year with a studio band and Raphael on harmonica. He paid for it himself as he was currently between labels. Was suggested they play the tape of 'Undo The Right' for his friend, the head of Island Records Chris Blackwell, the man who had been instrumental in exposing Bob Marley – and in the process reggae in general – to white, mainstream rock audiences in the early 70s. The pair visited Blackwell at his home in Jamaica to determine whether he would be interested in signing Nelson to the label. He was, but it was not really the reggae version of 'Undo The Right' that convinced him. Blackwell knew his reggae inside out and was unlikely to have been bowled over by the performance, which was on the formulaic side. 'We went out and did it with Don Was originally,' recalls Mickey Raphael, 'but the players weren't true Jamaican reggae guys. [They were] studio players trying to play in that way.' Nelson continued to record reggae versions of his songs in Los Angeles throughout 1996 and 1997 and continually mentioned the project in the press, but Island seemed increasingly reluctant to release it. The album, called *Countryman*, finally slipped out in the summer of 2005, and was not a successful meeting of cultures.

The music that had really seduced Chris Blackwell was much more traditional. While in Jamaica, Nelson had also played the Island boss a completed version of a self-produced album he had recently made in Pedernales: it was called *Spirit*, and it was mesmerising. The record had grown out of a long period of re-examination, both personally and musically. He had recently published *Willie Nelson: The Lyrics 1957–1994* and overseen the release of his *Classic And Unreleased* box-set, and both projects involved trawling through hours and hours of old music. As a result, he was more than usually aware of all the dusty corners of his back catalogue, as well as the quality of much of it. He was being reminded of awkward concepts like 'personal standards', 'history' and 'legacy'. He was looking to measure up to himself.

The process of rediscovering his muse began in the spring of 1995, when he'd 'accidentally' recorded an album with his old 60s band the Offenders: Jimmy Day, Johnny Bush and David Zettner. On one level it was simply a few old friends revisiting the glory days, but it also signified a symbolic blowing away of the cobwebs.

David Zettner: That was one of the funniest things we ever did. Jimmy Day had set it up. Jimmy wanted to record a steel guitar [album] and so we got all the musicians. Then I said, 'We'll get Baby John up here, Johnny Bush, he can really have fun on all those old tunes.' So we got Johnny up there. I guess we'd done about two things, waiting on a piano player, and here comes Willie walking in unannounced. He just looked around and said, 'My God, the old band's here, man!' I saw that little light go off in his head. All of a sudden, him and Jimmy were back there [chatting], and after that little discussion it was a Willie album. We had to practise a couple of them to remember how to do them. God we had fun. Jimmy came to me and said, 'Is this still my album?' and Willie said, 'How much do you want for it?' Jimmy Day said, 'Ummm, err, I've gotta pay off the car and . . .' He paid Jimmy a lot of money and said, 'We'll just call this The Offenders.' He bought the rights and everything and Jimmy was very happy.

Those sessions, which went on to provide material for the albums *Me And The Drummer* and *Can't Get The Hell Out Of Texas*, had been engineered by Joe Gracey. They led almost directly to the *Spirit* album, which couldn't have been more diametrically different in tone but which also had its genesis in the past. Four of the songs on the album had been written in the late 70s: 'I Guess I've Come To Live Here In Your Eyes' was recorded for the *Honeysuckle Rose* soundtrack, while 'Your Memory Won't Die In My Grave' had been cut in Bolugusa in 1976 and ended up on *The Hungry Years*. 'She Is Gone' was on the same album and 'I'm Not Trying To Forget You' was also recorded for Columbia. The rest of the material, however, heralded a long-overdue return to sustained, quality songwriting, written in a six-month burst in 1995.

Joe Gracey: I got a call from him saying he wanted to do some song demos. I went up there and set up a mic for his vocals and a mic for 'Trigger'. No amp. We didn't talk about it, we just did it, as usual. I put a little two-track DAT tape in the mastering machine and pointed at him to start singing and he did, and at the end of the day he realised it was really a record. He had just published a book of all of his early songs and he was dusting some of those off and then he had some new stuff he had written and pretty soon he had Gimble and Sister and [Jody Payne] in there to play along with him on stuff and we were making a record. I was sweating bullets, because when you record directly to two-track masters, you have no way to correct a mistake or revise a bad mix. It is all right there and all live to tape and you better get it right. I assure you, I didn't want to have to go out there and ask him to do it all over again because I forgot to turn something up, or on.

Spirit was as dry and spare as anything he had ever done. 'Barren,' he called it: no bass, no drums, no electric guitar, no fat or expendable notes or nuances. No rhythm. It was the sound of a dustbowl string quartet playing Tex-Mex chamber music, and it reflected upon a period of concomitant aridness in his spiritual life. Nelson's much-repeated mantra that he discards any negative songs was given short shrift here, giving some credence to Neil Reshen's claim that 'Willie only writes when he's sad. Most of the great songs that he wrote were when he was miserable.' The album is the sound of a 62-year-old looking back at his life and facing up to certain indisputable facts and creeping doubts; the new songs simply couldn't have been written by a younger man.

Much of the time the listener feels he is eavesdropping as Nelson recounts conversations he has had with God following the emotional upheavals of the last few years: 'Too Sick To Pray' makes his apologies for his absence and urges his maker to 'think of the family, Lord'; 'I Thought About You, Lord' is a wide ranging meditation on the the way he lives his life and the way he loves. The record is book-ended by the desolate instrumental 'Matador', conjuring up an ominous image of one man facing a powerful and dangerous opponent: for the matador it is merely the bull. For Nelson it is life itself.

Spirit is a quiet masterpiece, and again prompted comparisons with *Red Headed Stranger*, which Nelson himself positively encouraged. In an interview just before he made *Spirit* he gave a clue as to why he was still somewhat obsessed with his 1975 classic, and in doing so he touched on one of the most important and revealing strands of his own survival instinct.

Willie Nelson: To me, on that album, the ending isn't a happy ending. It was just an ending. Even though he had gotten away with those things, he had to live with them. No matter what you [do] you don't get away with it, because you know what you did. Is there life after that? Can you still go on after you've done something as horrible as that? The answer is always that you can, if you can forgive yourself. That's the big one. We all fall and we try to get up. That's life.[10]

Spirit is the sound of Nelson falling and trying to get back up. It is a much more personal album than *Red Headed Stranger* and a far greater triumph in songwriting terms. There is no narrative, no concept, no hiding behind cowboy personas or bravado. The closest it comes to an outlaw declaration is on 'We Don't Run', a matter-of-fact, Woody Guthrie-ish strum of defiance: 'We don't run/ We don't compromise/ We don't quit/ We never do,' he sings, and he means it. A further seductive strand of the record is the beauty and clarity of the musical performances, especially Nelson's sweet, sinewy, utterly unique guitar playing, which has never been better captured.

In concert his guitar is often too loud in the mix, the muddy sound accentuating only the booming lower notes, but here he reels off a masterclass which encompasses everything from ominous Spanish rumbles and almost classical figures to folk strums and tight blues. In all, *Spirit* is up there with the finest forty minutes of his career.

Willie Nelson: *Spirit* is my favourite. It's my over-all, all-time favourite, because it is so sparse. It was [a personal album]. It covered a long period of time and it was good to do it and simplify it, with just a few instruments. It made it less-is-more.[11]

Spirit came out in June 1996, the first country album Island had ever released. It was not marketed well. Chris Blackwell had left the company soon after Nelson signed, which had a negative impact on the record. Some people found it difficult to locate in record stores, while radio play proved almost impossible, to the extent that Nelson personally delivered it to a small station in Arkansas in order to get it on air. He was facing an uphill battle commercially. The ear of the world had turned away again following his wayward dalliances pace-*Across The Borderline*, and there was nothing on the new album that could really be called a single. Radio had changed to such an extent that none of the country legends were getting any airplay. It was all tied up in demographics, record company politics and money. You could turn the dial for a long time before you heard George Jones or Hank Williams on the airwaves. Or Willie Nelson.

Coincidentally, 1996 marked the twentieth anniversary of *Wanted! The Outlaws*, which had sold over two million copies in the intervening years. He and Waylon cut a new song with Steve Earle called 'Nowhere Road' for a CD reissue of the album on RCA. The irony was obvious for all to see. He was once again at odds with the establishment who cared little that he was making some of the best music of his life. It was nothing new – he well remembered the times when he couldn't get played on the radio. *Spirit* didn't get anywhere near the pop charts and reached only No. 21 on the country charts. He wasn't really bitter, just a little bemused and amused.

Willie Nelson: These days it's ridiculous who-all can't get played. [I] knew that radio-wise I was getting into a little bit of trouble when I heard some guy say, 'Boy, I wish they'd play some of those old guys again like George Strait and Randy Travis!'[12]

He really believed in *Spirit* and went the extra mile for the record. He gave a lot of interviews and even changed his well-worn live set-up to include a suite of songs from the album. On 10 July 1996 he played almost the entire album without Bee Spears or Paul English – just piano, guitar and harmonica – during a three-hour show at New York's Supper Club, to great acclaim. He dropped some of his reggae tunes into the live show – most often Jimmy Cliff's 'The Harder They Come' and 'Sittin' In Limbo' – and even strapped on an electric guitar for a medley of blues tunes like 'Texas Flood' and 'Milk Cow Blues'.

The leaps in energy levels in both band, audience and star were tangible on the new material, and though it did not herald the dawn of a new era on the stage, he performed in the quartet format on and off for the next couple of years, a seismic reconfiguration within the limited confines of the Nelson universe. A mammoth concert at London's Barbican in 1998, part of the Inventing America series, was illustrative: he would cling to his tried and tested set for the first ninety minutes before changing tack and throwing some curveballs, including songs from *Spirit*, a solo performance of 'A Song For You', and new songs such as 'Everywhere I Go' and 'Somebody Pick Up My Pieces', the latter a classic old country weepie, both of which would end up on his next record. In Ohio he previewed a song called 'A Whore With A Heart of Gold', written for a film called *Outlaw Justice* he had just finished making in Almeria, Spain with Kristofferson and Travis Tritt.

Spirit had stuck with him. He did not just cut it and lay it aside, as he did so many other of his records. Instead, he proposed to build on it, and planned a new album which would continue its themes of spirituality and doubt and musical minimalism, though in the end it didn't quite come out that way. He had heard – and heard good things about – Daniel Lanois, a Canadian musician and producer who had worked with everyone from Dylan and Emmylou Harris to Peter Gabriel and U2. Nelson had cut a song with U2 in Dublin called 'Slow Dancing' in 1997, and he was aware that Lanois was working on Bob Dylan's latest record and had recently made Emmylou Harris's acclaimed *Wrecking Ball*.

Daniel Lanois: There was a phone call out of the blue from Mark Rothbaum. Mark had been aware of my work and brought it to Willie's attention. We met and got along great and decided to make a record.

Nelson had four new songs, which had originally sounded a lot like the ones he had written for *Spirit*. 'Everywhere I Go', 'I Love You All Over The World', 'Somebody Pick Up My Pieces' and the instrumental 'Annie' were all promising, and he invited Lanois to rummage around in his back catalogue to select some more songs to make up an entire album. Lanois had just completed work on Dylan's tour-de-force *Time Out Of Mind*, released in September 1997, which was heavily rhythmic, thick with percussion and atmosphere, and he saw this album almost as a 'continuation, a cousin' to the Dylan record: as such, old Nelson songs like 'Three Days' and 'I Never Cared For You' appealed to him. He envisaged a much tougher rhythmic basis to the songs than Nelson had initially imagined, with the drums sparring off Nelson's Tex-Mex guitar. Lanois had a small repertory of musicians and his set-up included a drum kit which could accommodate two drummers playing simultaneously side by side. In the end the album took on a sound of its own, influenced by the material, Nelson's guitar style and, not least, the evocative location.

Daniel Lanois: He was fascinated with Django Reinhardt and it put a bit of a Spanish twist to the record. I wanted to play up the rhythmic side of things. My studio at the time was in an old Mexican theatre called El Teatro, so it all sort of came into focus.

Lanois' studio was an old porn theatre in Oxnard, southern California, which gave the album its name: *Teatro*. He had removed the seats from the middle of the theatre and built a level stage in the middle, facing the screen. On this stage he put all the recording equipment, amps, instruments and the musicians. Guitars were everywhere, including one Dylan had left behind. When the musicians played there were no headphones, no separation, everything was designed to be cut live with as much depth of sound as possible. Added to Lanois' studio crew, Nelson brought Bobbie and Mickey Raphael to the sessions, reflecting his desire to recreate the pared-down feel of his live show. There was never any talk of using the full Family Band. Lanois suggested getting a backing singer in and Nelson said, 'Well, Emmylou's the best. She should come in and we'll work her little tail off!' Harris hooked up with Nelson and Lanois in Las Vegas and they rode the bus together to California, picking songs and rehearsing harmonies on the way. Lanois kept phoning ahead to the studio to let them know what they were doing, and as soon as they arrived they were ready to go.

Daniel Lanois: As soon as Willie walked in, we recorded. He would keep his trailer out back of the theatre, he had his wife and his two young kids with him, and in between songs he would just go out there and relax and smoke pot. I would listen to the song we just did, do a little mix right on the spot and then move on – start rehearsing the band for the next one. When I thought they were ready to get through it I'd go and get Willie out of his trailer and we'd knock out the next one.

For Nelson it was almost like making a movie, except it took only 4 days, during which they recorded 22 songs. Some of the takes on Nelson classics were close to definitive: 'Home Motel', with Brad Meldhau's superb piano accompaniment, was spine-tingling and tear-inducing, a 'Danny Boy' for those suffering from a terminal case of self-pity. 'Three Days', 'Can't Let You Say Goodbye' and 'I Never Cared For You' all fitted the rhythmic structure perfectly. The clean, clear version of 'I've Just Destroyed The World' was an easy joy, but other transformations and song choices weren't quite so successful. The ghost of Nelson's original 'Spirit Mk II' concept could still be sensed in the inclusion of the two instrumentals that opened and closed the record, including a painstakingly rehearsed version of Django Reinhardt's 'Ou Est Tu, Mon Amour?' for which, said Nelson, 'my left hand hates me'.[13]

Rather than being a companion piece to *Spirit*, as originally intended, *Teatro* was instead an evolution, moving out of stark sorrow and pushing up into the overground. 'A stretching out', as Nelson put it,[14] from low spirits to high ones. What the record had in common with its predecessor was not its final feel, but its unity and coherence of sound, its brash sense of purpose. It was driven, full of rhythm and energy, largely down to the manner in which it was recorded.

Mickey Raphael: He was the most minimalistic producer we've worked with. We would go over the song maybe two or three times. Willie would come in and we'd play the song, and it could change with Willie there. Then listening to playback was the mix! Several times I wanted to either fix a part of mine or I thought I could do it better, and it was like, 'Nope – we're keeping that.' With Daniel every [take] could be it. You want the spontaneity too, it doesn't have to be perfect.

At the end of the four days Nelson got back on the bus and drove away with a completed album, fully mixed, in his pocket. Even by his standards, it was quick and instantly rewarding, and provided robust confirmation that he was still moving forwards. There is, however, a lingering sense that the purity of Nelson's hopes for *Teatro* were muddied a little by Lanois' firm hold of the reins. He has probably the most distinctive sound of any producer working today, heavy on the reverb, draping a smoky, sweaty patina over almost everything he touches.

In a sense, the degree to which you loved or hated *Teatro* depended largely on how much you loved or hated Lanois' trademark auteur flourishes. Nelson let himself be directed. Lanois saw him as 'old school, as a lot of folks from his era are: Sinatra, Ray Charles, they just walk in and sing', and the producer duly built a distinctive musical home for him to inhabit. Nelson himself admitted that the album 'extended . . . out into Daniel Lanois' spiritual journey a little bit',[15] but he seemed happy with the finished product, and it certainly put him back in the centre ground. It sold well and was critically acclaimed.

Willie Nelson: The stuff that Daniel is doing is on-the-edge stuff, and I like it.[16] When you have a producer, you've really got to trust him. You've got to say, 'OK, take it.'[17]

Soon after the release of *Teatro* in September 1998 he received a momentous recognition, the Kennedy Center Honors for a lifetime achievement in performing arts, presented by President Bill Clinton. It is the highest accolade in the country for an artist: Dylan had received it the previous year. Nelson arrived at the December ceremony in Washington in black tuxedo, black cowboy hat, black boots and black velvet braiding on his hair, still wondering aloud whether they had got the right 'Nelson'. Later, his bus, the *Honeysuckle Rose* was driven onto the reinforced stage and the likes of Kris Kristofferson, Dwight Yoakam, Lyle Lovett and Shelby Lynne serenaded him with his own songs as Don Was's 'Willie Nelson Tribute Band' provided backing.

It was a sweet moment, but not definitive. He was 65-years-old, and although now an elder statesman he remained almost impossible to pin down. He duetted with Beck for a movie soundtrack, filmed a genuinely amusing cameo as a songwriter hired to write an anti-Albanian propaganda song in the anti-war satire *Wag The Dog* ('Albania's hard to rhyme') and featured in a charity wrestling match with 'Tex' Cobb, which he threw himself into with gusto. 'I lived through it, which was the main thing,'[18] he later laughed. He had taken up tae kwon do alongside his wife and kids – 'you know what they say, the family that kicks together sticks together' – and was still running and looking after himself, drinking special water from Houston made from aloe vera. He would park in the grounds of the ranch, within sight of his $4m home, and watch TV with his two boys on the bus. And for those who mentioned the dread word 'retirement', Nelson fired off a well-oiled one liner: 'All I do is play golf and play music – which one do you want me to give up?'

I HAVE NO REASON TO THINK ABOUT
QUITTING ANYTHING

Willie Nelson is talking about the end.

'Well, I think there's probably that thing where, you know, nobody wants to be the first one to admit that it's time to quit,' he says a little hesitantly. 'I definitely don't want to be that guy.'

He is 72-years-old and he looks it. Tired, worn, but strong. His arms are tough as teak. His eyes are a little droopy and glazed, but that will be the dope. His hair is thick and long and still auburn in places. His trainers are white. His brain is still receiving and transmitting clearly, although he veers between saying things that make perfect sense to everyone and things that simply make sense to him. That might be the dope as well.

Men half his age grow tired of this life: of buses, stages, aeroplanes and cold hotel rooms exactly like this one, handing out autographs and endlessly shaking hands with strangers. Yet there is a defiance about him. He shows no signs that he will be turning around and heading back down the road at this late stage.

'My health is good, I think my attitude is good, and I have no reason to think about quitting anything,' he says. 'Whatever the opposite of that is, I guess, is where I'm at. I have a lot of energy. That can be a problem or . . . ha ha ha!'

What he means is that the road keeps him out of trouble, gives him a purpose. He could play his music in one solitary spot but it wouldn't work.

He is still capable of twisting and turning for a few more miles down the road. He thinks for a second. 'Right now I'm working on about six different albums: we've got about six albums going on.'

Six albums. How could he stop? Why would he want to? He inspires devotion and love and can feel it every time he walks into a room. Typically, he turns it around. 'Well, I think I have a lot of devotion toward a lot of people that I feel like I've been obligated to through the years as well,' he says. 'I feel like I owe them something. So I don't mind admitting that.'

He pauses and finally allows himself to consider the other side of the equation. When he walked into the lobby of the hotel earlier today he reduced one woman to tears of surprise and joy. Perhaps he is thinking about her now. Perhaps it's someone else.

'I'm sure there are people out there who maybe feel the same way about me,' he says. He smiles the Willie Nelson smile and locks into deep eye contact. He is thinking about why he is here, in this room, in this city, in this country, in the world. Tonight he will step out of the bus, walk onto the stage with his friends, throw his hands out towards the mass of humanity that has gathered in one place to see, hear and feel him, and he will be back home again.

He breathes out, long and slow.

'And that's great too.'

14. 1999–2005

Willie Nelson: Once you've reached that point where it seems like you've been through the fires and you're still here, then that in itself is a miracle – that you survived all these things. There is enough reason there for jubilation, I think.[1]

Johnny Bush has a saying: 'Old age takes care of a lot of the things the preacher takes the credit for.' The manner in which Nelson has burrowed into the twenty-first century stands in simultaneous agreement and defiance of this statement. He is still living an extraordinary life for a father, husband, grandfather and great-grandfather well into his eighth decade on earth. His antics might still concern the average preacher, as he criss-crosses the country for eight or nine months each year, fervently smoking the kind of dope which floors men half his age and twice his size after barely a puff, still taking the occasional sip of tequila and inviting a little madness to descend.

On the other hand, he is a black belt in tae kwon do, preaches peace to his children and has become increasingly vocal about political, environmental and military issues: he waxes evangelical about the merits of Biodiesel, an alternative fuel source he endorses, and recently wrote a furious diatribe against the Iraq War entitled 'Whatever Happened To Peace On Earth?', asking rhetorically of fellow Texan, President George

W. Bush: 'How much oil is one human life worth/ How much is a liar's word worth?' In some lights he passes for a conventional member of liberal society.

More and more of his down time away from the road is nowadays spent in the house in Spreckelsville, Hawaii, where his wife Annie lives permanently and the boys go to school. He long ago learned not to count his chickens domestically, but the incessant womanising appears to have stopped – he now characterises himself as an admirer rather than a participator in these matters. But he is still wrestling with the eternal dilemma that has no resolution: his deep spiritual need for a home and a family, and the refusal of his road fever – and all the attendant trouble that brings – to dissipate. As long as he walks that line – and he always will – he knows that everything is endlessly open to question.

Willie Nelson: I am married. She may not hang onto me, but so far, so good. So far, so good.[2] We've got two teenage boys. They are great kids. Sweet kids. They don't like it when I leave to go on tour. For that matter, neither do I. But that's the way my job is. I tried quittin' for a while but I just couldn't handle it.[3]

He has become an elder statesman: part cartoon character, part eternal rebellious schoolboy, part mystic. He is beyond cool and above hip, although he intersects with those concepts now and then. In the last five years in particular, a confluence of factors have draped a kind of culturally relevant patina over Nelson and his work. *Teatro* was embraced by a younger audience and, according to him at least, the girls at the shows 'have been getting younger and prettier', although that may just be a mirage brought on by age.

Another member of the band was heard to comment excitably in 2003 that 'It's like 1975 all over again.' Not quite. He isn't selling anywhere near as many records, for a start. He may still be playing 150 shows a year and is almost universally loved, but with his scattergun approach to record making, no radio play and his refusal to really promote a new record where it counts – on stage – he is never likely to return to the kind of commercial peak he enjoyed in the 70s. And after all, you can't re-invent the wheel.

He followed up *Teatro* with a couple of genre records, both occupying territory he'd been edging towards for some time. *Night And Day* in 1999 was a sprightly instrumental album, heavy on the Django, and it denoted a final shift away from the voice as his primary tool of expression. He had always loved the guitar over anything else, and those listening to his shows could now plainly hear that his interest in it was taking precedence over his singing: even at his age, his voice could still be a beautifully expressive instrument in the studio, but on stage it was harder to cut through and increasingly he raced through the lyrics in order to reel off a volley of those improvised, bouncing, clambering guitar runs that so defined him. He has become bored with the parameters of vocal melody. An instrumental album was a logical step.

Merle Haggard: He's mastered his singing more than his guitar. It's a lot harder for him to play guitar than it is for him to sing. He has reached that plateau with his singing, as long as his body is able to do it he's got it figured out. The guitar is a greater challenge for him.

Milk Cow Blues in 2000 was an equally predictable move, a foray into the blues, but less successful. He had recorded the basic tracks in the mid-90s with the house band from Antones, the famous Austin blues club, and then added cameos from the likes of B.B. King, Dr John and Kenny Wayne Shepherd, and in all it sounded a little stale and disjointed. However, his audiences weren't coming to hear him play songs from his new records, but to participate in something akin to living history. Johnny Cash was undergoing an even more momentous reinvention. Having been dropped by Columbia years ago and hitting the skids in his career, Cash had suddenly become the coolest name to drop in all the right places thanks to his brilliant and stark series of *American Recordings* records made with Rick Rubin, which absolutely resurrected him as a giant of music in the late 90s and into the noughties.

Nelson was enjoying a low-voltage, off-Broadway version of the same treatment. A quirk of record industry shuffling after *Milk Cow Blues* had resulted in him being signed to Lost Highway Records following the Universal Music Group's takeover of Island and several other record companies. It gave him an added edge: the label was home to artists such as Ryan Adams and Lucinda Williams, the kind of hip names who combined raw country with bluesy rock and who naturally viewed Nelson as a pioneer.

The likes of Uncle Tupelo, Gillian Welch, Lambchop, Smog, Adams and Williams were inadvertently spearheading the retrograde alt.country movement, which had skipped the slick vapidity of the Garth Brooks generation and headed back to the sounds of Steve Earle and Emmylou Harris, then further back to Nelson, Haggard, Cash and Gram Parsons, and back even further still to Hank Williams, bluegrass, Appalachian and folk, for their musical inspiration. The Mantera compilation *Beyond Nashville* became a switched-on shorthand guide to the riches of the past and the glories of the present. If you screwed your eyes up tightly enough it was almost a cyclical return to the forces which enveloped Austin in the early 70s, except now Nelson was Lefty Frizzel, the benchmark of old-time authenticity, and someone else was busy fighting all those old battles that never really went away and were never really won.

He was in a good place, and a series of unconnected landmark appearances and events underscored his status as a national icon for young and old. He turned up at the thirtieth anniversary of Woodstock in the summer of 1999, opening up on Sunday morning after the previous night's headliner Limp Bizkit had left all the karma and feng shui in a mess. Nelson invited a select group of small farmers into the VIP area, sang 'Amazing Grace' and generally seduced and soothed everyone within earshot. In 2000 he appeared in *The Simpsons*, a sure sign of immortality; there was a Lifetime Achievement Grammy the same year, and an induction into the Songwriters Hall of Fame in 2001. He led the choir after the bombing of the World Trade Center on 11 September with 'America The Beautiful' and somewhat controversially, used the atrocity as a platform to lobby for a reintroduction of farmers' subsidies, usually only enforced during wartime. 'Well it's wartime again, let's bring it up,' he argued.

There was a degree of mythologisation, even canonisation, going on, and he played his part. To celebrate his 69th birthday, hardly a traditional landmark, he threw a party at the Ryman in Nashville on 14 April 2002. Alongside the usual suspects like Ray Price, Emmylou Harris and Keith Richards; Jon Bon Jovi, Sheryl Crow, R&B singer Brian McKnight, Norah Jones, Ryan Adams and Matchbox 20 also came along for the ride. The line-up betrayed the fact that the concert, called 'Willie Nelson and Friends: Stars and Guitars', was really a launch party for his new Lost Highway album, *The Great Divide*, and the night was an uneasy mix of voices, the sounds of Bon Jovi playing 'Always On My Mind' and Adams and Nelson stumbling through 'The Harder They Come' rubbing up against Nelson's sublime duets with Harris on 'Til I Gain Control Again' and Price on 'Night Life'. It was all good fun nonetheless and heartwarming recognition from a whole generation of younger artists, something he had never really experienced before. Nelson had always been feted across musical boundaries by his own peer group – hence the appearances of Dylan, Simon, Raitt, Crosby and Kristofferson on *Across The Borderline* – but he had not always been taken entirely seriously as an influence upon future generations, partly because of some of the artistic missteps he'd taken in the 80s. Such *en masse* admiration from his musical children was long overdue.

Ryan Adams: He kind of did his own thing, and that makes me think I can kind of do my own thing. Immediately, we're like fifty per cent more cool than we were three hours ago.[4]

He enjoyed the experience so much he repeated the birthday concert concept in the following two years: in 2003 at the Beacon Theatre in New York and in 2004 at the Wiltern Theater in Los Angeles. The New York show celebrating his seventieth birthday was a genuine and justified event, but even then it fell prey to bafflingly wayward quality control. For instance, Wyclef Jean performing 'To All The Girls I've Loved Before' over a soporific reggae beat was a tribute to nothing but sheer misguidedness. Nelson grinned beatifically throughout but only really found the heart and soul of the night in a version of 'A Song For You' with Ray Charles and Leon Russell.

The milestone was celebrated elsewhere. Predictably, Nelson covered all angles. He turned up to be honoured by the Senate in Washington just before the big day, but on 30 April itself, the night of his seventieth birthday, he could be found out on the road, playing another joint, in this case the Horseshoe Casino in Bossier City, Louisiana. It was a beautifully illustrative example of a life that has stretched like a skin over the whole expanse of the North American continent, book-ended by the most powerful people in the land at one end and the rank and file at the other. Both doffed their caps, but on the night he chose to be with his own kind.

It was also an opportune time for some reflection and reappraisal of his music. Most of his classic records were reissued on compact disc, and a 41 song career-spanning retrospective, *The Essential Willie Nelson*, sailed to No. 1 in the country album charts. He had both the distant past and the immediate present wrapped up: Sugar Hill Records released his Nashville demos from 1961–1966, including the earliest versions of 'Crazy', 'Three Days' and 'I've Just Destroyed The World', while he won a Grammy for his rather slick duet with Lee Ann Womack on 'Mendocino County Line' – he'd shot the video on horseback on Congress Avenue in Austin and had closed the street for the best part of the day, the equivalent of shutting down The Mall in London. No one else could have got away with it.

Even more improbably, in June 2003 he was back at the top of the country music singles charts for the first time since 1989. He had cut a duet of 'Beer For My Horses' for Toby Keith's hugely successful album *Unleashed*. Keith was an ex-footballer and swaggered across the rickety line between devout patriot and knee-jerk redneck. His considered response to the 9/11 bombings was expressed in a song called 'Courtesy Of The Red, White And Blue (The Angry American)', which contained the line: 'You'll be sorry that you messed with the US of A/ 'Cause we'll put a boot in your ass it's the American way.' Keith seemed an unlikely bedfellow for Nelson, but the two were friends and 'Beer For My Horses' was an absolute smash, hitting No. 1 for four weeks in June and staying in the charts for 25 weeks. It later won four CMA awards and crept into Nelson's live set. All of this said more about Keith's huge commercial pull than it did about Nelson's, but he wasn't complaining. He had come from the Nashville system and he knew the value of a hit single. Besides, he loved the title.

To date, Nelson has written two truly great songs since the onset of the new Millennium, which is probably two more than we have any right to expect. Each provided the title of his two Lost Highway albums, *The*

Great Divide and *It Always Will Be*, and each was the best thing on them by a considerable distance.

The timing of *The Great Divide*, released in early 2002, in theory couldn't have been better. He was on a sympathetic label and with the prevailing winds in his favour it was a perfect opportunity to release something iconic, spare and authentic, a bone-dry country classic, something in the line of Cash's dark, stripped back, almost Gothic *American Recordings*. Instead, Nelson seemed to be chasing the dollars and was happy to let his new friends run the show. *The Great Divide* was in essence a pale retread of the formula that had resurrected the fortunes of Santana in 1999, helping them sell 11 million records with their *Supernatural* album. The records shared the same producer in Matt Serletic, the same central guest in Rob Thomas from Matchbox 20, and the same glutinous, promiscuous spread of duets from all corners of the contemporary landscape, cynically designed to rope in buyers from every demographic.

Thomas had befriended Nelson after attending a number of his shows and had subsequently written three songs for the record. Serletic had worked with Celine Dion and Aerosmith and was the kind of producer who couldn't let the listener forget for one minute that a record is indeed being 'produced'. *The Great Divide* was really his baby. He co-wrote some of the songs, chose the duet partners, and displayed an utter misunderstanding of the rhythms, nuances and elasticity of Nelson's music.

All but five of the tracks were duets and as a rule they jettisoned emotion for schlock. Nelson was singing the kinds of songs that somehow took five people to write and which creaked under the weight of their own self importance. Bernie Taupin, Elton John's regular lyricist, weighed in with overwrought lyrics on 'This Face', a horribly self-referential rehash of a sentiment that Nelson had effortlessly and eloquently expressed forty years earlier in one of his greatest songs, 'The Face Of A Fighter'. On the awful 'Last Stand In Open Country' he was up against rap-metal flash-in-the-pan Kid Rock, although he may not even have known it at the time he was singing the song. Nelson had recorded most of his parts by early 2001, but the album took another year to come out, by which time he had little idea what kind of record he was putting his name to.

Willie Nelson: I'm not sure what to call it – maybe a 'way out there' production. He wants to get folks like Kid Rock, 'N Sync, Sheryl Crow and Rob Thomas to come in and do harmony and background vocals. I don't know what all they're going to put on there – strings, horns . . . I'll have to wait and see like everyone else![5]

It was a depressing statement. After his positive experiences with Lanois and Was, on *The Great Divide* Nelson was finally and firmly let down by his producer. He sounded uncomfortable, at sea, overpowered by the gratuitous cacophony surrounding him. In truth, he was just another guest on his own album, and Serletic played with his voice as he would a new toy.

There were precisely three good performances on the record: a knowing, beautifully stripped-down version of the psychedelic classic '(I Just Dropped In) To See What Condition My Condition Was In' and the pleasantly reflective 'Recollection Phoenix' both escaped virtually unscathed. And somewhere buried within Serletic's self-satisfied mess was the mesmerising title track, where Nelson somehow shakes off the attentions of the echoing drums and overkill on display everywhere else and quietly commands attention with a brooding, virtuoso performance. 'The Great Divide' is a classic, musically a sequel to 'I Never Cared For You', with its Spanish-style minor chords and stark, lovelorn atmosphere. Even lyrically, its use of the elements gone somehow awry – 'Summer sun/ No prettier than summer rain' – seems to hark back to its mother song from almost forty years before. It is a complex, dark lyric about a love affair that can never be fulfilled and yet can never be cut loose, and it is the sound of an artist who has not yet given up on his muse, and furthermore has not yet quite surrendered his will to positivity. The title track alone, however, was not enough to rescue the fortunes of *The Great Divide*, which didn't quite emulate *Supernatural*'s 11 million sales. It sold under 400,000 copies and was not reviewed favourably.

His other recent landmark composition, 'It Always Will Be', is a much gentler, more philosophical take on the nature of love. 'There are some things I think about/ And every time I do they break my heart,' he sings, and the listener can conjure up Myrle, or Connie, or Billy, or the IRS. Like all his best songs, it is personal and universal all at once. Merle Haggard considers the song as being 'as great as anything he's ever written', and he is not alone.

Johnny Bush: 'It Always Will Be' is so good that I study it. I don't know yet if he's singing about a woman, a wife, or maybe one of his children. I haven't figured it out yet. It doesn't matter, it's the feeling and the emotion.

In fact, Nelson says the song was written about a love affair, but he doesn't specify who or when. 'There was nothing that could be done about it, but it doesn't diminish the fact that it was a very sad situation,' he says softly. 'The song is about that. One particular thing: "Sometimes I think that love/ Is somewhere living on an island all alone." Sometimes I think that.' It is the opening and standout track on an album which is more unified than its predecessor, although again Nelson was less than fully involved in the recording process. The basic tracks were recorded under producer James Stroud's supervision in Nashville and then vocals were added at Pedernales. However, it utilises a much more low-key, sympathetic modern country sound than its predecessor, and although it again features a handful of duets, the artists and the songs are well chosen: a pair of jazzy ballads with Lucinda Williams and Norah Jones, and a bluesy affair with his daughter Paula, the latter the latest instalment in an ongoing process to make his records a little more family orientated.

Having spent so long playing and recording with his other 'family', he now seemed to recognise that almost all of his children were involved in music in some way, and so endeavoured to involve them in his own music: Lana is the on-tour mother hen and almost constant companion alongside sister Bobbie, documenting his tours for his website, adding photos and diaries. Connie's daughters Paula and Amy are both musically inclined: Paula and her band supported Nelson a few times in the early 2000s, and she and Amy were both present when Nelson made his first proper 'family' album, *The Rainbow Connection*, recorded in early December 2000. It was a real home-cooked affair. David Zettner had installed some computerised, digital recording equipment in Nelson's studio at his Western town and Nelson's grandson-in-law, Matt Hubbard, came along to help out. Hubbard had played with Paula in her band and later married Lana's daughter Martha. Paula was also there, as were Susie and Amy, and in three days they cut an album. Zettner has since calculated that it cost $16.50 to make.

Amy wrote and sang two tracks on *The Rainbow Connection*, while the title song came from the 1979 film *The Muppet Movie*, thus making Nelson perhaps the only performer ever to cover songs made famous by Hoagy Carmichael, Frank Sinatra, Ray Charles, Hank Williams and Kermit the Frog in a single live show. Amy had been trying to get him to do the song since she was a little girl twenty years ago, and he had finally relented. In the end *The Rainbow Connection* was a family album with a twist, ending with a cover of Mickey Newbury's 'Thirty-Third Of August' which concluded: 'Though the demons dance and sing their songs within my fevered brain/ Not all my God-like thoughts, Lord, are defiled.' Sweet dreams, indeed.

Three years later on *It Always Will Be*, Nelson duetted with Paula on the song 'Be That As It May', a tough, bluesy number that she had also written. It meant a huge amount to her.

Connie Nelson: I knew he had heard the song before, but I called Willie and said, 'Listen, I swear to you I'm not trying to get you to do it because it's our daughter, but I just really think you should listen to that song again because I can hear you doing it.' Next thing I knew, Paula was calling me a couple of days later: 'Oh my God, oh my God, Dad's going to do my song! And he's got me singing it with him!' Which I didn't ask him to do. So he did listen to it again. It was fabulous.

Elsewhere on the record, Nelson's eldest son Lukas wrote and played guitar on 'You Were It', a neat little tearjerker – 'I once had a heart/ Now

I have a song' – which suggested he was well acquainted with his father's back catalogue and also had a viable future ahead of him as a musician. He wrote it when he was twelve. Lukas has become a seriously talented guitar player, specialising in sinewy blues in the Stevie Ray Vaughn vernacular. His younger brother Micah plays the drums. Back in Hawaii Nelson has his own little family bar band, and they go out and play for fun. 'I'm very proud of them,' he says. Despite the fact he raises them from a distance most of the time, he is close to his boys.

As the Millennium rolls on, inevitably the shadows of mortality have begun to lengthen over Nelson and his gang. Many of his closest friends haven't made the distance. The great Jimmy Day, the engine of the band in the 60s and one of the all time legendary steel players, passed away from cancer in January 1999. In the following years Nelson has lost a whole host of others who were close to him. Grady Martin, his old guitarist, died in 2001, while Waylon Jennings had been suffering for some years and seemed only to keep going through force of will and love of music. In December 2001 his left foot was amputated and by the following February he was gone, a victim of complications arising from diabetes. Nelson said little, but let the music reach out to his soulmate. He prefaced one of the gospel songs in his set with a quiet, 'This one's for Waylon,' and kept his own counsel.

Two months later Paul Buskirk was also dead, but not before Nelson had made one final record with his old Houston buddy, a retread of *Without A Song* called *Nacogdoches*. Johnny Cash, too, finally slipped away on 12 September 2003, and in July 2004 Ray Charles passed on; he sang a tearful 'Georgia On My Mind' at his funeral. His oldest pal, Zeke Varnon, is also dead, and there have been other brushes: Hank Cochran underwent triple heart bypass surgery in March 2005, while Billy Joe Shaver lost his son Eddy to a heroin overdose on New Year's Eve 2000. Eddy and Billy were due to play a show that night at Poodie Locke's Hilltop Bar and Grill in Austin, and Nelson stepped in to help Shaver make it through the night.

Billy Joe Shaver: Willie put a band together and insisted that I come down there. I guess If I'd stayed at home there's no telling . . . I held it together long enough to go up there and do a few songs, and Willie did a bunch. I didn't do many because I really wasn't capable of it. He was the best one I could have run into. I spent the night over at his house and we talked and he talked me into not doing anything about it, because I was so mad I was going to run out and kill a bunch of drug dealers. He told me it's best to let God take care of it. He paid for Eddy's funeral. I couldn't make him take the money. I'll never be able to repay him for it, but if I mention it he gets real mad at me. He did what a real friend is supposed to do.

Nelson himself is beginning to take on a little wear and tear. Most recently he was struck with a severe bout of flu which caused him to cancel an Australian tour in early 2005. Under strict doctor's orders, he was forced to stop smoking, stop talking and stop singing for a few weeks. 'It was educational!' he says, but his friends are a little concerned that he is beginning to wear himself out.

Merle Haggard: I disagree with the length of his show and the amount of time he gives people autographing. I think he's paying for it. He has given of himself more than any human being is ever required in life. I've told him that. I just don't understand it. He's the hardest working man I've ever known. Shit, he's Willie Nelson, he don't have to show up in the afternoon and sign autographs, but that's his business and not for me to judge.

In the past few years he has also suffered serious nosebleeds which hospitalised him, and a bronchial infection which turned into pneumonia. In May 2004 he was forced to undergo carpal tunnel surgery on his left hand after experiencing severe pain for much of the previous year. The doctor diagnosed acute nerve damage through age and overuse and recommended surgery, but Nelson's fear of hospitals ensured he tried every available alternative before relenting to an operation. It took nearly three months out of his touring schedule, and even when he returned to the stage in July he couldn't play guitar for a short time. Lukas backed him up on guitar, and Micah and Annie also joined the tour in the summer holidays.

None of his illnesses have succeeded in slowing him down for any length of time. Immediately after his recovery from surgery he was back on the road, this time with Bob Dylan, undertaking a co-headlining tour of minor league baseball parks through August and September. It was the first time they had gone on the road together, although the two had a long history. Nelson had played the Houston date on Dylan's legendary Rolling Thunder Revue on 8 May 1976, joining in on the encore of 'Will The Circle Be Unbroken', but the quiet alliance between them had really begun with Farm Aid, an overdue meeting of minds between two of America's finest songwriters.

The 2004 tour was a logical seal on a growing friendship and mutual appreciation. Their instincts and art were not as far apart as might be supposed: each refused to be backed into a corner, and each boasted a bottomless knowledge and appreciation of the American songbook, everything from traditional folk songs to Stephen Foster, Woody Guthrie, Jimmie Rodgers, Hank Williams and Paul Simon was devoured; each had a love of Broadway, Tin Pan Alley and the timeless art of Cole Porter, Hoagy Carmichael and the great songwriting teams of Cahn and Van Heusen, Rodgers and Hart *et al.* Each could now comfortably take their place in that lineage. If Nelson's lyrical gift was flatter, more prosaic and succinct than Dylan's, at its best it was no less spellbinding. Both had voices which could divide a room, with those poor, misguided souls who thought that neither of them could sing – in the way that, say, Mariah Carey could sing – being condemned to the dunces' corner.

Dylan was the undisputed, if reluctant, sovereign of the well-educated, middle-class, liberal cognoscenti, each morsel of his life and lyrics endlessly swallowed, regurgitated and re-consumed. Nelson's status was equally deified among the less culturally visible members of the country's blue-collar population, but he was largely free from the attentions of such overwrought analysis, principally due to plain old snobbery. Both were regarded as leaders, as teachers, and while Dylan has strained every sinew trying to deconstruct and re-assemble his myth into new and unsettling shapes, deep down there is the sense that Nelson is happy with his role and really does regard himself as being born for a singular purpose; that he might really be, as one of the magician-priests on his Hawaiian island home of Maui once claimed, an Old King born to bring native races together. In the words of Dylan, 'he is a philosopher-poet who gets to the heart of it in a quick way'.

On tour, it was an interesting contrast: Dylan mixing it up every night, throwing in obscurities from his back catalogue, messing with the arrangements, playing the piano rather than the guitar. Then there was Nelson, throwing down an hour of greatest hits, so ingrained in his mind that he virtually breathed it, although because of his recent surgery he was playing less guitar and things sounded a little different. He even opened with 'Living In The Promiseland' instead of 'Whiskey River', the kind of thing that makes the superstitious consult the skies for strange and ominous signs. Dylan allowed no one backstage, insisting on a clear run from dressing room to stage, whereas it would take Nelson thirty minutes to get through the autograph hunters, smiling all the way. They hung out a little together, Dylan enjoying the fact that Nelson had his children with him on the bus and on stage.

Above all, the tour was a gratifying, almost moving experience. To see two of the genuine musical greats from the past half-century doing what they do best without any fuss or fancy embellishment was to jump aboard a rolling exhibition of living musical history, for between them Dylan and Nelson cover almost all the ground of the past fifty years of American music, rap and hip hop excluded. And as the recent years of bereavement indicated, it was an opportunity to glimpse a dying breed in their natural habitat, like seeing two rare old birds take flight together. They enjoyed it so much they repeated the exercise again in the summer of 2005, a more worthy use of Nelson's time and talents than his role as Uncle Jesse in the witless big screen version of *The Dukes Of Hazzard* which came out around the same time.

For some the lure of the highway is endless, and at the final end what Nelson is left with is the road. The bus, the band, the songs and the road.

It is virtually impossible to over-emphasise just how much of his life has been spent touring. A glance at his itineraries from as far back as 1986 make for exhausting reading. Nearly two hundred days of his life neatly typed up and accounted for between April and December, for instance, is a typical example – the 'days off' marked on early drafts soon filling up as more and more dates are added. The name of the hotel and the nearest golf courses and jogging tracks are marked on the sheets. A 24-hour restaurant might be flagged up. On the page it looks utterly daunting: Humboldt, California one week, Fayetteville, North Carolina the next, and on and on, as spring turns to winter, as 1986 turns to 1987, as the 80s turn into the 90s and on into the new Millennium, which also fails to stop the show. In 2005 he played around 150 dates, which doesn't account for the off-days inbetween the shows which are also spent travelling.

To most observers it looks like life with all the sharp corners cut off, but it is the meat of his existence nonetheless. Everything he does, every record cut, every song written, every love affair conducted, every movie shot, every TV show visited, is done in the shadow of the big bus tumbling down the road. Everything else is done only with permission; he is leased out and quickly called back. It is the one true constant in his life, providing the backdrop to everything he has done for the last thirty years. It is his only real home and it is the reason he doesn't really have a home. He has a sign which reads: 'He who lives by the song will die by the road,' and he seems hell-bent on proving it. It will be a most unkind conspiracy of fate if he ends up taking his leave anywhere other than on his bus or on a stage.

David Zettner: Every time he has a birthday I ask him, 'Well this year Willie, what's your words of wisdom?' On his sixty-ninth birthday he said, 'At this age you buy licence to be senile automatically at will. You don't have to remember shit!' This year I asked him, 'How do you want to be found, Will? How do you want to go out?' That kind of set him back a little bit. I thought, uh oh! Then he said, 'You know, I think I'd rather be found lying backstage between the third and fourth set.' And that's it. Cool. I notice he didn't get mad at me this time about negativity. He wants to rock – out. We'll get a phone call one day.

Things have changed out there, of course. It's calmer now. Most of the band don't even smoke marijuana any more; Mickey Raphael might have half a glass of wine with his dinner, but he is more likely to be jogging, using the hotel gym or doing his laundry than anything else. That's not to say that the crew don't still have a little wildness in them and around them, but the scene is nothing like it once was. Paul English is still the band leader, the man who commands instant respect, the ultimate moral policeman, but he is no longer feared. He no longer rules with an iron fist. Nowadays his bond with the band has settled into a paternal relationship of mutual affection.

Paul English: I call them my boys, my young boys, because they're always getting squabbling and I'm the one who tries to straighten them out. They love me, I know that, and they know that I care about them too. When I go home, I'm with one family but I'm away from my other family. I really have no friends at home. I have my family. Out here, I have my friends and family. We've got a lot of good guys. They've grown up out here. Mickey was 21 years old. David Anderson was 18 years old, now he's about 57. Poodie Locke has been with us 28 years, Buddy Prewitt [lighting director] 26 years. Tom Hawkins, the piano tuner, 26 years. We've got a couple of bus drivers: Gator Moore, he's been with us some thirty-odd years, and Tony Sizemore, he's been with us 25 years. Billy, my younger brother, has been with us now 21, 22 years, and he's a new member of the band! I've seen them grow up, that's what I mean. We've been out here all of our lives.

Life is a sight more comfortable compared to the days when Nelson would squeeze himself up onto the dashboard of a station wagon and will himself to sleep, or when they would all lie in the back of a Winnebago in sleeping bags with no air conditioning. His bus is as well equipped as any hotel: state-of-the-art stereo, satellite TV, Internet, good food. His personal quarters have all the relaxed trappings of his home, with paintings of Native American art, beads, necklaces, flags, photos of his boys, a hand-carved wooden king-size bed, guitars, music, books. He keeps up with current innovations, listening to XM and Sirius satellite radio so he can still hear Hank Williams, and reading Dan Brown's blockbuster *The Da Vinci Code*, which touched on mystical, quasi-religious themes like Rosicrucianism which are close to his heart. The book became a minor obsession. 'He loves conspiracies,' says Raphael. 'Even though it was the No. 1 *fiction* bestseller, that was fact – historical fact. It was great, because [Willie] was digging through the Internet to prove and find these different theories. He loves that stuff.'

His door remains open. Any of the band might want to knock and come in and hang out for a while, but most have their own interests. Nelson still takes good care of himself, jogging every day, eating well, drinking lots of water. Golf, meals and getting on stage to play their music remains the primary source of interaction. They have seen every corner of America and much of the world but have absorbed almost none of it. Bee Spears, who has spent over 35 years on the road playing bass with Nelson, plans to return to the road with his wife and an RV in his retirement and investigate all the places they have been. That is, if retirement day every arrives. As Spears himself admits, 'You can't quit. Even if you die you don't quit.' As the years roll on and the pace keeps rolling relentlessly on, there is an increasing sense of a destiny having to be fulfilled at whatever price. The road is a pact that can't be reneged upon, a deal with the devil which has no crossroads.

David Zettner: I've been in touch with band members and even they are saying, 'God Almighty, we're just at our wits end sometimes because he just *will not stop*. And when he does, that throws us all in a bind because we've got to sit and twiddle our thumbs. None of us know how to live at home.' I saw a sadness in that. I thanked myself for getting away from that bubble. I think I'd have been very unhappy, making all this money and not being able to do nothing with it except keep making more, until you get sick and die – what's left? That's their life. I think the band at this point, I couldn't say for sure, but it feels like they're at the point where they just can't give up the race. They gotta finish! They don't care about losing their health, they've come this far and they have to finish.

It is an extraordinary life. The hotels and venues might be bigger and better but the basic shape is the same: another night, another town, another gig, the same old songs by and large, and then back on the bus to sleep through the night until the morning brings another town, another scene, a new beginning. The family he is closest to and chooses to spend the majority of his time with is the one he keeps on a payroll: 5 men and 1 woman, the youngest at 53, the oldest at 75, living in a bus for a good part of the year, all there to fulfil the timeless passion of one man.

Although some band members maintain a much clearer sense of their own identity – both personal and musical – than others away from the bus, all of them are defined by Willie Nelson's lifestyle. Their lives are lived through his own. Then there is the crew, more than two dozen men spread over three buses. All still paid by the show. No show, no dough. The old way.

He is full of energy. In light of his schedule and his age it is remarkable that he gets so much work done, and in light of how many shows he plays, it is above all incredible that he takes so few chances on stage. Unlike Bob Dylan, who keeps up a tour schedule which is almost as punishing as Nelson's but who is constantly changing his set and – for good or ill – chiselling away at the structure of his songs, he is content to stick to a tried and tested formula. It has, in some ways, destroyed him as a creatively vibrant and relevant artist. His records occasionally take the listener down new avenues, but a harsh critic might conclude that in concert he has become his own tribute band, reeling off the oldies to the converted.

Underneath the surface of the songs all the band are improvising, playing with their own little parts each night, while Nelson toys with the melodies of his best-loved songs, snapping them often, working his guitar hard. No one on stage is locked in or told what to do. You have to listen hard but things do move around. Nonetheless, the lingering sensation is of a remarkably gifted man who has been content to let himself stand still on stage for the last twenty years as the musicians around him have tried to maintain an interest in the proceedings. There is no question that the repetition of the set grates a little.

Mickey Raphael: The set is the same. I get tired of 'Whiskey River', but I'm not the guy in the middle. I asked him one time jokingly, 'When do I get to stand in the middle?' He said, 'Anytime that you want!' But he does love the songs. What's weird is, we finally mutinied one time and said 'We gotta do some different songs!' He changed the whole set-up and the audience, like, attacked him! It was heresy, because they're used to a set pattern, they're used to these songs. He's got so many great songs other than those, but they wanna hear these songs, and they really turned on him.

In many ways his strengths are also his biggest weaknesses: his ability to communicate, his desire to please, his energy and his charisma – the very things that make him such a wonderful and regular draw into his 70s have also held him back. He could spend more time on his records and his songwriting and less on the road and the results would be more interesting, but that would deny him the intimate connection he craves.

His touring brings genuine happiness to many people and has provided a lifestyle and a purpose for hundreds of those around him. He reflects and emits warmth. He has changed perceptions with Farm Aid but mostly he is the soundtrack to a good time. 'It's like this guy is plugged permanently into this cosmic groove,' says Bob Geldof. 'And the minute they start playing it's right there: there's no preamble, no warm-up. It's fucking – bang! Amazing.'

Nelson has a complicated, mysterious relationship with his music. He claims to receive messages from angels and archangels and other wavebands, some in languages unknown to the human race. The standard set list is like an extended mantra, a connection of emotions and moods which works for him. 'I like the old stuff better,' he says. 'It's already proven itself to be good for me.' A change of structure or the introduction of a new song has to be carefully thought through, for it is almost an interruption of something that has become a recitation, a form of healing, a prescription that he knows will work to soothe and mend. He has to think long and hard before he feels sure it will work. Mostly he doesn't take the risk.

The shows are really a mix of the very personal and the joyously communal. He is working through the mantra in his head, and at the same time he needs the adulation, the warmth coming back at him, to really make it work. It is a duet. And when it does work, as it did at London's Shepherd's Bush Empire in April 2005, it is dependent on a convergence of the will of the venue, the crowd, the atmosphere, and Nelson's energy levels. On these nights his set remains a wondrous train of music, each carriage carrying another chapter of the great American hymn sheet, from Hank Williams to Rodney Crowell, Hoagy Carmichael to Methodist gospels, not forgetting his own immense canon. The critic suddenly sees and hears why he needs to keep going. He hasn't reached the destination yet.

Mickey Raphael: I don't think he cares if it's Berlin or if it's Beaumont – it's a gig. As long as the fans want to see him, I don't think he cares where he goes, really. He's the kind of guy who would be content playing in a hotel lobby bar, in a Holiday Inn, if there were five people in the audience. He truly would be comfortable doing that.

One of his oldest friends explains that he sometimes looks up at the afternoon sun and takes comfort in the fact that he knows Nelson is somewhere out there underneath it with his band, still moving, still receiving his education from the nation he loves. It's a romantic but nonetheless beguiling notion: the sun shining down on Nelson and the vast numbers of lives inextricably connected with his own.

In his home town of Abbott, his house stands empty almost all of the time, watched by Jimmy Bruce, his next-door neighbour and friend of nearly seventy years. Not all that long ago someone broke in and stole the answering-machine tape with Nelson's welcome message on it. Bruce sits in the old cotton gin down by the railroad, reading his paper, wondering if he's made Annie Nelson mad over some domestic matter. In the post office they admit he hasn't been around much lately, not since Zeke Varnon died. Jack Clements got a call at Christmas but hasn't seen him for a while.

A hundred miles or so south down the I-35 Larry Trader sits outside the golf course at Pedernales, chewing the fat with the regulars, cadging a cigarette, criticising golf swings from afar, taking it easy, talking about all the good times, all that he has learned from Nelson. 'It's been most enjoyable,' he says slowly. 'It's going to be a sad day when we all leave this planet and go to another one. They'll never make another one like him. I've been trying to figure it out, really, but I think his whole life revolves around trying to make people happy. Understanding people.' Just behind him stands the recording studio where the majority of his music has been made over the last three decades. There is a lifetime's worth of it still in there that nobody has ever heard.

Over by the sixth fairway is Bobbie Nelson's house, the woman who knows him better than anyone, who has played music with him almost every night since the days when they shared a house in Abbott. She represents, of course, the mother figure neither of them ever really had. They gather strength and protection from each other, living together on the road and less than a mile apart in Austin. It is a silent bond, a mysterious and lifelong pact that neither can really define.

David Zettner: I could never fathom what they had to go through. His son died, and Bobbie lost her sons in a matter of years. All this tragedy, and these two old people just hang on to each other and just keep getting bigger and bigger. And they smile! I told Bobbie one day, 'If I wished for anything it would be able to have that kind of mindset. That you people are able go through any tragedy, anything on this earth, and know how to survive it. How do y'all do it?' She said, 'Oh, I don't know if we're doing that very well.' They're real humble people. These two guys have got it figured out. They don't talk about it much. He never likes us to talk about any recollection of negativity. Sometimes he'll just blow me off if I'm talking about something like an ex-wife. I kind of have to watch myself, even today, not to ever say anything that would connotate a negative thing. He don't want to hear about that.

A few hundred yards down the hill in his condo, Bob Wishoff is up in his tiny engine room, an electronic crow's nest at the end of a step ladder filled with a dizzying array of computers and memorabilia and books. This is Outlaw Radio HQ, the place where all manner of chaos has been dreamed up over the years. Nelson has had a high internet presence since he launched his web site in the late 90s and recently launched www.livewillie.com, where many of his shows can be downloaded.

Wishoff's home is surrounded by other condos where many of the crew live when they are off the road. The area is called Spicewood, but he calls in Space Weed, or sometimes Spice Weird. It is a tight little community, rough around the edges and fuelled on humour and eccentricity and dope and devotion to the cause. Nelson has a business office which takes care of day-to-day interests, but this is where the dreaming happens, where the connections occur.

Less than a mile away up the hill, the black gates to Nelson's sprawling 700-acre ranch swing open. Just out of sight behind the almost anonymous entrance stands the old tour bus, painted with heroic images of an Indian warrior and Nelson's face morphing into an eagle and taking flight, a visual representation of his karma. They were painted by David Zettner, who lives on the grounds in his little cabin, painting, making posters and pondering Nelson's ideas for everything from Biodiesel to building a new venue at Carl's Corner near Abbott.

Today the $4m ranch house, added to and expanded through the years, stands empty. Annie and the boys are in Maui; they don't come around much. Nelson recently wrote a new song called 'Love Gets Lost In The Big House'. Sometimes when he is here he can be found sitting in the main building, the World Headquarters, in the Western town he built on the ranch, quietly playing chess. He likes to spend his home time on the golf course, or in the little cabin he built behind the house, or in the more homely confines of Zettner's own cabin.

David Zettner: He loves coming to my old place, with insulation hanging out and nothing on the floor but boards. He loves coming there and just sitting for hours, like it was before [fame]. He never has been able to get people to understand that, because they all think: If I do this for Willie it will make me look better. What can this [do] for me?

Zettner slips down to the Broken Spoke in Austin, orders a chicken fried steak and sees a picture of himself nearly forty years ago, boarding an aeroplane with Nelson, Paul English and Jimmy Day. He's glad he made it back. Later, the old honky-tonk will fill with waistcoats and smoke and music and laughter, and the owner James White will point with pride at the pictures of Nelson on the wall, his old Stetson, his gold records. In the back room, Cornell Hurd and his ten-piece band plays 'San Antonio Rose' and people dance the same way they've been dancing here for the past forty years.

It's a mere snapshot of the world Nelson has helped create and the one he so frequently leaves behind. He is still out there, rolling around in his big tin can somewhere on the endless highway, insisting that the world is turning his way, playing almost the same songs for different people every night, moving and sitting still. He is constant dialogue with his sprawling, loving, slightly dysfunctional family: faxes, telephone calls, e-mail, but one day he won't return at all and you wonder if anyone has really thought about what will happen then. It sometimes seems like it is a dependent relationship, his friends relying on Nelson as, for want of a better word, employer and absentee landlord, and on one level it is: everything here is designed with his best interests in mind. But on a deeper level it is all about co-dependence. Nelson needs to know they are there, just like he needs to know that his wife and kids are there. They all give him the capacity to be alone and yet feel that he is not alone. Most of all, they give him a reason to keep going.

The song playing in the background during Nelson's latter years is Bob Dylan's 'I Can't Wait', the one where he sings 'It doesn't matter where I go any more/ I just go.' His life is held together and defined by movement. He has created a way of life that keeps him out of trouble and keeps him from sinking into unhappiness. 'If it wasn't for the bus and this weed, I'd be at the bar right now, doing serious harm to myself,' he once admitted.[6] He lives the life he does through the instinct of self-preservation. In one sense it has become an extended meditation, an escape from the inevitability of who he really is. There is a lot going on beneath the skin of the smiling, benevolent troubadour, kept at bay by a constant dose of marijuana which inevitably blunts his stimuli, takes some of the sharp edges away.

There is a dichotomy at his heart: he defines himself as a 'hippie cowboy', but you could easily add a whole host of other opposing terms to describe him, a man who has sufficient love to reach around the whole world yet not quite enough to allow anyone to hold him too closely. Perhaps he said it best himself in 1974 on 'Pick Up The Tempo': 'Well I'm good and I'm bad, I'm happy and I'm sad and I'm lazy/ I'm quiet and I'm loud/ And I'm gathering a crowd.' He is all these things and has nothing left to prove. He need not write another song, though he will. He is a one-off, a force beyond contrivance or marketing, and the fact that he somehow became a superstar so firmly on his own terms should be endlessly celebrated, for such a strange occurrence is unlikely to ever happen again.

Connie Nelson: I remember sitting just offstage with Kris Kristofferson one time. Kris had opened the show, then Willie comes out. It was back in the days where he was wearing overalls and he had pigtails, and Kris was shaking his head. He said, 'You know, I come out here and I try to look really cool and be as sexy as I can be, and Willie comes out in overalls and pigtails and sings 'All Of Me' and the crowd goes nuts. I just don't get it!' It was one of the funniest moments. If you tried to manufacture that it wouldn't work. It would look contrived.

He has released far too much music, although he would balk at the very possibility of such a notion. 'All music is gospel,'[7] he says, and that is really it. He is a point of communion, a church at which all the other millions worldwide who chafe with their own internal contradictions can congregate. He plugs into something so honest and fundamental it really defies definition. 'Soul' is the closest term. He has not allowed anything as awkward as reasoning or logic to get in his way, trusting his intuition all the way down the line. He will not stop now. 'However you want things to be, create them in your own mind and they'll be that way,' he once said.[8]

Perhaps his greatest achievement – in a life studded with hard-won victories, landmark acts of creativity and immense rewards, alongside desperate lows and more pain than he allows himself to acknowledge – has been convincing so many people to come and join him in the world he has built using only the sound in his mind.

NOTES ON SOURCES

All quotations throughout the book have been drawn from the author's own interviews, except where indicated in the text or referenced below.

CHAPTER ONE: 1933–1950
1. Nelson, Willie and Shrake, Bud – *Willie: An Autobiography*, Cooper Square Press, 2000
2. ibid
3. Scobey, Lola – *Willie Nelson: Country Outlaw*, Zebra Books, 1982
4. *St Louis Post Dispatch*, 19 March, 1991
5. *People*, 3 May, 1976
6. Nelson, Willie and Shrake, Bud – *Willie: An Autobiography*, Cooper Square Press, 2000
7. Interview with Todd Copeland
8. *Esquire*, August 1981
9. Nelson, Willie and Shrake, Bud – *Willie: An Autobiography*, Cooper Square Press, 2000
10. Interview with the author, 2005
11. *Pickin' Up The Tempo*, May 1975
12. Interview with the author, 2005
13. *Esquire*, August 1981
14. *Gallery*, March 2001
15. Nelson, Willie and Shrake, Bud – *Willie: An Autobiography*, Cooper Square Press, 2000

CHAPTER TWO: 1950–1957
1. *Pickin' Up The Tempo*, May 1975
2. Nelson, Willie and Shrake, Bud – *Willie: An Autobiography*, Cooper Square Press, 2000
3. ibid
4. ibid
5. Nelson, Susie – *Heartworn Memories*, Eakin Press, 1987
6. *The Baylor Line*, Spring 2001
7. *People*, 3 May 1976
8. *Houston Chronicle*, August 1988
9. Nelson, Willie and Shrake, Bud – *Willie: An Autobiography*, Cooper Square Press, 2000

10. Nelson, Susie – *Heartworn Memories*, Eakin Press, 1987
11. *New York Times*, 5 December 1980
12. Digital Interviews, August 2000

CHAPTER THREE: 1958–1961
1. *Hartford Courant*, 30 January 1994
2. Scobey, Lola – *Willie Nelson: Country Outlaw*, Zebra Books, 1982
3. *Houston Press*, 29 June 1995
4. Scobey, Lola – *Willie Nelson: Country Outlaw*, Zebra Books, 1982
5. Kienzle, Rich – *It's Been Rough And Rocky Travellin'*
6. *Record Collector*, August 1986
7. *Commercial Appeal*, 4 May 1997
8. *Country Music*, February 1976
9. Nelson, Willie and Shrake, Bud – *Willie: An Autobiography*, Cooper Square Press, 2000
10. *The Commercial Appeal*, 4 May 1997
11. *Austin-American Statesman*, 17 August 1995
12. *Associated Press*, 7 April 2003

CHAPTER FOUR: 1961–1965
1. *Chicago Tribune*, 26 March 1985
2. Nelson, Willie and Shrake, Bud – *Willie: An Autobiography*, Cooper Square Press, 2000
3. *Hartford Courant*, 30 January 1994
4. *Charleston Daily Mail*, 5 September 1998
5. Nelson, Susie – *Heartworn Memories*, Eakin Press, 1987
6. *New York Times*, 10 October 1993
7. *Columbus Dispatch*, 20 February 1993
8. Nelson, Willie and Shrake, Bud – *Willie: An Autobiography*, Cooper Square Press, 2000

CHAPTER FIVE: 1966–1970
1. Nelson, Willie and Shrake, Bud – *Willie: An Autobiography*, Cooper Square Press, 2000
2. *Pickin' Up The Tempo*, May 1975
3. *New York Daily News*, 4 May 1997
4. *People*, 3 May 1976
5. *Pickin' Up The Tempo*, May 1975
6. Nelson, Willie and Shrake, Bud – *Willie: An Autobiography*, Cooper Square Press, 2000
7. ibid
8. Nelson, Susie – *Heartworn Memories*, Eakin Press, 1987
9. Nelson, Willie and Shrake, Bud – *Willie: An Autobiography*, Cooper Square Press, 2000

CHAPTER SIX: 1970–1972
1. Author interview with David Zettner
2. *Esquire*, August 1981

3. Interview with author
4. Nelson, Willie and Shrake, Bud – *Willie: An Autobiography*, Cooper Square Press, 2000
5. *Country Music*, February 1976

CHAPTER SEVEN: 1972–1973
1. *Washington Post*, 4 July 1987
2. *Esquire*, August 1981
3. Interview with author
4. St John, Lauren – *Hardcore Troubadour: The Life And Near Death Of Steve Earle*, Fourth Estate, 2002
5. *Esquire*, August 1981
6. *Rolling Stone*, 12 April 1973
7. *Country Music*, June 1977

CHAPTER EIGHT: 1974–1976
1. *Pickin' Up The Tempo*, May 1975
2. Opdyke, Steven – *Willie Nelson Sings America*, Eakin Press, 1998
3. *Washington Post*, 4 July 1987
4. *Associated Press*, 27 April 1993
5. Nelson, Willie and Shrake, Bud – *Willie: An Autobiography*, Cooper Square Press, 2000
6. ibid
7. *Country Music*, June 1977

CHAPTER NINE: 1976–1978
1. *Washington Post*, 25 April 1978
2. *Crawdaddy*, October 1978
3. ibid
4. *Associated Press*, 27 April 1993
5. *Esquire*, August 1981
6. Nelson, Susie – *Heartworn Memories*, Eakin Press, 1987
7. Nelson, Willie and Shrake, Bud – *Willie: An Autobiography*, Cooper Square Press, 2000
8. ibid

CHAPTER TEN: 1978–1984
1. UPI, 18 October 1983
2. *Texas Monthly*, May 1991
3. ibid
4. Nelson, Willie and Shrake, Bud – *Willie: An Autobiography*, Cooper Square Press, 2000
5. *Chicago Tribune*, 15 December 1985
6. *Country Weekly*, 1980
7. *Texas Monthly*, April 1998
8. *New York Times*, 18 July 1980
9. Nelson, Willie and Shrake, Bud – *Willie: An Autobiography*, Cooper Square Press, 2000

CHAPTER ELEVEN: 1985–1990
1. *Associated Press*, 7 August 1989
2. Nelson, Willie and Shrake, Bud – *Willie: An Autobiography*, Cooper Square Press, 2000
3. *Associated Press*, 22 September 1985
4. Nelson, Willie and Shrake, Bud – *Willie: An Autobiography*, Cooper Square Press, 2000
5. *Texas Monthly*, April 1998
6. UPI, 31 March 1988
7. Opdyke, Steven – *Willie Nelson Sings America*, Eakin Press, 1998
8. *Associated Press*, 2 March 1990
9. *Associated Press*, 22 May 1990

CHAPTER TWELVE: 1990–1992
1. *Chicago Tribune*, 31 May 1991
2. *Texas Monthly*, May 1991
3. ibid
4. ibid
5. ibid
6. *Texas Monthly*, April 1998
7. *New York Times*, 23 February 1995
8. *Penthouse*, late 70s
9. *New York Times*, 23 February 1995
10. *Chicago Tribune*, 8 March 1992
11. ibid
12. *Associated Press*, 9 October 1991
13. *St Louis Post Dispatch*, 1 December 1992

CHAPTER THIRTEEN: 1993–1998
1. *Plain Dealer*, 24 April 1993
2. Opdyke, Steven – *Willie Nelson Sings America*, Eakin Press, 1998
3. *Plain Dealer*, 24 April 1993
4. *Denver Westwood*, 15 August 1996
5. *Dallas Observer*, 7 August 1997
6. *Chicago Sun Times*, 18 May 1993
7. *Knoxville News-Sentinel*, June 12 1994
8. *Dallas Observer*, August 1997
9. Opdyke, Steven – *Willie Nelson Sings America*, Eakin Press, 1998
10. *Los Angeles Times*, December 1995
11. ibid
12. Opdyke, Steven – *Willie Nelson Sings America*, Eakin Press, 1998
13. *Knoxville News-Sentinel*, 28 August 1998
14. *Dallas Morning News*, 24 September 1998
15. *Cox News Service*, 10 December 1998
16. *Knoxville News-Sentinel*, 28 August 1998
17. *Digital Interviews*, August 2000
18. *Daily News of Los Angeles*, 29 July 1997

CHAPTER FOURTEEN: 1999–2005

1. *New York Times*, 27 April 1993
2. *The Tennessean*, 15 March 2003
3. *Pittsburgh Post Gazette*, 21 July 1999
4. *Austin-American Statesman*, 9 May 2002
5. *San Antonio Express News*, 14 February 2001
6. *Texas Monthly*, April 1998
7. *Denver Westwood*, 15 August 1996
8. *Texas Monthly*, April 1998

BIOGRAPHICAL NOTES

Listed below are brief biographical sketches of the characters whose voices are heard throughout the book. Their roles are explained in reference to their relationship with Willie Nelson.

Dwayne Adair: Childhood friend from Abbott.

Ryan Adams: Musician. Nelson's label mate at Lost Highway Records.

Richie Albright: Drummed with Waylon Jennings from 1964 until his death in 2002. Also Jennings' collaborator and co-producer.

Chet Atkins: Musician, producer and executive at RCA Records. Produced the bulk of Nelson's 60s output.

Barry Beckett: Keyboard player with the Muscle Shoals Band. Worked with Nelson on *Phases And Stages*.

Johnny Bush: Country musician and close friend of fifty years. Band member until 1968. Wrote Nelson's signature tune 'Whiskey River'.

Paul Buskirk: Friend and Houston-based musician who bought some of Nelson's earliest original songs, including 'Night Life' and 'Family Bible'.

Jack Clements: Childhood friend from Abbott.

Jessi Colter: Country musician and third and final wife of Waylon Jennings. Appeared on *Wanted! The Outlaws*.

Pat Croslin: Barmaid at Tootsie's Orchid Lounge, Nashville.

Rodney Crowell: Musician, songwriter and former member of Emmylou Harris's Hot Band.

Bob Dylan: Friend, musician and icon. Collaborated with Nelson on Farm Aid, *Across The Borderline* and toured with him in 2004 and 2005.

Paul English: Drummer in the Family Band since 1966.

Fred Foster: Nashville producer and founder of Monument records. Worked with Nelson in the 1960s and 1980s.

Bob Geldof: Musician and activist. Founded Band Aid and Live Aid.

Tompall Glaser: Country musician. Appeared on *Wanted! The Outlaws*.

Joe Gracey: Influential Austin DJ appearing on KOKE-FM in early 1970s. Friend, producer and musician, married to Kimmie Rhodes.

Merle Haggard: Friend and country legend. Duetted with Nelson on 'Pancho And Lefty'.

David Hood: Bass player with Muscle Shoals Band. Worked with Nelson on *Phases And Stages*.

Dennis Hopper: Actor and friend.

Nick Hunter: Record executive. Worked in Atlantic Records country division from 1972 to 1974. Later worked for Nelson's manager Neil Reshen.

Waylon Jennings: Close friend, country musician, and prominent member of the outlaw movement. A co-member of the Highwaymen, Jennings died February 2002.

Booker T. Jones: Musician and producer. Has worked with Nelson sporadically from 1970s until present.

Buddy Killen: Musician, songwriter and legendary Music Row figure in Nashville. Later President and CEO of Tree Publishing.

Kris Kristofferson: Friend, country musician, and co-member of the Highwaymen. Still recording.

Daniel Lanois: Producer who has worked with Bob Dylan, U2, Peter Gabriel and Emmylou Harris. Worked with Nelson on *Teatro*.

Don Light: Member of the *Grand Ole Opry* house band in Nashville in the 1960s.

Jack Loftis: Nelson's friend during his brief time at Baylor University in 1954. Loftis became editor and later editor emeritus of the *Houston Chronicle*.

Bruce Lundvall: Joined CBS Records in 1960 and became president in 1976. Left for Elektra in 1982 and is now CEO at Blue Note Records. Signed Nelson to CBS in 1975.

Bobbie Nelson: Elder sister and piano player in the Family Band.

Connie Nelson: Third wife. Married 1971, divorced 1988. Mother of Paula Carlene and Amy Nelson.

Lana Nelson: Daughter. Born 11 November 1953.

Martha Nelson: First wife. Married 1952, divorced 1962. Died 1989.

Myrle Nelson: Mother.

Shirley Nelson: Second wife. Married 1963, divorced 1971.

Susie Nelson: Daughter. Born 20 January 1957.

Tim O'Connor: Former member of Nelson's road crew and later his business partner. Now he is CEO of Direct Events which operates, owns or manages some of the biggest clubs in Austin, such as The Backyard and Antones.

Sydney Pollack: Film director, producer and actor. Friend. Worked with Nelson on *The Electric Horseman, Honeysuckle Rose* and *Songwriter*.

Ray Price: Country music legend and close friend. Gave Nelson hirst break in Nashville by inviting him to join the Cherokee Cowboys in 1961. Still recording.

Charlotte Ramsay: Daughter of Dr Ben Parker, the founder of KBOP radio station where Nelson worked from 1954 to 1955.

Mickey Raphael: Harmonica player in Family Band since 1973.

Neil Reshen: Nelson's manager from 1972 to 1978.

Keith Richards: Musician, songwriter and friend. Living embodiment of rock 'n' roll.

Mark Rothbaum: Manager.

Darrell Royal: Close friend, patron and football coach at UT from 1956 to 1976.

Billy Joe Shaver: Friend and Austin-based musician. Writer of 'Willie The Wandering Gypsy And Me'.

Billy Sherill: Songwriter, staff producer and director of A&R at CBS Nashville.

Paul Simon: Musician and friend. Worked with Nelson on *Across The Borderline*.

Bee Spears: Bass player in Family Band since 1970.

Larry Trader: Close friend and golf professional at Pedernales Country Club.

Zeke Varnon: Childhood friend. Now deceased.

Jerry Jeff Walker: Friend and Austin-based musician. Wrote the standard 'Mr Bojangles'. Albums include *Viva Terlingua*.

Jerry Wexler: Legendary record executive and producer of Ray Charles, Aretha Franklin and many more. Worked with Nelson on his Atlantic albums *Shotgun Willie* and *Phases And Stages*

James White: Owner of the Broken Spoke honky-tonk in Austin, Texas.

Eddie Wilson: Co-founder of the Armadillo World Headquarters in Austin, Texas.

Bob Wishoff: Friend and founder of Outlaw radio. Based at Pedernales and known as Computer Bob for his expertise in all technical matters.

Faron Young: Friend and country star who recorded 'Hello Walls' in 1961. Committed suicide in 1996.

David Zettner: Close friend, musician, artist and producer. Member of Nelson's band from 1967 until 1970. Lives in the grounds of Nelson's ranch near Austin, Texas.

BIBLIOGRAPHY

The newspaper and magazine articles referred to during the research and writing of this book are too numerous to mention individually. Any direct reference in the text to a particular publication is covered in the *Notes on Sources* section. In addition, two articles were especially helpful in documenting certain short periods of Willie Nelson's life. Both appeared in *Texas Monthly* magazine: Robert Draper's excellent 'Poor Willie' essay appeared in the May 1991 issue, while Gary Cartwright's rumination on 'Willie At 65' appeared in the April 1998 issue. The draft copy of the 1987 Farm Aid report was also a useful reference document.

Books used for reference include:

Bane, Michael – *Willie Nelson*, Dell Publishing, 1984

Brown, Jim – *Willie Nelson: Red Headed Stranger*, Quarry Music Books, 2001

Edmonds, Ben – *What's Going On?*, Mojo Books, 2001

Hicks, Bill – *Love All The People*, Constable, 2004

Jennings, Waylon – *Waylon: An Autobiography*, Warner Books, 1998

Kienzle, Rich – *It's Been Rough And Rocky Travellin'*, Companion book to Bear Records box-set of the same name

Kienzle, Rich – *Nashville Was The Roughest*, Companion book to Bear Records box-set of the same name

Milner, Jay – *Confessions Of A Mad Dog*, University Of North Texas Press, 1998

Nelson, Susie – *Heartworn Memories*, Eakin Press, 1987

Nelson, Willie – *The Facts Of Life And Other Dirty Jokes*, Random House, 2003

Nelson, Willie and Shrake, Bud – *Willie: An Autobiography*, Cooper Square Press, 2000

Opdyke, Steven – *Willie Nelson Sings America*, Eakin Press, 1998

Reid, Jan – *The Improbable Rise Of Redneck Rock (New Edition)*, University Of Texas Press, 2004

Richmond, Clint – *Willie Nelson: Behind The Music*, VH-1 Books/Pocket Books, 2000

Scobey, Lola – *Willie Nelson: Country Outlaw*, Zebra Books, 1982

Sounes, Howard – *Down The Highway: The Life Of Bob Dylan*, Doubleday, 2001

St John, Lauren – *Hardcore Troubadour: The Life And Near Death Of Steve Earle*, Fourth Estate, 2002

Taraborrelli, Randall J. – *Sinatra: The Man Behind The Myth*, Mainstream, 1997

Turner, Steve – *The Man Called Cash*, Bloomsbury, 2005

Films used for reference include:

American Masters: Willie Nelson: Still Is Still Moving, produced by Thirteen/ WNET New York for PBS, US (2002)

South Bank Show on Willie Nelson, first aired 19 September 2004 on ITV1, UK (2004)

Lost Highway – 4-part BBC series (2003)

ACKNOWLEDGEMENTS

This is not an authorised biography. Willie Nelson was not granted – nor did he ever ask for – any veto rights or copy approval in respect of the final product. He did, however, make himself available to be interviewed at length specifically for this book, and for such a generous donation of his time and energy I thank him warmly. I also extend my gratitude to his manager Mark Rothbaum for overcoming his initial scepticism, and for his subsequent patience in coordinating the interview.

The members of the fabled Family Band were also generous and forthcoming to a fault: to Paul English, Bee Spears and especially Mickey Raphael – thank you. Thanks also to Buddy Prewitt for access to his vast library of photographs.

Connie Nelson provided a remarkably honest insight into her life with Willie Nelson and was consistently charming and helpful thereafter. I thank her for it. This would have been a considerably lesser book without her input.

I spent a very enjoyable and illuminating few weeks in and around Nelson mission control in Texas, made all the more worthwhile by the company I kept. At Pedernales, Bob Wishoff proved an entertaining and insightful guide to life in and around the ranch; he also came to my aid when requested during the writing of the book. I owe him one in The Diggers. Likewise David Zettner, an amusing and thoughtful interviewee, not to mention a true gentleman. Thanks also to Larry Trader for sharing almost forty years' worth of memories.

Todd Copeland at Baylor University was hugely helpful and hospitable and I pass on my gratitude for a fun foray around Waco, Abbott, West and Hillsboro, as well as access to his valuable interview notes on some of Abbott's oldest and most colourful characters. Still in Texas, Katie Salzmann from the Southwestern Writers Collection at the University of Texas, San Marcos was diligent and patient. To all at the Austin Motel on South Congress and the secretarial staff at Abbott High School – thank you.

Aside from those listed already, I owe a debt of gratitude to everyone who kindly agreed to be interviewed for the book between 2002 and 2005. Their memories and insights were shared without condition, and they form the heart of the biography. Thanks to: Ryan Adams, Richie Albright, Barry Beckett, Jimmy Bruce, Johnny Bush, Jessi Colter, Jackie Clements, Rodney Crowell, Chris Ethridge, Fred Foster, Bob Geldof, Joe Gracey, Merle Haggard, David Hood, Dennis Hopper, Nick Hunter, Mary Suzanne Jackson, Booker T. Jones, Buddy Killen, Daniel Lanois, Don Light, Jack Loftis, Bruce Lundvall, Bill Mack, Chips Moman, Turk Pipkin, Sydney Pollack, Ray Price, Charlotte Ramsay, Neil Reshen, Kimmie Rhodes, Billy Joe Shaver, Roger Sovine, James Talley, Jack Tarver, Larry Trader,

Jerry Jeff Walker, Jack Walrath, Jerry Wexler, James White, Lucinda Williams, and Eddie Wilson. Special thanks to Keith Richards.

Arranging interviews can be a logistical nightmare. I extend thanks to the following for their general help and assistance smoothing my path: Martha Moore, Richard Wootton, Barbara Charone, Nicole Hegeman, Jennifer Tipoulow, KSP Wilson, Braden Kuhlman, Nikki Mitchell, Tamara Saviano, Kay Clary, Jeanne Meyer and Amanda Conroy, Tresa Mumba and Geoff Andrew. There have been many more helping hands along the way, and each one was appreciated.

Closer to home, a big thank you to my agent Stan for all his encouragement throughout, and his tenacity (above and beyond the call of duty) in every aspect of my work over the past year. Thanks to Stuart Evers for his input and enthusiasm in the latter stages.

Thanks also to the editors at all the publications I write for, especially those who published some of my work-in-progress on Willie Nelson in 2005: Gordon Thomson at *Time Out*, Mark Ellen at *The Word* and Keith Bruce at the *Herald*.

As always, love and thanks are due to my mother, father and brother. Most of all, this biography comes with love and appreciation for my wife Jen. Not only for her constant support, but also for colluding in the notion that this is somehow a perfectly acceptable way to make a living.

INDEX